ECONOMICS

The World as One Economy

Rudolf Steiner

NEW ECONOMY PUBLICATIONS
Rudolf Steiner Archive Series

This book comprises lectures and discourses given by
Rudolf Steiner in 1922 in Dornach, Switzerland,
to a gathering of economics students and others.

The original German texts, from shorthand reports
unrevised by the lecturer, are published in German as
Nationalökonomischer Kurs, GA 340 (the lectures) and
Nationalökonomischer Seminar, GA 341 (the discourses),
Rudolf Steiner Verlag, Dornach, Switzerland.

The lectures were originally translated in 1936
by Owen Barfield and T Gordon-Jones*;
the discourses in 1981 by Petra Evertz (1,2,4,5,6)
and Frank Sellinat (3).

In all cases the translations have then been edited and brought
up-to-date by Christopher Houghton Budd, who
has also supplied the introductory material and notation.

(* Published as *World Economy*, © Rudolf Steiner Press, London, 1972.)

A CIP catalogue record for this book
is available from the British Library.

© New Economy Publications 1993

ISBN 0 948229 16 0

Printed by Booksprint
Bristol, England

CONTENTS

ACKNOWLEDGEMENTS

Thanks are due to the translators, both those we have borrowed from and those we used directly, for their work in getting Steiner's texts into the English language. This was no mean feat, as anyone will confirm who knows the two languages concerned, let alone the adventurous use made of German by Steiner himself - for example by creating words to express himself where none existed before. Mention should be made also of the proof reader, who prefers to remain anonymous, but without whose efforts the reader would have been confronted by much unschooled text. A similar debt is owed to Fowler; his book on use of English* has proved a faithful desk companion (and a great read in its own right). Thank you, too, to the management of Rudolf Steiner Press for their help in this project, particularly their granting of the right to work from the original translation. Lastly, a word of gratitude to all those who have helped in the financing of this book.

* A Dictionary of Modern English Usage, H M Foster, OUP, 1978.

EDITORIAL INTRODUCTION

This book, the transcript of a course on economics given some 70 years ago, may leave an odd impression on today's economist. With its penchant for statistics, coupled to a second-guessing of the future, modern economics proceeds along paths quite different to those taken by Rudolf Steiner. Moreover, it can be argued that so much has happened in the development of economics, and so greatly has the world changed since Steiner's time, that his relevance to the current situation is hard to credit. It is not surprising, therefore, that Steiner's contribution to economics is so little known. So why publish?

The degree of historical progress since 1922 may seem substantial, but appearances can be deceptive. Many of the events now taking place put one in mind of the very times when Steiner delivered his lectures. The "Balkan situation", for example, is no more resolved now than it was at the end of the First World War. Events in Iraq are hardly more than the product of that country's artificial creation in the same period, essentially as a Western oil reserve.

More fundamentally, economic nationalism now permeates the whole of the modern economic world, at a time in history when internationalism should be the order of the day. And on the conceptual level, despite the best efforts of Keynes and notwithstanding the current fashion for monetarism, we are no nearer a clear understanding of inflation, money or the role of gold than we were in 1914 - when the stability of the 19th century finally passed into history. Daily one hears in the news and from the mouths of politicians everywhere glib, unthinking statements about inflation being "Public Enemy No.1", while unemployment presumably ranks second. We are told that we need to rid ourselves of these menaces, although, so feeble is our thinking about them, that it is no wonder that they persist! They will continue to do so as long as we do not realise that our greatest economic problem is the way we think about economics.

The need to understand the nature of economic life in this century, and especially in the next, has never been more pressing. Rudolf Steiner's contribution would, indeed, be an irrelevant anachronism if it did not address this issue head-on. As it is, this is precisely the goal he set himself. The course he gave was an attempt to deal with the two main aspects of this problem. First of all, he sought to draw attention to the fact that, in the decades leading up to the First World War, the national economies of Adam Smith's era had coalesced into a single global economy. Secondly, for that reason 20th century economic life simply cannot be understood or made to work properly on a basis of nation state economies and narrow Smithian concepts. It needs to be conceived as a worldwide affair, the common task of humanity as a whole, with its proceeds their common wealth - to be shared, not colonised.

This, of course, directly challenges most people's motivation, for ours is a selfish, acquisitive culture that mistakenly equates spiritual well-being with material prosperity. Above all, the emergence of a single global economy confronts the way we think about economic life. For the most part we do not think economically, but in expression of our political and cultural prejudices and interests. This is natural enough, but it neither makes for accuracy in economics nor, in the end, will it serve as an excuse.

Insofar as we need to change the motives and methods underlying our conduct of economic life, we need to rethink what the economy represents and how it functions. In a word, we need to think from the economy outwards, and no longer treat the economy as if it were the adjunct of our political or cultural interests. This requirement is as real now as it was in 1922.

However daunting this task might be, it remains to be tackled. If it is left undone, economic life worldwide will gradually become unviable - a fact that is already beginning to make itself known. We have to get back to basics, back to that moment when the national economies were overtaken by global economics and when economic reality transcended the framework constructed for it by 18th and 19th century ideologies. In their stead, an 'economics first' approach is called for.

Notwithstanding the extensive literature within economics produced in the interim, the science of economics as a whole lacks the kind of perspective offered by Steiner. The object of this publication is, therefore, to make Steiner's approach more widely accessible by means of an up-to-date English-language version.

It is my conviction that the relevance of Steiner's contribution has not been diminished by the passage of time. The problems he addressed in the early

1920s have been little more than glossed over in the decades since, and are now re-emerging and calling once again for a viable solution. The principal purpose in publishing this material is to show how Rudolf Steiner, usually known as a seer, dealt with such "earthly" matters as inflation, speculation and the general ills of modern economic life.

Believing that muddled thinking was everywhere an unseen cause of our many social problems, Steiner placed great emphasis on clear thinking. It is not an easy path. There are no set formulae, and merely reactive thinking is insufficient, indeed dangerous. This book illustrates the kind of thinking Steiner himself brought to bear on the complex issues of modern social life.

Economics is derived from fuller German editions of uncorrected notes of the course that Steiner gave to students of economics. The present texts were first translated into English in a form that closely followed the original. They have then been reproduced in a looser, more English style in order to overcome certain editorial problems that would otherwise result. For example, the lectures involve a degree of repetition that does not suit the English palate, or indeed make for a 'comfortable' read. While in the case of the discourses, Steiner's style is discursive, places frequent reliance on his listeners' knowledge of economics, and addresses particular nuances on the part of his questioners.

Concerning style, in German precision of meaning often depends on the elaboration of words, whereas in English verbal economy is the path to the same end. A certain amount of condensation of the original has been made, therefore, but without lessening in any way the clarity or particularity of Steiner's comments. Indeed, in the English language, economy of words often enhances their meaning. As regards content, throughout the lectures and discourses some details, left unspecified by Steiner, have been introduced. In the same vein, the events then under discussion cannot be assumed to be present in the mind of today's reader, still less an interpretation of them that diverges from the traditional Allies' version, in which most Westerners have been schooled. To overcome this difficulty, factual information has been supplied when it seemed appropriate to do so.

One aspect of this revision needs specific mention - the use of italics. The original English translation was somewhat liberal with its use of italics to stress points and it also used this device where the German texts did not. Moreover, in the German version, it being unrevised by the lecturer, the use of italics was a judgement on the part of the stenographer or publishing editor. Valid as this technique is, it can also be a hindrance. In this version I have made sparing use of italics and then rarely to stress meaning. That is best left to emerge from the sense of the sentence or from the reader's own reading of it.

The greatest liberty (but also the greatest care) has been taken with respect to abridgements. In some cases I have left out whole sentences, in others I have supplemented them - and even invented one or two! Either way, my purpose has been to make the sense and direction of Steiner's approach clearer and more understandable than is possible by literal translation. To this end, I have not clung to verbatim translation, where in my judgement to have done so would have been to cloud the point being made, for example. Nor have I pedantically retained every word uttered by Steiner. My guide in this has been to get across the way he thought, rather than to ensure that everything he said gets into English.

Rendering Steiner's texts in this way, risks, of course, putting certain words into his mouth, while taking others out! It would have been possible to italicise every such amendment, but this would have led the reader down a very bumpy road, full of interruptions and detours. A smoother passage was considered more helpful, and this has been possible to achieve without infidelity to Steiner. On the contrary, the whole exercise is intended to help the English mind come closer to Steiner's contribution to economics, one that merits far greater consideration than it has enjoyed to date. In the process, I hope in some measure to have opened the door to the further content he had intended to offer.

Finally, in retaining the lecture format, rather than effecting a more wholesale revision, I am aware that the presentation is not to be compared to that which a book would have made possible. The choice was deliberate, therefore, to use a format which, on the one hand, smoothes the reader's passage and thus allows him to follow closely Steiner's thesis, and in particular the way he unfolds it, while on the other preserving the text for what it is - an important, valuable, and still valid, historical document. After all, Steiner did not write a book, so it would be unwise to give the impression that he had. To have reproduced these texts as if they were a written work would have been too presumptive a task. Moreover, what would have bene the point?

However convenient it may be to regard Steiner as a seer, whose preoccupation with things spiritual unsuits him to economic debate, unprejudiced and careful study of his analysis does not support this view. Many a conundrum in today's economic world can be answered by the perspective he helps to unfold. If this publication serves in any way therefore to clarify humanity's thinking about economic life it will have achieved its purpose.

Christopher Houghton Budd
Vernazza, Italy

RUDOLF STEINER
Economist

Christopher Houghton Budd

RUDOLF STEINER, ECONOMIST

The subject of this book is a course of lectures given by Rudolf Steiner in 1922 to an audience of students of economics. The course was intended to be a specific contribution to a specialist subject. After some of the lectures he conducted short discussions, during which he was able to deal in greater depth with some of his themes. Taken together, the lectures and discourses provide a rich mine of information and thinking, both as regards economic history to date and in respect of present problems and future developments.

English translations of the lectures have to date been entitled *World Economy*. Though understandable, this choice of title - referring to a central theme of Steiner's work - can also be misleading for two reasons. Firstly, it lessens attention to the fundamental rethink of economics that the lectures presuppose. Secondly, the expression "world economy" is now part of the vocabulary of economics, but without having the meaning Steiner gave to it. Most importantly, Rudolf Steiner regarded reciprocity in both economic and social relationships as the necessary context of world economy, but this idea is notably remote from the term as used today. As a title, "World Economy" is possibly more catchy than "Economics", but it detracts from the work in that there are many other, equally cardinal, themes in the course - such as the three kinds of money, the factors of price formation, and the economics of cultural work.

ECONOMIC THINKING

But a greater detraction still lies in that a partial title plays into the hands of those who either believe economics can be grasped on the basis of current thinking or taken further in its evolution by so many armchair discussions. Steiner was insistent that the thinking used in economics was unable to recognise living organisms and yet, in his view, the economy was precisely such an organism. He pointed out that the kind of thinking needed to understand economics died away just at the time when so-called economic science began to emerge. He was of the view that a genuine science of economics had yet to be created, and that to do so would require quite different thinking to that employed in natural science, making the latter unsuitable as a model for economic science.

Seen as a whole, the lectures and discourses are an expression of the kind of thinking advocated by Steiner. The reader is ill-advised to read them piecemeal, therefore, lest he give attention mainly to those aspects which appeal most easily to his powers of comprehension or, to be frank, merely to his prejudices. To experience the thinking Steiner was after, it is necessary to read the course in its entirety and only afterwards to dip down into any one section. No doubt a partial study will yield interesting ideas and lead to valuable debates; but it will not give one the experience of thinking in which Rudolf Steiner placed so much store. If, on the other hand, one is able to grasp Steiner's economics as a whole, then one will be able to create within oneself the thinking from which they derive and of which they are an expression.

It cannot be over-emphasised that Steiner's work illustrates *a way of thinking* and does not constitute a prescription, or set of prescriptions. Indeed, endless difficulties await those who treat his works in an external way. Steiner was more concerned with promoting economic thinking than providing recipes for economic reform. He was convinced that economic thinking of itself leads to the kind of action that is needed in modern economic life - action that proceeds from an accurate perception of concrete events, rather than from a wish to apply prescriptions based on preconceptions. It is all too easy to overlook the role played in life by thinking as an activity in itself. Behind Steiner's approach lies a kind of thinking which transcends its subject matter and has thereby a pan-historical quality, such that the thinking itself does not become dated by the passage of time, even if the matters it deals with may do.

One who sees Steiner's work within the context of economics generally will see, then, not the ideas only, but the thinking that gives rise to them. It is a thinking which goes beyond Steiner and which anyone is capable of. One needs, therefore, to distinguish sharply between the ideas Steiner formulated and the thinking he used to do this. The ideas may well be shown to be peculiar to him and conditioned by the times he lived in. They may even be "wrong." But it is the type of thinking Steiner employed that matters, a kind of thinking attainable by anyone who wants to think and not just have thoughts.

Keynes once described this kind of thinking with characteristic succinctness when he likened economists to "Euclidean geometers in a non-Euclidean world, who, discovering in experience that straight lines apparently parallel often meet, rebuke the lines for not keeping straight as the only remedy for the unfortunate collisions that are occurring. Yet there is no remedy except to throw over the axiom of parallels, and to work out a non-Euclidean geometry. Something of the kind is required in economics."[1]

THE RESPONSIBILITY OF ECONOMISTS

Steiner's works on economics are full to bursting with ideas, observations, concepts and even practical suggestions not only for economic science, but also for the conduct of economic life itself, demonstrating his conviction that economics is both an ethical and a practical science. But it will take more than intellectual discourse to value these ideas to the degree they merit. They were given to economists who, it must be presumed, reckoned to use their training to give shape to economic life. They were given, moreover, at a time when the German economy was in shreds - ruined by the cost of the First World War and the subsequent bankruptcy visited on Germany by the so-called reparations, vindictively exacted by the Allies. In this sense Steiner's ideas belong more to kinetic than to potential economics; they are in movement and call to be led over into action. They are wasted on those who neither wish to act, nor to change their way of acting. That is as true now as it was in 1922, and so the question remains: How are such ideas to be put into practice? And, by whom?

Steiner answers the first question early on in the course, when he speaks of the need to get inside the retort of the economic process. To study it from outside was for him worthless; economics can get nowhere as a merely contemplative activity. But to enter the retort means nothing less than to observe, in the first place, one's own experience of economic life - or, rather, of the economic process that underlies it. It is this objective organic process that *Economics* describes. No other contributor has done this, making it Steiner's unique contribution. As a living process, the economic process takes its reality from the fact of the human being. It is not a process of interest or relevance to birds or beasts. It is for this reason that everyone could now, and in the distant future probably will, understand the economic process, just as today everyone learns Euclidean geometry in elementary school, whereas once it was instruction strictly reserved for would-be initiates, to use the nomenclature of the time. Its expression will always be comprehensible to the human being and not at odds with him; at least, not with his higher, non-egotistical nature.

It will be in very definite contradiction, however, to all that proceeds from him as selfishness with regard to economic life. Steiner makes no bones about his conviction that egoism in economic life must be "extirpated, root and branch." In answer to the question "who?", therefore, those who most usefully take up Steiner's ideas and endeavour to give them practical expression will be those who are intent on abating their own egoism in economic life, people whose concern will be to ensure that their contribution to society, even if they earn their living from it, is of benefit to society generally and not undertaken merely as a means of getting money. Such people are not so far away; anymore than is the realm in which such motives come to the fore. Many more people than is ordinarily supposed would, and in some cases already do, live this way. Those who actually enjoy, rather than endure, the deeply materialistic economic life of today are not to be found in legions: They are comparatively few when one surveys the entirety of humanity.

The fundamentally anti-social tone of modern economic life is due to the influence of materialistic economics. Those who create the ideas and develop the practices of modern economic life provide, more or less knowingly, profound and far-reaching leading thoughts for the whole of humanity. They know that Marx was right when he drew attention to the powerful formative force exercised over humanity by the relations of production. Today the productive forces have been harnessed unequivocally to the narrowly defined and, therefore, narrowly beneficial purposes of self-interest. Self-interest is not out of place or harmful when it arises on the way to full self-awareness, the birth of the independent ego in the human being. But once this consciousness has been attained, such self-interest, if persisted in, becomes egoism.

As regards economic life - something in which everyone shares - ego-hood must give rise to a sense of service to the community. More than any other factor in modern society, economics brings to expression the human egoism that so often afflicts us today. In refusing to throw over the axioms it has borrowed from capitalism, economics gives people the ideas by which, for the most part, they conduct their economic affairs and, more importantly, in terms of which they organise their thoughts.

With due reason, Rudolf Steiner expected much of his listeners. He knew the need to break the spell that materialistic economics, with its pretence of science, has cast over humanity. The profession would no doubt experience many curtailments of salaries and much drying-up of grant funds if it were to take the path urged upon it by Steiner. Nevertheless, over against these selfish and short-term considerations must be placed the responsibility that attaches to economists in our time. Like the high priests of olden times who gave out ordering impulses for the entire social life through the medium of religion, today it is the economists who shape the entire social life, but now through the medium of economics.

RUDOLF STEINER *QUA* ECONOMIST

Many lay people endeavour, and to some extent manage, to translate Steiner's ideas into practice; but it rests with the economists of our time to lead the way - to render the technicalities and complexities of economic life amenable to selflessness and a sense of common wealth. This begs the question: What is an economist? And what credentials does Rudolf Steiner have in this respect?

When one looks at the state of economic science, and considers the long list of people who claim to be or are credited with being economists, one cannot reliably conclude much more than that an economist is one who applies his mind sincerely to the nature of economic life. On this basis, Rudolf Steiner is as much an economist as Smith, Ricardo, Marx, Keynes or Friedman. It is also clear that the content of his works in economics could not proceed from anything other than a thorough grounding in the history of the subject. This background resulted in the main from Steiner's own studies, research carried out over a long period before he felt able to share its results.

He gave his lecture course in 1922, but its contents are an elaboration of certain cornerstone concepts that eventually found expression three years previously in his book *The Threefold Social Order*, first published in April 1919.[2] These concepts unfold in turn from a consideration of the key issue, that has accompanied the development of capitalism ever since its emergence: With the emancipation of capital, how is human labour to be treated so that the human being is not dragged into the economic process -a process that is anathema to him? This question was central to Steiner's work in the social sciences. His response to it was always predicated on a clear understanding of the meaning of labour and the reforms necessary to avoid human work becoming a form of spiritual slavery.

One final credential can perhaps be claimed for Steiner as an economist.

From 1920 to 1923 he was chairman of "Der Kommende Tag",[3] a grouping of companies and cultural institutions that sought to generate profits with which to underwrite scientific research, especially medical research. The events that befell this endeavour, undertaken as it was in the teeth of Germany's rampant inflation, must have been powerful teachers. There is no doubt that they bore considerable fruit in the 1922 lectures.

THE THREEFOLD SOCIAL ORDER

Before continuing, a potted version of what Steiner meant by the threefold social order, mentioned earlier, may be of some use. Steiner's conception of social evolution turns on the idea that society comprises three distinguishable (though not separable) spheres - economic life, the life of rights, and cultural life. In ancient times the three spheres were contained one inside the other, as it were. The ancient theocracies governed not only the cultural life, but political and economic matters also. In Roman times the life of rights emancipated itself somewhat, but the economy remained a subordinate element. The emergence of capitalism marks the emancipation of the economic life, as an element in its own right.

With the emancipation of the economic life, the relationship between the three spheres of society could then develop in one of two directions. It could either evolve on a basis where each sphere had a degree of autonomy, albeit harmonised with and interdependent in respect of the others. Or it could develop as a reverse image of theocracy, into a form of society in which the cultural and political life become subsumed in the economic. The former is what Rudolf Steiner refers to when he speaks of the threefold social order. The latter is the course actually taken in history, ushered in by the economic materialism of the 19th century, something that is by no means peculiar to Marxism alone, but which also provides the underpinning of capitalism.

THE TREATY OF VERSAILLES

In my essay *The Consequences of the Peace for Economics*,[4] I sought to treat in detail the history of economics since the Treaty of Versailles, the fulcrum of modern history. In the essay, I express the view that in the years since, economics has done little else than gloss over the problems it already faced at the advent of the First World War. To paraphrase Keynes, modern economists are still rebuking supposedly parallel lines for their stubborn intent on convergence. But, although he might not agree with me, even

Keynes only turned 'Euclidean economics' upside down; when what is needed is to turn it inside out - to flipe it, as one would a glove.

Alas, the idea of turning thinking upside down is a catch-phrase through which both Keynes, and Marx before him, have been credited with greater achievements than is perhaps their due. In reality, what has happened is that humanity, through efforts of sheer will, has held life's real circumstances at bay for over seven decades, cocooning a frail and actually formless economic life within a hard and over-formed, but increasingly brittle shell - a social structure consisting of over-stretched theory and thin treaties. In due course this husk must implode, as surely as the force of will that sustains it must, in the end, also give out. At that point, it will become clear how formless is the life we have harboured for so long, and how great is the need for inherent ordering.

Whether the external forces of "law and order" prevail over the inner ordering power of such ideas as Rudolf Steiner would have us take up, remains to be seen. The choice between the two is not, however, a new development in history, but marks the return of the very same problem that arose with the First World War, but which humanity baulked at and shied away from.

Against this background, Rudolf Steiner gave many lectures on the genesis of the social and economic problems of the twentieth century. He also referred frequently to these problems in the course of many other, often unrelated, lectures. What follows is an aphoristic resumé of the picture that gradually and quietly unfolds from these many indications. It is, however, a personal survey of history for which the writer of this essay, not Rudolf Steiner, should be held responsible.

THE EVOLUTION OF CONSCIOUSNESS

Steiner describes history in essentially spiritual terms - that is to say, in terms of the development of consciousness and the inner evolution of humanity, as told by the outer events that clothed them. He describes how the social life of humanity has always been based on a threefold order and that this could not be otherwise, given that the human being is himself a threefold being and that his social order is nothing more than a description "from outside" of this being. The three spheres that constitute human society are those that concern the development of the individual, the rights between people, and the means whereby they provide for their material existence - cultural life, rights life and economic life, respectively. Against this backcloth, stands the evolution of human individuality. As this inner evolution progresses, the form of the threefold order changes, reflecting faithfully the stages reached by the development of human consciousness.

The evolution of individuality is such that the human being passes out of a condition in which he is part of the community, subservient to it and dependent on it, through the processes whereby the ego emancipates itself from the community, and thence into a condition in which the independent ego either goes off on its own, or recreates human community out of itself. The twentieth century marks the time when, the latter stage having been reached, people will either sunder themselves from one another and from the world in the most horrible ways imaginable; or they will strive for and create a new sense of community from out of their egohood - a community that champions freedom of the individual, for the reason that the free individual places the highest value on his fellow human beings and on the material world, recognising that in reality it is on them that he depends. Even the crassest egoist has to admit to this fact of life - unless he lives truly alone on an island, importing nothing, neither goods nor human companionship.

In consequence of the development of self-consciousness, two souls reside within the modern human breast. Like Shakespeare's Lancelot Gobbo, the human being is caught between his conscience and the fiend. Albeit heavily overlain and pressed into the background by the economics of our time, a veritable struggle must needs ensue in everyone, between the social and anti-social tendencies within him. We are trapped in a dualism that has long been in the making, but one that has access to human affairs only because the newly-won egohood of modern humanity will not take itself seriously, and declare itself the arbiter of human deeds and the measurer of their validity.

The emergence of the State, with its characteristically omnipresent and seemingly unbreakable power, is itself a reflection of our timidity with regard to ourselves. The State thrives on this lack of self-conviction on the part of the individual, taking its origins and maintaining its essential being from his lack of courage. However, "external" and "real" the State and other outer authorities may become, they all rely for their effect on conditions wherein the human being, dithering and teetering at the brink, is afraid to try his new wings, and denies, in fact, the inner principle whereby he exists at all. For no-one can attribute his essential self to the outer world. The outer world may provoke the emergence of the human ego, but it cannot beget it.

THE 'COVENANT'

These are inner facts, to do with free will, which it is unrealistic to attempt to prove externally. Everyone can find them in himself. Against this background, Steiner describes the development through centuries of conditions which, positively seen, have no purpose other than to engender human ego-hood; but which, when seen negatively, bode ill indeed for our future freedom. In our age it is all too easy to home in on, and even feel at home in contemplation of the negative side of life. Advisedly, therefore, I intend to focus my remaining remarks only on the positive aspects of this version of history, mindful that to do so requires a greater effort of will.

It can be imagined that, long ago, the human being resolved to tread the path away from immersion in the community towards independent individuality, and that, as he did so, he made an "covenant" that, as and when he declared himself no longer in need of the community or any other guiding element outside himself, the props on which he had previously relied should be removed in one way or another and thenceforward denied him. It would then be up to him to create afresh the community life on which he had hitherto depended.

Having made such an agreement, he set out on his way - a path well marked in history and identifiable by certain large landmarks. The first is the passage from Plato's ancient world of the Orient to Aristotle's modern world. In the ancient world the threefold nature of the human being was well known, but in order to be guided on his way, the human being was to lose remembrance of this fact. He was to go all the way to the point where he would declare himself to be undifferentiated, and create a monolithic social order to prove it. For this reason, when in the fourth century Julian the Apostate sought to turn modern civilisation back to its pre-history, he was rudely dealt with. Humanity's face was to be set away from these things, away from the "light of the East" towards whatever was to issue from the West. Thus it was also that in 869AD the Council of Nicea declared the human being no longer to be a being of body, soul and spirit, but of body and soul only. Those who hankered after the, now heretical, threefold conception were treated as roundly as was Julian. Finally, through their promulgation of the materialist conception of history, it was Marx and Engels who effectively declared the human being to be mere body, and his social life a matrix of material forces alone.

This development was mirrored in the evolution of society's threefold ordering. In Plato's time the threefold order was a unity, with cultural life predominating over rights life and economic life. But as the human being went his way these two spheres emancipated themselves. As human personality developed, the impulses connected with Rome came to the fore, giving a powerful impetus to the rights life. Subsequently, with the emergence of capitalism, the economic life emancipated itself - mirroring the dawn of individuality. At this stage the three spheres of society could, like the human individuality they reflected, go one of two ways. Either they could be held in a kind of reciprocal tension, each one autonomous; or the tendency would arise to centralise them, to make them into a monolith. The deciding factor would be the direction taken by the human ego. If, as described earlier, the ego came to rest in itself, the three spheres would balance one another in a threefold social organism. But if the ego failed to assume its proper place or, worse yet, abdicated its position, then the social order, for all its emancipated development, would become centralised through the agency of the State. The State, in this sense, comes about when a weak ego refuses to take responsibility for its own activity.

A NEW TESTAMENT

This inner, spiritual history of the human being is capable of detailed elaboration, although that cannot be the task of this essay. Suffice it to say that, when the human being had reached this point in his evolution the materialist conception of history proclaimed to him in a synthesised form the "gospel" by which the ego had reached its goal: through the denial of all that was given to it, the ego came to selfhood. In this sense, the materialist conception of history is as true and as real as is the Old Testament, in that both refer to conditions that were once valid, but that ceased to be so once the event they anticipated had come to pass. At that point, in both cases, a tremendous reversal took place. Just as Christ overthrew the Mosaic Law by which His appearance on earth had been made possible, so human individuality, once it has asserted its independence, can, and for its own sake must, reverse its egoism and seek to serve others - albeit out of an inner freedom, rather than in obedience to external social factors. A "new testament" is needed to replace the outdated scriptures of materialism, especially the documents produced by, or in consequence of the thought processes to which Karl Marx became wedded.

In many details of his life, Rudolf Steiner sought to counter the error of Marx, especially what he called the "colossal piece of nonsense" of Marx's doctrine on labour value. But Steiner strove in vain. False ideas, sectarian interests and, above all, the machinations of capitalism, conspired to provide a path into modern consciousness that was not sufficiently critical and, therefore, allowed the ideas of Marxism to gain a currency that may well have dismayed even Marx himself. For, whatever else one may say or think about Karl Marx, the charge that he had an uncritical mind and was intellectually lazy would not stick for a moment. One can by no means be sure that he would have let his ideas go unmodified by the events subsequent to his death.

The First World War was the inevitable consequence of the triumph of external forces over weak egos. Rudolf Steiner did his utmost to avert the fate he sensed would befall Germany, and with her all humanity, if she were held responsible for the War. He felt there could be no greater untruth than this. Nevertheless, he had to watch, as from out of the West, in place of the light of the East, there came not light, but machinations, deviousness, and the strongest possible contradictions of individual freedom. Lenin's return to Russia is one profound example. Organised by the West, it diverted the Russian peoples from their inherent sense of social purpose. Lenin, who even in the shape of his head, strikes one as someone representative of a poisonous intellectualism, inspired by vengeance. Moreover, this same vengeance also underlies the Treaty of Versailles, the most serious of all the events responsible for the diversion of modern humanity from its best path. To this day, this treaty is the source of the economic nationalism that everywhere dogs our existence.

From "the West" (I am being careful not to say "the Americans" or "the English", for I do not mean that) came the procedures and the personalities whereby, precisely at the moment in history when the ego should have become master of the economic process, and when a single world economy should have been created, the economic process rose to rule over the human being instead, and the world economy became sundered by national interests. We have fought ever since over the proceeds of the world's economy. We have made treaty after treaty with an insincerity, paucity of conviction and dishonesty of intention that everyone seems content to overlook. And none of it so that we shall be happy and blessed of material plenty; that could only be said of a very small part of humanity. Moreover, those who make up this minority know in their heart of hearts that as long as their wealth is had at the expense of the rest of humanity, it is ill-gotten and may be taken away at any time.

Thus, the economic process reigns over the human being, who should be its master, because that is the directly opposite condition of human freedom. Before this fact, whether one is capitalist, communist, or anything else, is of limited significance. Indeed, the 20th century picture of humanity at odds over whether to be capitalist or communist is a false and quite inaccurate appraisal of our condition, as is, one should now add, the notion that the demise of the Soviet Union is a vindication of capitalism.

Who can say where the human being will now take himself or find himself taken? But I am certain that it was in view of these outer and inner historical facts that Rudolf Steiner gave the course on economics published here. Whether one approaches its content for its own sake and derives impulses to elaborate it entirely from out of its intensive thinking, or whether one is moved to take it up by considerations such as I have sought to make in this essay, this book stands there as a "new testament" oriented to the future and to humanity as a whole, and away from the past and the events that separate us. If taken up without prejudice and with a readiness to follow through its consequences for one's own life, it has the power not only to render modern social problems understandable, but to loose the human being from their tenacious grip.

Before closing, I would like to say that I thought carefully before introducing the somewhat religious notions of 'covenant' and 'testament', lest I gave rise to the criticism, which Rudolf Steiner himself made, that economic science needs no imported morality. I am aware that the empty and amoral content of modern thought-life - especially as it manifests in economics - does not like what it regards as religious sentiment. Yet one cannot help thinking that somewhere in this fashionably empty world, a hint of conviction about and even passion for one's ideas may not be a bad thing, and, when expressed consciously in regard to economics, will not be experienced as moralic acid. In this spirit, what I have presented here is not put forward so much to support the economics Steiner describes, as to illustrate the personal reasons that encourage me to take up the challenge he offers.

It is the supreme paradox of modern economic science that, whereas its content is best crafted at a remove from moral precepts, nevertheless its practitioners need a viable ethical foundation.

ECONOMICS

The World as One Economy

The Lectures

SYNOPSIS OF THE LECTURES

1: FROM INDUSTRIALISM TO WORLD ECONOMY (24.7.22)

Contrast between England and Germany in 19th century - Instinctive and conscious transitions to industrialism - Virgin soil of India and old middle-European agrarian economy - Emergence of the State in German economics instead of 1830's and 1840's ideals (Liberalism) - Inability to enter world economy - Absence of life's contrasts, in particular the contrast between cultural, rights and economic life - The threefold social order - Insufficient thinking in economics - Comparison of economics to a complete theory of light - Expansion beyond single personalities - Intelligence (infra-red)/Land (ultra-violet) - Unsuitability of natural scientific concepts - Invalidity of economics of isolated regions - World as a whole economic and social organism.

2: THE ECONOMIC PROCESS (25.7.22)

Economic process in perpetual motion - Exchange as essence of economics - Price - Fluctuation in price - Unreality of definitions - Ordinary doctrine of land, labour, capital - Animal economics - Apparent labour - Human labour connected to providing for more than oneself - Value created by elaboration of land by labour - Nonsense of Marx's view of labour - Economic irrelevance of labour in itself - Labour directed by intelligence also creates value - Exchange of values - Price and interplay of values - Cannot observe at rest what is in flux.

3: ECONOMIC SCIENCE (26.7.22)

Proper form of economic science - Ethics and natural science - Religion and economics in early history - Distinction between commandment and law - Distillation of law and appearance of labour and emancipation from religious life - Rise of egoism and search for democracy - Division of labour - Individual works for community - Economic impossibility of egoism - Division of labour requires altruism - Egoism contradicts facts of world economy - Labour exchanged "for a living" - Mean price - Trader.

4: DIVISION OF LABOUR AND CREATION OF VALUE (27.7.22)

Cheapening effect of division of labour - Origin of capital through division of labour - Intelligence emancipates capital from land - Money - Capitalism and finance - Money as realised intelligence - Intelligence envalues capital - Investments - Borrowings - The circulation of capital - "difference of level" in terms of capacities - Diversity of capacities - Relation of two value poles to commodities and money - Essential nature of commodity and money - Mobility of thinking.

5: THE PRODUCTION AND CONSUMPTION OF VALUES (28.7.22)

The polarity of production and consumption - The economic process as an organic process - Envaluation and devaluation - Value-creating tension and value-creating movement - Analogy to kinetic and potential energy - Personal credit and the rate of interest - Real credit - Congestion of capital in land and its disappearance in intelligence - Land has no value - Real and apparent values - Associations - Distribution of the workforce - Variety of skill.

6: "TRUE PRICE" (29.7.22)

"True price" formula - Capitalised land opposes production of goods - Two rates of interest - The economic significance of freed activity - Pure consumption - Goods and payment - Capital and lending - Cultural life and giving - Gift as 100% interest on land.

7: THE FACTORS OF PRICE FORMULATION (30.7.22)

Purchase, loan and gift as three factors of price formation - The factors of rest - Fiction of purchase of labour - Reciprocal determination of values - Products of labour - True price and falsification of price - Origin of rent - Rent as compulsory gift - Creation of rent inherent in economic process - Agriculture as a single entity - Industrial capital constantly undervalued - Tendency of industrial capital to devalue - Self-provision with agriculture, not with capital - The need to establish equilibrium - Means of production - Industrial capital - Commodities - Goods - Need to be *within* process only possible in associations.

8: ON SUPPLY AND DEMAND (31.7.22)

The idea of supply and demand - Supply, demand and price as primary factors - The role of rights - The role of individual faculties - Economic impossibilities - Economics and natural science - Associations for production, consumption and distribution - The economics of barter, of money and of human faculties.

9: THE FORMS OF CAPITAL (1.8.22)

Concept of "internal economies" - Distance between outlay and return - Role of gift - Association - Trade, loan and industrial capital - Loan capital and authority - Industrial capital - Raw materials and concepts of might - Markets and intelligence (wise or cunning) - Trade capital and competition - The rise of banking - The withdrawal of financial control from the human being - "Pure money business" and "objectless imperialism".

10: ON ASSOCIATIONS (2.8.22)

Circulation of values - Profit - Exchange creates value - Transformation of commodity into money - Associations - Advantage (profit) as pressure - Loan capital (enterprise) as suction - Interest, human mutuality and lending - Imagination and economic judgement - Associations - Public spirit - Threefold social order.

11: THE CONDITIONS AND CONSEQUENCES OF A WORLD ECONOMY (3.8.22)

Evolution of economic life - Private economies - National economies - State economies - State as economic and cultural organism - Profit by consolidation of economies - Ricardo and Smith - England as leader of world trade - Origin of gold-based currencies - Transition from world trade to world economy - World economy as the end of consolidation - The falsity of Versailles and after - World economy as a closed economy - Relation of commodities and money - The non-depreciation of money - Total consumption by all humanity - Unsuitability of national economic thinking for world economy - Closed economic domains presuppose free gifts - Non-capitalisation of land - Relation of food production to free gifts to cultural life.

12: MONEY (4.8.22)

Money and price - The envaluation of money - Money as a medium of exchange - Purchase money (exchange money) - Loan money - Gift money - Correcting the function of money - The ageing of money - Associative management - Money and control of the economy.

13: THE ECONOMICS OF THE SPIRIT (5.8.22)

Valuing intelligence - Premise of cultural needs - Freed activity as saved labour - Inherent compensatory balances.

14: KEY CONCEPTS FOR WORLD ECONOMICS (6.8.22)

Modern economic science - Living concepts - Parallelism of real and false values - World-wide book-keeping - Medium of exchange as proper quality of money - The polarity of spent labour and saved labour - Land and its elaboration as the basis - Stored up labour requires saved up labour - Money as sum total of means of production - Ratio of population to land - Relation of currency to land and to gold - Prices.

1: FROM INDUSTRIALISM TO WORLD ECONOMY
24 July 1922

Today I intend a kind of introduction. In tomorrow's lecture we shall begin to try to give a more or less complete picture of the socio-economic questions which humanity today must set before itself.

Economics, as understood today, is actually a very recent creation. It did not arise until the economic life of modern peoples had become extraordinarily complicated in comparison with earlier conditions. As this course is intended primarily for students of economics,* this peculiarity of modern economic thinking needs to be pointed out at the outset.

After all, we need not go very far back in history to see how much economics has changed, even during the nineteenth century. Consider this one fact: During the first half of the century, England, for example, already had what was practically the modern form of economic life. The economic structure of England in the course of the nineteenth century changed comparatively little. The great social questions which arise out of economic questions in modern times were being asked in England as early as the first half of the nineteenth century, and those who wanted to think of social and economic questions in the modern sense could pursue their studies in England at a time when in Germany - for instance - such studies must have remained unfruitful. In England, above all, the conditions of trade and commerce on a large scale had already come into being by the first third of the nineteenth century. Through this development England already had a foundation in the shape of trade capital. The English had no need to seek for any other starting-point for modern economic life. They simply had to apply the trade resulting from the consolidation of trade and commerce. From the first third of the nineteenth century on, everything took place in England with a certain logical consistency. However, we must not forget that the whole of this English

* The German has "Volkswirtschaft", political economy. The fact that economics was originally called "political economy" is due to its origins in the period of national economies. This is emphasised by the German word in a way that is not possible in English, though we are reminded of it by the title of Adam Smith's book, *The Wealth of Nations* (see Note 14).

economic life was only possible on the basis originally given by England's relation to her colonies, especially to India. The entire English economic system is unthinkable without the relationship of England to India. In other words, English economic life, with all its facility for evolving large sums of capital, is founded on the fact that there lies in the background a country which is, as it were, virgin economic soil. We must not overlook this fact, especially when we pass from England to Germany.

The economic life of Germany in the first third of the nineteenth century essentially corresponded to economic customs which had arisen out of the Middle Ages. Economic customs and relationships within Germany in this period were essentially old; consequently the whole tempo of economic life was different from what it was in England during the first third, or even the first half, of the nineteenth century. In England, at that time, there was already what we may call a reckoning with quickly changing habits of life. The main character of economic life remained essentially the same, but it was already adaptable to change.

In Germany, on the other hand, habits of life were still conservative. Economic development could afford to advance at a snail's pace, for it had only to adapt itself to technical conditions, which remained more or less the same over long periods, and to human needs, which hardly changed. However, a great transformation took place in the second third of the nineteenth century, when the development of the industrial system rapidly brought about an approximation to English conditions. From being an essentially agrarian country, Germany was rapidly transformed into an industrial one - and this far more quickly than any other region of the earth.

But this was connected to something else: In England the transition to an industrial condition of life took place instinctively. Nobody knew exactly how it happened; it occurred like an event of nature. In Germany, on the other hand, while the outer economic conditions were taking their accustomed course in a way that might almost be called medieval, human thinking was undergoing a fundamental change. It came into the consciousness of people that something altogether different must now arise, that the existing conditions were no longer true to the time. Thus the transformation of economic conditions in Germany took place far more consciously than in England. In Germany people were far more aware of how they entered into modern capitalism; in England people were not aware of it at all. If you read today all the writings and discussions in Germany during that period concerning the transition to industrialism, you will get a remarkable impression of how people in Germany were thinking. They looked upon it as a real liberation of humanity. They called it "Liberalism", "Democracy". They regarded it as the great opportunity to escape from the old binding links, the old kind of corporation, and pass over to the freedom (as they saw it) of the individual within the economic life. Hence in England you will never meet with a theory of economics such as was developed by those who received their education in Germany at the height of the period which I have just characterised. Schmoller[5], Roscher[6] and others derived their views from the heyday of liberalism* in economics. What they built up was altogether in this sense, and they built it with full consciousness. An Englishman would have thought such theories stale and boring. He would have said: "One does not trouble to think about such things." Look at the radical difference between the way in which people in England talked about these things (to mention even a man like Beaconsfield[7], who was theoretical enough in all conscience) and the way in which Richter[8] or Lasker[9] or even Brentano[10] were speaking in Germany. In Germany, therefore, this second period was entered into with full consciousness.

Then came the third period, essentially that of the State. As the last third of the nineteenth century drew near, the German State was consolidated purely by means of force. That which was consolidated was not what the idealists of '48 or even of the 1830's had desired, but the "State", achieved moreover by means of sheer force. And this State, by and by, requisitioned the economic life with full consciousness for its own purposes. Thus, in the last third of the nineteenth century, the structure of economic life was permeated through and through by the very opposite principle to before. The ideas of liberalism gave way altogether to the idea of the State. This was what gave Germany's economic life as a whole its stamp.

Certainly, there were elements of consciousness in the whole process, and yet in another sense it was quite unconscious. But the most important thing is that through all these developments a radical contrast, an antagonism of principle, was created, not only in thought but in the whole conduct of economic life itself as between the English and the Mid-European economies. On this contrast the manner of their economic intercourse depended. The economy of the nineteenth century, as it evolved into the twentieth, would be unthinkable without this contrast between Western and Middle Europe, right into the way goods were sold, marketed and produced.

* This does not refer to the British political philosophy of the same name.

This was the course of development. First, the economic and industrial life of England was made possible by her possession of India; then her whole economic activity was extended on the basis of the contrast between Western and Mid-European economic life. Thus, economic life is founded not on what one sees in one's immediate surroundings, but on the great reciprocal relationships in the world at large.

It was with this contrast that the world as a whole entered upon world economy... and could not enter! For the world continued to depend on that instinctive element which had evolved from the past, the existence of which I have just indicated in describing the antithesis between England and Mid-Europe. Come the twentieth century, though the world was unaware of the fact, we stood face to face with this situation. The antithesis became more and more immediate; it became deeper and deeper. We stood before this great question: The economic conditions that had evolved out of these contrasts were carrying them ever more intensely into the future, and yet, if they were to go on for ever increasing, economic intercourse would become impossible. The contrast between England and Middle Europe had created the economic life, which in turn reinforced the contrast to the point when it needed resolution. The question was how? The further course of history was destined to show that human beings were incapable of finding the answer.

It would have been practical to talk in words like these in 1914, in the days of peace. But, instead of the much needed world-historic solution, there was failure. Economically considered, such was the disease which then set in.

Of course, the possibility of all evolution always depends on contrasts. To take but one example, the fact that English economic life had been consolidated far earlier than the Mid-European, meant that the English were unable to produce certain goods as cheaply as was possible in Germany. Thus, there arose a great competition, epitomised in the slogan 'Made in Germany'. So that when the War* was over, people said: "Now that we have knocked each other's heads in, rather than resolve the contrasts, what is to be done?"

At this time I could not but believe in the possibility of finding people who would understand the contrasts which must be brought forth in another domain, if those of economic life were not to degenerate into conflict. For life depends on contrasts, and can only exist if contrasts are there, interacting with

* All references to "the War" in these lectures are to the First World War.

one another. The question is which are the right contrasts for our time? And in 1919 I sought to draw attention to the real contrasts towards which world-historic evolution is tending, namely, those that arise between the economic life, the rights life and the cultural life when these are seen as distinct but coordinated aspects of the social order as a whole.[11]

What, after all, was the actual situation when we believed that we must bring the threefold idea into as many human heads as possible? I will only describe it externally today. The most important thing would have been to bring about a consciousness of the threefold idea as soon as possible before the economic consequences ensued which afterwards took place.[12] You must remember that when the threefold social order was first mentioned, we did not yet stand face to face with the monetary difficulties of today. On the contrary, if the threefold social order had been understood at the time, these difficulties could never have occurred. Yet once again we were faced by the inability of people to understand such a thing as this in a really practical sense. When we tried to bring the threefold social order home to them, people would come and say: "Yes, all that is excellent, but surely we need first to counteract the depreciation of the currency." To which one could only answer: "That is implicit in the threefold order. Set to work with the threefold order. It is the only means of counter-acting the depreciation of the currency." People were asking how to do the very thing which the threefold social order was meant to do. They did not understand it, however often they declared that they did.

The position is now such that we can no longer speak in the same forms as we did then. Today another language is necessary; and that is what I want to give you in these present lectures.

Thus, on the one hand, we can characterise a certain period - that of the nineteenth century - in terms of world-historic economic contrasts, but we might also go still farther back to the time when human beings first began to think about "political economy", as it was then called. If you take the history of economics you will see that everything before that time took place instinctively. It was only in modern times that there arose that complexity of economic life, in the midst of which people felt it necessary to think about these things.

Since I am speaking to students of economics, trying to show the way into this subject, let me relate the most essential thing on which it all depends. The time when human beings had to begin to think about economics was just the time when they no longer had the thoughts to comprehend such a subject. They simply no longer had the requisite ideas. I will give you an example from natural science to indicate that this is so.

We as human beings have our physical bodies, which are heavy just like any other physical bodies. Your physical body will be heavier after a midday meal than before; we could even weigh the difference. That is to say, we partake in the general laws of gravity. But with this gravity, the property of all ponderable substances, we could do very little in our human body; we could at most go about the world as automatons, certainly not as conscious beings. I have often explained what is essential to any valid concept of these matters, what the human being needs in order to think. On its own the human brain weighs about 1,400 grammes. Were the weight of these 1,400 grammes to press on the veins and arteries, which are situated at the base of the skull, it would destroy and kill them. You could not live for a single moment if the human brain were pressing downward with its full 1,400 grammes. It is indeed a fortunate thing for the human being that the principle of Archimedes holds good. I mean, that every body loses as much of its weight in water as is the weight of the fluid which it displaces. If this is a heavy body, it loses as much of its weight in water as a body of water of equal size would weigh. The brain swims in the cerebro spinal fluid, and thereby loses 1,380 grammes: for such is the weight of a body of cerebro spinal fluid of the size of the human brain. The brain only presses downward on to the base of the skull with a weight of 20 grammes, and this weight it can bear. But if we now ask ourselves: What is the purpose of all this? then we must answer that with a brain which was a mere ponderable mass, we could not think. We do not think with the heavy substance, but with the bouyancy. Substance must first lose its weight. Only then can we think. We think with that which flies away from the earth.

But we are also conscious in our whole body. How do we become thus conscious? Our body contains 25 billions of red blood corpuscles. These corpuscles are very minute; nevertheless they are heavy for they contain iron. Every one of these 25 billions of red corpuscles swims in the serum of the blood, and loses weight exactly in accordance with the fluid it displaces. Once again, therefore, in every single blood corpuscle an effect of bouyancy is created - 25 billion times. Throughout our body we are conscious by virtue of this upward driving force. Thus we may say: Whatever foodstuffs we consume, they must first, to a very large extent, be divested of their weight; they must be transformed in order that they can serve us. Such is the demand of the living body. To think thus and to regard this way of thinking as essential, is the very thing human beings ceased to do just at the time when it became necessary to think economically. Thenceforward they only reckoned with ponderable substances; they no longer thought of the transformation which a substance undergoes in a living organism - as to its weight, for example, through the effect of bouyancy.

And now another thing. If you call to mind your studies of physics, you will remember the physicist speaks of the spectrum. This band of colours is created with the help of the prism: Red, orange, yellow, green, blue, indigo, violet. So far (from the red to the violet) the spectrum appears luminous. But, as you know, before the region which shows a luminous effect, what are called the infra-red rays are assumed to exist; and, beyond the violet, the ultra-violet rays. If, therefore, one speaks merely of light, one does not include the totality of the phenomena. We must go on to describe how the light is transformed in two opposite directions. We must explain how, beyond the red, light sinks into the element of warmth and, beyond the violet, into chemical effects. In both directions the light, as such, disappears. If, therefore, we give a theory of light alone, we are giving a mere extract. (The current theory of light is in any case not a true one. It is significant that in the very time when humanity had to begin to think consciously in economics, human thinking upon physics was in such a condition as to result, among other things, in an untrue theory of light.[13])

I have mentioned this matter here with some reason: For there is a valid analogy. Consider for a moment not the economy of human beings, but, let us say, the economy of sparrows or the economy of swallows. They, too, after all, have a kind of economy. But this - the economy of the animal kingdom - does not reach far up into the human kingdom. Possibly in the case of the hamster we may indeed speak of a kind of animal capitalism. But what is the essence of animal economics? It is this: Nature provides the products, and the animal as a single creature takes them for himself. The human being does indeed reach down into this animal economy, but he has to emerge from it.

The true human economy may be compared to that part of the spectrum which is visible as light. That which reaches down into nature would then be comparable with the part of the spectrum which extends into the infra-red. Here, for example, we come into the domain of agriculture, of economic geography, and so forth. The science of economics cannot be sharply defined in this direction: It reaches down into a region which must be grasped by very different methods. That on the one hand.

On the other hand - precisely because of today's very complicated relations - it has gradually come to pass that our economic thinking fails us once more in another direction. Just as light ceases to appear as light as we go into the ultra-violet, so does human economic activity cease to be purely economic. I have often characterised how this came about. The phenomenon began only in the nineteenth century. Until then, the economic life was still more or less dependent on the capability and efficiency of the individual human being. A bank prospered if some individual in it was a thoroughly capable person. Individuals were still of real importance. I have often related the amusing story of the ambassador of the King of France who came to Rothschild to raise a loan. Rothschild happened to be in conversation with a leather merchant. When the French ambassador was announced, he said: "Ask him to wait a little." The ambassador was terribly upset. Was he to wait, while a leather merchant was in there with Rothschild? When the attendant came out and told him, he simply would not believe his ears. "Go in again and tell Herr Rothschild that I am here as the ambassador of the King of France." But the attendant brought the same answer again: "Will you kindly wait a little?" Thereupon he himself burst into the inner room: "I am the ambassador of the King of France!" Rothschild answered: "Please sit down. Will you take a chair?" "Yes, but I am the ambassador of the King of France!" "Will you take two chairs!"

You see, what took place in the economic life in that time was placed consciously within the sphere of the human personality. But things have changed since then; and now, in the great affairs of economic life, very little indeed depends on the single personality. Human economic working has to a very large extent been drawn into what I am here comparing with the ultra-violet. I refer to the workings of capital as such. Accumulations of capital are active as such. Over and above the economic, there lies an ultra-economic life, which is essentially determined by the peculiar power inherent in the actual masses of capital. If, therefore we wish to understand the economic life of today, we must regard it as lying between two regions, of which the one leads downward into nature and the other upward into capital. Between them lies the domain which we must comprehend as the economic life proper.

From this you will see that human beings did not even possess the necessary concept to enable them to define the science of economics and set it in its proper place within the whole domain of knowledge. For, as we shall presently see, it is a curious thing, but this region alone (which I have compared with the infra-red) - this region which does not yet reach up into the sphere of economics properly speaking - this alone is intelligible by the human intellect. We can consider, with ordinary thinking, how to grow oats or barley and so forth; or how best to obtain the raw products in mining. That is all we can really think about with the intellect which we have grown accustomed to use in the science of modern times.

This is a fact of immense significance. Think for a moment of what I have just indicated as the concept which we need in science. We consume heavy substances as food. That they can be of use to us, depends upon the fact that they continually lose weight within us. That is to say, within the body they are totally transformed. But that is not all. They are changed in a different way in each organ; it is a different change in the liver from that in the brain or in the lung. The organism is differentiated and the conditions are different for each substance in each single organ. We have a perpetual change of quality along with the change from organ to organ.

Now, it is approximately the same when, within a given economic domain, we speak of the value of a commodity. It is nonsense to define some substance as carbon, for example, and then to ask: "How does it behave inside the human body?" The carbon, even as regards its weight, becomes something altogether different from what it is here or there in the outer world. Likewise, we cannot simply ask: "What is the value of a commodity?" The value is different depending on whether the commodity is lying in a shop, or is transported to this place or that.

Ideas in economics must be altogether mobile. We must rid ourselves of the habit of constructing concepts capable of absolute definition. We must realise that we are dealing with a living process, and must transform our concepts along with that process. But what economists have tried to do is to grasp such things as value, price, production, consumption and so forth with ideas taken from ordinary science. And these are of no use.

Fundamentally speaking, therefore, we have not yet attained a true science of economics. With the concepts to which we have grown accustomed hitherto, we cannot answer the question, for instance: "What is value?" Or, "What is price?" Whatever has value must be considered as being in perpetual circulation. Likewise we must consider the price, corresponding to a value, as something in perpetual circulation. If you simply ask: "What are the physical properties of carbon?" you will still know absolutely nothing of what goes on in the lung, for example, although carbon is also present in the lung. For its whole configuration becomes quite different in the lung. In the same way, iron, when you find it in the mine, is something altogether different from what it is in the economic process. Economics is concerned with something quite different from the mere fact that iron "is" iron. It is with these constantly changing factors that we must reckon.

Forty-five years ago, I came into a certain family. They showed me a picture. I think it had been lying up in a loft for about thirty years. So long as it lay there, and no one was there who knew any more about it than that it was the kind of thing one throws away in a corner of a loft, it had no value in the economic process. But once its value had been recognised, it was worth 30,000 gulden - quite a large sum of money in those days. What did the value depend on in this case? Purely and simply on the opinion people formed of the picture. The picture had not been removed from its place, only people had arrived at different thoughts about it. And so in no case does it depend on what a thing immediately "is". (That is, on what it is physically. - Ed.) The conceptions of economics are the very ones which you can never evolve by reference to mere external reality. You must always evolve them by reference to the economic process as a whole, and within a process everything is perpetually changing.

Therefore we must speak of the economic process of circulation before we can arrive at such things as value, price and so forth. In the economic theories of today, you will observe that they generally begin with definitions of value and price. However, the first thing needful is to describe the economic process. Only then do the things emerge with which we otherwise today begin.

Now, in the year 1919, when everything had been destroyed, one might have thought that people would realise the need to begin with something fresh. Alas, it was not the case. The small number of people who did believe that there must be a new beginning, very soon fell into the comfortable reflection: "There is nothing we can do." Meanwhile, the great calamity was taking place of the devaluation of money in the countries of Central and Eastern Europe, and with it a complete revolution in the social strata. For it goes without saying, that with each progressive devaluation of money, those who live by what I have here compared to the ultra-violet must be impoverished.

And this is happening today, far more perhaps than people are yet aware of. And it will happen, more and more completely.

Here, above all, we are directed to the idea of the social organism. For it is evident that this devaluation of money is caused by the old state frontiers and limitations interfering with the economic process. The latter must indeed be understood, but we must first gain an understanding of the social organism. Yet all economic theories - from that of Adam Smith[14] to the most modern - reckon, in the end, with small regions as if they were complete social organisms. They do not realise that, even if one is only using an analogy, the analogy must be correct. Have you ever seen an elaborate or full-grown organism - such as the human being, for instance, in this drawing - and immediately beside it a second one, and here a third, and so forth? (See Sketch 1.*) They would look quite pretty - these human organisms, sticking to one another in this way; and yet with elaborate and full-grown organisms there is no such thing. But with the separate states and countries, this is the case. Organisms require an empty space around them, empty space between them and other organisms. You could at most compare the single states with the cells of the organism. It is only the whole earth which, as a body economic, can truly be compared with an organism. This ought surely to be taken into account. It is quite obvious, ever since we had a world economy, that single states or countries can at most be compared only with cells.

The whole earth, considered as an economic organism, is the social organism.

Yet this is nowhere being taken into account. It is precisely owing to this error that the whole of economic science has grown so remote from reality. People seek to establish principles that only apply to certain individual cells. Hence, if you study French economics, you will find it differently constituted from English or German or other economics. But as economists, what we really need is an understanding of the social organism in its totality.

So much for today by way of introduction.

---

* For ease of reference, all sketches are reproduced on a pull-out flap at page 245.

2: THE ECONOMIC PROCESS
25 July 1922

In the sphere of economics the first conceptions and ideas which we need to develop cannot but be a little complicated, for the perfectly genuine reason that the economic process is a thing of perpetual movement. As the blood flows through the human being, so do goods flow by every conceivable channel through the whole economic body. We need to realise that the most important thing within the economic process is all that takes place in consequence of buying and selling. That, at least, is true of economic life today. Whatever else there may be - and we shall of course have to consider the most varied impulses contained in the economic life - the subject of economics comes home to one directly one has anything to buy or sell. In the last resort, the instinctive thinking of every naïve person on economic matters culminates in the process taking place between buyer and seller. Fundamentally, this is what it all comes to.

What is it that counts when buying and selling are considered in the economic process? It is always the price of the commodity, the price of the goods in question. All the most important economic considerations and all the impulses and forces that are at work in economics culminate at length in the question of price. We shall, therefore, have to consider the problem of price first, although it is by no means a simple one. You need only consider the most simple case: At a given place, A, we have a certain commodity. At place A it has a certain price. But suppose it is not bought there but is first transported to another place, B. Our endeavour will then be to add to the price whatever transport charges had to be paid to get it from A to B. Thus the price changes in the process of circulation. There we have the simplest - if I may put it so, the flattest - instance; but of course there are far more complex cases. Assume, for instance, that at a given date a house in a large town costs "x". Fifteen years later the same house may perhaps cost six or eight times as much. We need not imagine that the main cause of the rise in price lies in the devaluation of money. On the contrary, let us assume that this is not the case. The rise in price may simply lie in this: That in the meantime many other houses have been built around it, greatly increasing its value. Indeed, there may be ten or fifteen other circumstances accounting for the rise in price. In reality, we are never in a position to apply some general statement to the single case - to say, for instance, that the price of houses, or iron, or cereals, can be uniquely determined, at a given place, from certain specified conditions. To begin with, we can do little more than observe how price fluctuates with place and time. Then, perhaps, we can trace some of the conditions whereby at a given place a given price actually emerges. But there can be no such thing as a general definition stating how the price of a thing is composed. That is an impossibility. Again and again one is astonished to find price discussed in economics as though it were possible to define it. We simply cannot define it, for a price is always concrete and specific. In economic matters, it is altogether impossible to get anywhere near the realities by means of definitions.

I once witnessed the following case. In a certain district land is very cheap. There is a society with a more-or-less famous man in its midst. The society buys up all the cheap plots of land, and prevails upon the famous man to build himself a house there. Then the plots of land are offered for sale. They can be offered at a considerably higher price than they were bought for, for the simple reason that the famous man has been persuaded to build himself a house there. Such instances will show you how indeterminate are the conditions on which the price of a thing depends in the economic process. Of course, you may say such developments must be counter-acted. Land reformers and people with similar aims try to resist these things. Through various artificial measures they desire to establish a kind of just price for all things. Of course that can be done; but, economically considered, the price is not changed thereby. In the above example, when the plots of land are sold at a higher price, we can take the money away again, in the form of a higher property-tax. Then the State will pocket the difference; but the reality remains as before, the increase in price has taken place just the same. You can take preventative measures, but they will only obscure the issue. The price will still be what it would have been without them. You only bring about a redistribution; and it is not true economic thinking to say that the land has not increased in price during the last ten years, simply because you have obscured the matter by artificial measures.

Economic science must stand firmly on its feet, on a basis of reality. In economics we can only speak of the conditions obtaining at a given time and at the actual place to which we are referring. Needless to say, anyone who desires the progress of humanity will still come to the conclusion that such things have to be changed. But, to begin with, things must be observed in their immediate reality at the particular moment. From all this you will see how impossible it is to approach such a concept as this - the most important in economics (I mean the concept of price) - by seeking to grasp it with sharply defined notions. In the science of economics we can make no progress by this means; quite other ways must be adopted. We must first observe the economic process itself. Within this process the problem of price is of cardinal importance, however, and all our efforts must be directed to understanding it. We must observe the economic process, and try, as it were, to catch the point where the actual price of a given thing results from all the underlying economic causes.

Now if you take the ordinary economic doctrines, you will generally find three factors mentioned - three factors, through the interplay of which the whole economic process is thought to take its course. They are:- land[15], labour and capital. Certainly to begin with, tracing the economic process reveals these three factors - that which comes from land, that which is achieved by labour and that which is derived from, or directed by means of capital. But if we take land, labour and capital simply side by side in this way, we shall not grasp the economic process in a living way. On the contrary, we shall be led to many one-sided points of view - a fact to which the history of economic theory bears eloquent witness. Some say that all value is inherent in land and that no special value is added to the substance of natural objects by labour. Others believe that all true economic value is really impressed on goods[16], on commodities, by the labour which, as they sometimes say, is crystallised in the commodity. Or again, the moment you place capital and labour merely side by side, you will find people saying, on the one hand, in reality it is capital which alone makes labour possible and that the wages of labour are paid out of accumulated capital. On the other side it is said that the only thing that produces real value is labour, and that all that capital obtains for itself is the surplus value abstracted from the yield of labour.

The fact is, consider things from the one point of view, and the one is right; consider them from the other point of view, and the other is right. The reality is not unlike that of book-keeping - put the item here and this will be the result; put it there, and that will. One can speak with strong apparent reasons of surplus value, saying that this is abstracted from the wages of labour and allocated by the capitalist to himself. But one can say with equally good reasons, that, in the whole round of economic life, everything is due in the first place to the capitalist, who can only pay his workers from what he has available for the wages of labour. For both these points of view there are very good and very bad reasons. In fact, none of these ways of thinking comes near the reality of economics. Excellent as they may be as a basis for agitation, they are of no importance in a serious economic science. Quite other foundations must be found if one is to talk of progress in economics.

Up to a certain point, of course, all these systems have their justification. Adam Smith, for instance, sees the real, original value-forming factor in the labour that is expended on things. Here, too, excellent reasons can be brought forward in support of this view. Such a man as Adam Smith certainly did not think in a stupid or nonsensical way. Nevertheless, here again there is the underlying idea of taking hold of something static and giving it a definition, whereas in the real economic process things are in perpetual movement. It is comparatively simple to form concepts of the phenomena of nature - even the most complicated - as compared with the ideas which we require for a science of economics. Infinitely more complicated, variable and shifting, however, are the phenomena of economics; more fluctuating than those of nature, they are less capable of being grasped with any defined or hard-and-fast concepts. In effect, an altogether different method must be adopted. You will find this method difficult at the outset, but as a result of it - as I hope to show - you will discover the only real and possible foundation for economic science.

To begin with, we may say that three things contribute to this economic process: Land, labour and (considering, to begin with, its purely external aspect) capital. But this is only the beginning! For consider at once the middle one of these three - labour. Try to form a conception of labour by going down, as indicated yesterday, into the sphere of animal life, by observing, instead of the economy of peoples, the economy of sparrows, for example, or the economy of swallows.

Here you see at once, that land is the basis of economy. True, even the sparrow has to do a kind of work; at the very least, it has to hop about to find its food. Sometimes it has to hop about a very great deal in the course of a day to find what it requires. The swallow building its nest also has to do a kind of work, and it again has much to do to build it. Nevertheless, in the true economic sense, we cannot call this "labour". We shall make no progress in economic ideas if we do. For if we observe more closely, we shall have to admit that the sparrow and the swallow are organised precisely in order to do the very things they do, to fulfil the functions necessary to the finding of food, etc. They simply could not be healthy if they did not move about in this way.

It is part and parcel of their organisation, belonging to them, no less than their legs and wings.

In seeking to build up economic concepts, we can therefore leave out of account what we might here call "apparent labour". In such cases land is taken just as it is, and the single creature, merely to satisfy its own needs or those of its nearest kin, carries out the corresponding "semblance of labour". If, however, we wish to determine what is "value" or "a value" in the true economic sense, we must disregard this apparent labour. Thus, our first object must be to reach a real concept of economic value.

Consider the animal economy once more. There we may say:- Land alone is the value-forming factor. If we now ascend to the human being - that is, to economics proper - it is true we still have, from the side of land, the same starting point of "land value". But the moment human beings no longer provide merely for themselves or for the nearest kindred, but for one another, labour, properly so called, comes into account. Indeed, the moment a human being no longer uses nature's products for himself, but stands in some relation to other human beings - if only to the extent of bartering his goods with theirs - what he then does becomes, in relation to land, labour. Here we arrive at the one aspect of value in economics. It arises where labour is expended on land, on the products of nature, and where we have before us in economic circulation nature's products transformed by labour. It is only here that a true economic value first arises. So long as nature's products are untouched, at the place where they are found they have no other value than they have, for instance, for animals. But the moment you take the very first steps to put a product of nature into the process of economic circulation, so transformed, it begins to have economic value. We may characterise this as follows: "An economic value, seen from this one aspect, is a product of nature transformed by labour." Whether the labour consists in digging or chopping, or merely moving nature's products from one place to another, is irrelevant. If we are seeking the determination of value in general, then we must simply say: "One value-forming factor is that of labour, transforming a product of nature so as to pass it into the economic process of circulation."[17]

If you consider this, you will see at once how very fluctuating are the values of goods circulating in the economic life. For labour is something always present, perpetually being expended on goods. You cannot really say what value is, you can only say: Value appears in a given place and at a given time, inasmuch as labour is transforming some product of nature. That is where value emerges. To begin with, we cannot and will not try to define value. We simply point out the place where it appears.

I will express this diagrammatically. (See Sketch 2.) Here, on the left side of the drawing, we have land, as it were in the background. Labour approaches land. What then becomes visible - appearing, as it were, through the interplay of land and labour - is the one aspect of value. It is by no means a faulty image if we think of a black surface or of anything black which, when seen through a luminous medium, appears blue. According as the luminous medium is thick or thin, you will see various shades of blue; according as you shift it, its density will vary. It is for ever fluctuating. So it is with value in the economic life; it is really none other than the appearance of land through labour. And that, too, is always fluctuating.

To begin with, we are gaining a few abstract indications and little more; but these will give us our bearings during the next few days and help us to reach more concrete things. After all, you are accustomed to this, for in all sciences one takes what is most simple to begin with.

Labour as such has no meaning at all in economics. Someone may chop wood, or he may use an exercise bike in the hope of getting thinner. The one who pedals the bicycle may be doing just as much work as the one who chops wood. To consider labour as Marx did, when he said that we should look for its equivalent in the amount that is consumed in the human organism by the labour, is a colossal piece of nonsense. For the same amount is consumed whether one chops wood or dances about on a bicycle. What happens in the human being is not the point in economics. We have already seen how the subject of economics borders on uneconomic matters. Purely economically speaking, it is quite unjustifiable to point to the fact that labour uses up the human being's forces. I mean it is unjustifiable in this connection, where, to begin with, we wish to establish an economic concept of labour. Indirectly it is of great significance, for on the other side human needs have to be cared for. But Marx's way of thinking at this point is a colossal piece of nonsense.

So, what do we need in order to take hold of labour in the economic process? Quite apart from the human being, it is necessary, to begin with to observe how labour enters into the economic process. The labour of the person on the bicycle does not enter it at all, but simply adheres to the cyclist himself. The chopping of wood, on the other hand, does enter the economic process. What matters is how labour enters the economic process. It does so by transforming land. Only in so far as land is transformed by labour do we create real economic values on this side. If, for instance, we find it necessary for our bodily health, having worked upon land in some way, to get some exercise, all this may of course be judged from another standpoint; but what we thus do cannot be described as labour in the economic sense, nor can it be regarded in any way as a factor creating economic values. Seen from another side, it may be creating values, but first we must get our concepts pure and clear concerning economic values as such.

Now there is a second, altogether different, possibility for economic values to arise. Turning our attention to labour as such, take labour as the starting point. To begin with, as you have seen just now, economically speaking labour is something neutral and irrelevant. But it becomes a value-creating factor the moment we let it be directed by our intelligence.[18] I must now speak in a somewhat different sense from before. Even in the most far-fetched cases, you can imagine something which would otherwise not be labour at all in the economic sense being transformed into labour by human intelligence. If it occurs to someone, in order to get thinner, to set up an exercise bicycle and practise on it, no economic value will ensue. But the moment a rope is wound round the wheel and used to drive some machine, at that moment, that which would not otherwise be labour at all in the economic sense, is turned to good account by intelligence. The person who rides the cycle will get thinner just the same, but the essential point is that through intelligence labour is given a particular direction and the various units of labour are brought into certain mutual relations.

This is the second aspect of value-formation in economics. (See Sketch 2, right-hand side.) In this case, labour stands in the background, and before it is intelligence which directs labour. Labour shines through intelligence, and in this way also creates an economic value.

As you will soon see, these two aspects are present everywhere as the two essential poles of the economic process. There are indeed no other ways in which economic values are created. Either land is modified by labour, or labour is modified by intelligence. The outer expression of intelligence, in this connection, is in the manifold formations of capital. Economically, intelligence must be looked for in the configurations of capital. These at any rate are its outward expression. We shall realise such things more clearly when we come to consider capital as such, and then capital in its monetary sense.

So you see, there can be no question of arriving at a definition of economic value. Once more, you need only consider on how many circumstances - on the cleverness or stupidity of how many different people - the modification of labour by intelligence in any given instance will depend. There is every kind of fluctuating condition, but one fact will always be in evidence: The value-creating factors in the economic process will always be found at these two opposite poles.

Suppose now that we find ourselves at any given point within the economic process. The economic process takes its course in the activity of buying and selling, essentially, that is, in the exchanging of values. There is, in fact, no other exchange than that of values. Properly speaking, it is incorrect to speak of an exchange of goods. The "goods" that play a part in the economic process - whether they appear as modified products of nature or modified labour - are always values. It is always an exchange of values. Wherever a process of buying and selling takes place, values are exchanged.

Now what is it that emerges in the economic process when value and value, at it were, impinge on one another in the process of exchange? It is price. For this reason you cannot think truly about price if you have in mind the exchange of mere goods. If you buy an apple for a penny, you may say that you are exchanging one good for another - an apple for a penny. But you will make no progress in economic thinking along these lines. For the apple has been picked somewhere and then transported, and it may well be that various other things have been done around it, all of which represents its modification by labour. What you are dealing with is not an apple but a product of nature transformed by labour, that is, an economic value. In economics we must always take our start from values. Similarly, the penny does not represent a good, but a value; for after all the penny is but a sign that there is present, in the one who has to buy the apple, another value which he exchanges for it.

Today I am anxious for you to get a clear insight into this fact: In economics we must speak of values, not goods, as the elementary thing. It is wrong to try to consider price in any other way than by envisaging the interplay of values. Value set against value gives you price. And if, as we saw, value itself is a fluctuating thing, incapable of definition, may we not then say that when you exchange value for value, price which arises in the process of exchange is a fluctuating thing raised to the second power?

From all this you may see how futile it is to try to take hold of values and prices with the idea of finding a firm and fixed ground in economics. It is still more futile, if your object is to influence the economic process in practice. Something altogether different is needed - something that lies behind all these things.

Simply consider for a moment: Land appears to us through labour. Suppose we obtain iron at a given place under extraordinarily difficult conditions. The value that is thus produced through labour is elaborated land. If at a different place iron is produced under far easier conditions, it may happen that an altogether different value will result. You see, therefore, that we cannot grasp the reality in the value itself, we must go behind the value. We must go back to that which creates it. Here alone can we gradually find our way to the more constant conditions on which we can exercise a direct influence. The moment you have brought the value into economic circulation, you must let it fluctuate with the economic organism as a whole. Consider the finer constitution of a blood corpuscle: It is different in the head and in the heart and in the liver. You cannot say: We will now seek the true definition of blood. The most you can do is to consider what are the more favourable foodstuffs in the one case and in the other. Likewise there is no point in talking round and round about value and price. The important thing is to go back to the primary factors, back to that which, if rightly formed, will actually bring forth the proper price. The proper price will then emerge of its own accord.

In the study of economics it is quite impossible to stop short at definitions of value and price. We must always go back to the real origins whence the economic process is nourished, on the one hand, and by which, on the other, it is regulated - land, on the one hand; intelligence on the other.

In all economic theories of modern times, this has been the difficulty: They always set out to try to hold fast that which is really fluctuating. It is not that one is confronted with wrong definitions thereby; scarcely any of them are wrong. (Although it is an exceedingly bad shot to say that the amount of labour corresponds to that which has been expended and has to be restored in the human body, to the expenditure, therefore, of substance. Such a statement really is a howler, and he who makes it has failed to see the simplest things.) No, the point is that even people of considerable insight, in developing their theory of economics, have stumbled again and again over this obstacle: They have tried to observe at rest things that are always in a state of flux. In observing nature one can and often must proceed in this way.

There, however, it suffices to observe the state of rest in a quite different way; and if we have to observe a state of movement, all we have come to do in today's natural science is to regard it as though it were composed of a multitude of tiny states of rest and jump from one to the other. We thus regard even movement as if it were composed of states of rest.

The economic process cannot be studied on the model of such a science. This, therefore, must be said: To grasp economics we must first consider how, on the one hand, value appears as land transformed by labour - land seen through labour - while, on the other hand, it appears as labour seen through intelligence. These two origins of value are real polar opposites: they differ as, in the spectrum, the one - the luminous or yellow pole - differs from the other - the blue or violet. You may well hold fast this picture: Just as in the spectrum the warm colours appear on the one side, so on one side of the economic process there appears the land-value which will show itself more in the formation of rents[19] - the side of land transformed by labour. On the other side there appears instead those values which are translated into capital. Labour transformed by intelligence. Then, indeed, price can arise, inasmuch as values of the one pole impinge on values of the other. Or again, the several values within the one pole come into mutual interaction. The point is that every time, wherever it is a question of price-formation, there will be a mutual interaction of value and value. We must therefore disregard everything to do with the substances and materials themselves; we must look away from all this and begin by seeing how values are formed on the one side and on the other. Then we shall be able to press forward to the problem of price.

3: ECONOMIC SCIENCE
26 July 1922

Economic science is essentially a taking hold of something that is forever fluctuating, namely the circulation of values and the mutual interplay of changing values in the forming of price.Our first need, therefore, is to discover what the proper form of economic science is. For a thing that fluctuates cannot be taken hold of by direct observation. The only sensible procedure is to consider it in connection with what really lies beneath it.

Take the example of a thermometer. We use it to read the degrees of temperature, which we have grown used to comparing with one another. We estimate 20° of warmth in relation to 5° and so on. We may also construct temperature curves, plotting the temperatures during the winter, followed by the rising temperatures of summer. Our curve will then represent the fluctuating level of the thermometer. But we do not come to the underlying reality until we consider the various conditions which determine the lower temperature in the winter, the higher temperature in the summer months, the temperature in one district, the different temperature in another, and so forth. We only have something real in hand when we refer the varying levels of the mercury to that which underlies them. To record the readings of the thermometer is in itself a mere statistical procedure.

It is not much more than this when, in economics, we merely study prices, values and so forth. It only begins to have a real meaning when we regard prices and values much as we regard the positions of the mercury - as indicators, pointing to something else. Only then do we arrive at the realities of economic life. This consideration will lead us to the true and proper form of economic science.

By ancient usage, as you are probably aware, the sciences are classified as theoretical and practical. Ethics, for instance, is called a practical science; natural science a theoretical one. Natural science deals with that which is; ethics with that which ought to be. This distinction has been made since ancient times: The sciences of that which is and the sciences of that which ought to be.

Clearly then, to arrive at any knowledge in economics we have to make observations, just as we must observe the readings of the barometer and thermometer in order to ascertain the state of air and warmth. To that extent, economics is a theoretical science. But at this point, nothing has yet been done. We only achieve something when we are really able to act under the influence of this theoretical knowledge.

Take a special case. Let us assume that by certain observations (which, like all observations, until they lead to action, will be of a theoretical nature) we ascertain that in a given domain the price of a certain commodity falls considerably, so much so as to give rise to acute distress. In the first place, then, we observe - "theoretically", as I have said - the actual fall in price. Here, so to speak, we are still only at the stage of reading the thermometer. But now the question arises: What are we to do if the price of a commodity or product falls to an undesirable extent? We shall have to go into these matters more closely later on; for the moment I will but indicate what should be done and by whom, if the price of some commodity shows a considerable decrease. There may be many such measures, but one of them will be to do something to accelerate trade in the commodity in question. This will be one possible measure, though naturally it will not be enough in itself. For the moment, however, we shall not discuss whether it is sufficient, or even the right measure to take. The point is: If prices fall in such a way, we must do something of a kind that can increase turnover.

It is in fact similar to what happens when we observe the thermometer. If we feel cold in a room, we do not go to the thermometer and try by some mysterious device to lengthen out the column of mercury. We leave the thermometer alone and stoke the fire; we get at the thing from quite a different angle; and so it must be in economics too. When it comes to action, we must start from quite a different angle. Then only does it become practical. We must answer, therefore, that the science of economics is both theoretical *and* practical, the point being how to bring the practical and the theoretical together. Here we have one aspect of the form of economic science.

To understand the other, we must go back a little way in human history. As I pointed out in the first lecture, in former times - even as recently as the 15th or 16th century - economic questions such as we have today did not exist at all. In oriental antiquity to a very large extent economic life took its course instinctively. Certain social conditions obtained - caste-forming and class-

forming conditions - and the relations between human beings which arose out
of these conditions had the power to shape instincts for the way in which the
individual must play his particular part in economic life. These things were
very largely founded on impulses of the religious life, which in those ancient
times were still of such a kind as to aim simultaneously at the ordering of
economic affairs. Study oriental history; nowhere will you find a hard-and-
fast dividing line between what is ordained for the religious life and what is
ordained for the economic. The religious commandments very largely extend
into the economic life. In those early times, the question of labour, or of the
social circulation of labour-values did not arise. Labour was performed in a
certain sense instinctively. In pre-Roman times, whether one man was to do
more or less never became a pressing question, not at any rate a pressing
public question. Such exceptions as there may have been are of no
importance, compared to the general course of human evolution. Even in
Plato's conception of social life, labouring is accepted as a complete matter
of course. Only those aspects are considered which Plato regards as wisdom-
filled ethical and social impulses, from which he excludes the performance
of labour.

In the course of time, however, things became more and more different. As
religious and ethical impulses became less effective in creating economic
instincts, as they became more restricted to moral life, mere precepts as to
how people should feel for one another or relate themselves to extra-human
powers, there arose more and more the feeling, expressed pictorially, that, *ex
cathedra*, nothing whatever can be said about the way a human being should
work! Only then did labour's incorporation in the social life become a
question.

The incorporation of labour in the social life is historically impossible,
however, without the rise of all that is comprised in the term "law" or "rights".
We see emerge at the same historical moment the assignment of value to
labour in relation to the individual human being and what we now call law.
Go back into very ancient times of human history and you cannot properly
speak of law or rights as we conceive them today. You can only do so from
the moment when law becomes distinct from commandment. In very ancient
times there is only one kind of commandment, that which included at the
same time all matters of rights. Subsequently, the commandment is restricted
more to the life of the soul, while law makes itself felt with respect to outer
life. This again takes place within a certain historic epoch, during which time
definite social relationships evolve. It would take us too far afield to describe

all this in detail, but it is an interesting study - especially as regards the first centuries of the Middle Ages - to see how rights relationships on the one hand, and on the other those of labour, became distinct from the religious organisations in which they had hitherto been more or less closely merged. I mean, of course, religious organisations in the wider sense of the term.

Now this change involves an important consequence. So long as religious impulses dominate humanity's entire social life, human egoism does no harm. This is a most important point for an understanding of social and economic life. The human being may be never so selfish; if there is a religious organisation (and these, be it noted, were very strict in certain regions in oriental antiquity) such that in spite of his egoism the individual is fruitfully placed in a social whole, it will do no harm. But egoism begins to play a part in society the moment human rights and labour emancipate themselves from other social impulses or social currents. Hence, during the period when labour and rights started to become emancipated, humanity unconsciously strove to come to grips with egoism, which then began to make itself felt and had in some way to be allowed for in the social life. Ultimately, this striving culminates in nothing else than modern democracy - the sense for equality, the feeling that each must have his influence in determining rights and in determining the labour which he contributes.

Moreover, simultaneously with this culmination of emancipation in regard to rights and labour, another element arises which, though it undoubtedly existed in former epochs of human evolution, had quite a different significance in those times, owing to the operation of religious impulses. In European civilisation, during the Middle Ages, this element existed only to a very limited degree, but it reached its zenith at the very time when the life of rights and labour were emancipated most of all. I mean the division of labour.

In former epochs the division of labour had no peculiar significance. It too was embraced in religious impulses. Everyone had his proper place assigned to him. But it was very different when the democratic tendency united with the tendency to division of labour - a process which only began in the last few centuries and reached its climax in the nineteenth century. Then the division of labour gained very great significance, for it entails a specific economic consequence.

Of course, we shall have to consider the causes and development of division of labour more fully. To begin with, however, if we think the division of labour abstractly to its conclusion, we must say that in the last resort it leads to this: No one uses for himself what he produces.

Economically speaking, what will this signify? Suppose there is a tailor, making clothes. Given the division of labour, he must, of course, be making them for other people. But he may say to himself: I will make clothes for others and I will also make my own clothes for myself. He will then devote a certain portion of his labour to making his own clothes, and the remainder - by far the greater portion - to making clothes for other people. Well, superficially considered, one may say: It is the most natural thing in the world, even under the division of labour, for a tailor to make his own clothes and then go on working as a tailor for his fellows. But, economically, how does the matter stand ?

Through the very fact that there is division of labour, and that we do not make all our things for ourselves but always work for others, the various products have certain values and consequently prices. Now the division of labour extends, of course, into the actual circulation of the products. Assuming, therefore, that, when traded, the tailor's products have a certain value, will those he makes for himself have the same economic value? or will they possibly be cheaper or more expensive? That is the most important question. If the tailor makes his own clothes for himself one thing will certainly be eliminated; they will not enter into the general circulation of products. Thus, what he makes for himself will not share in the cheapening due to the division of labour. It will, therefore, be dearer. Though he pays nothing for it, it will be more expensive. For on those products of his labour which he uses for himself, it is impossible for him to expend as little labour - compared to their value - as he expends on those that pass into general circulation.

This may require a little closer consideration, nevertheless it is so. What one produces for oneself does not enter into the general circulation which is founded on the division of labour. Consequently it is more expensive. Thinking the division of labour to its logical conclusion, we must say: A tailor, who is obliged to work for other people only, will tend to obtain for his products the prices which ought to be obtained. For himself, he will have to buy his clothes from another tailor, or rather, he will get them through the ordinary channels, buying them at the places where clothes are sold.

These things considered, you will realise that the division of labour tends towards this conclusion: No one any longer works for himself at all. All that he produces by his labour is passed on to others, and what he himself requires must come to him in turn from the community. Of course, you may object: If the tailor buys his suit from another tailor, it will cost him as much as if he made it for himself; the other tailor will not produce it any more cheaply nor more expensively. But if this objection were true, we should not have the division of labour - or at least the division of labour would not be complete. For it would mean that the maximum concentration of work, due to the division of labour, could not be applied to this particular product of tailoring. In effect, once we have the division of labour, it must inevitably extend into the process of circulation. It is in fact impossible for the tailor to buy from another tailor; in reality he must buy from a clothier and this will result in quite a different value. If he makes his own coat for himself, he will "buy" it from himself. If he actually buys it, he buys it from a clothier. That is the difference. If division of labour in conjunction with the process of circulation has a cheapening effect, his coat will, for that reason, cost him less at the clothier's. He cannot make it as cheaply for himself.

To begin with, let us regard this as a line of thought that will lead us to the true form of economic science. The facts themselves will, of course - all of them - have to be considered again later. Meanwhile it is absolutely true - and indeed self-evident - that the more the division of labour advances, the more it will come about that the individual always works for the rest of the community in general and never for himself. In other words, with the rise of the modern division of labour, the economic life as such depends on egoism being extirpated, root and branch. I beg you to take this remark not in an ethical but in a purely economic sense! Economically speaking, egoism is impossible. I can no longer do anything for myself; the more the division of labour advances, the more must I do everything for others. The summons to altruism has, in fact, come far more quickly through purely outward circumstances in the economic sphere than it has been answered on the ethical and religious side. This is illustrated by an easily accessible historical fact.

The word "egoism", you will find, is a pretty old one, though not perhaps in the severe meaning we attach to it today. But its opposite, "altruism," - to think for another - is scarcely a hundred years old.* As a word, it was coined very late. We need not dwell overmuch on this external feature, though a closer historical study would confirm the indication. But we may truly say:

* The OED attributes it to Auguste Comte in 1830.

Human thought on ethics was far from having arrived at a full appreciation of altruism at a time when the division of labour had already brought about its appreciation in the economic life. Taking it, therefore, in its purely economic aspect, we see at once the further consequences of this demand for altruism. We must find our way into the true process of modern economic life, wherein no-one has to provide for himself, but only for his fellow human beings. We must realise how by this means each individual will, in fact, be provided for in the best possible way.

This might easily be taken for a piece of idealism, but I beg you to observe once more: I am speaking neither idealistically nor ethically, but from an economic point of view. What I have just said is intended in a purely economic sense. It is neither a God, nor a moral law, nor an instinct that calls for altruism in modern economic life - altruism in work, altruism in the production of goods. It is the modern division of labour - a purely economic category - that requires it.

This is the other aspect of the form of economic science. In recent times our economic life has begun to require more of us than we are ethically, religiously, capable of achieving. This is the underlying fact of many a conflict. Study the sociology of the present day and you will find: The social conflicts are largely due to the fact that, as economic systems expanded into world economy, it became more and more needful to be altruistic, to organise the various social institutions altruistically. At the same time, in their way of thinking, human beings did not get beyond egoism and therefore kept on interfering with the course of things in a clumsy, selfish way.

We shall only arrive at the full significance of this if we observe not merely the plain and obvious fact, but the same fact in its more masked and hidden forms. Owing to this discrepancy in the mentality of present-day humanity - owing to the discrepancy between the demands of the economic life and the inadequate ethical and religious response - the following state of affairs is largely predominant in practice. To a large extent, nowadays, people are providing for themselves. That is to say, by virtue of the division of labour, our economic life is actually in contradiction to its own fundamental demand. The few who provide for themselves on the model of our tailor do not so much matter. A tailor who makes his own clothes is obviously one who mixes up with the division of labour something that does not properly belong to it. This is open and unmasked. But the same thing is present in a hidden form in modern economic life, wherever - though he by no means makes his products for himself - someone has little or nothing to do with the value or price of the products of his labour, when he simply has to contribute, as a value to the economic life, the labour of his hands. It amounts to this: Even today, every wage-earner in the ordinary sense is someone who provides for himself. He gives only so much as he wants to earn, for which reason he simply cannot be giving as much to the social organism as he might.

In effect, to provide for oneself is to work for one's earnings, to work "for a living." On the other hand, to work for others is to work out of social needs. To the extent that the demand which the division of labour involves has been fulfilled in our time, altruism is actually present, namely, work for others. But to the extent that the demand is unfulfilled, the old egoism persists. It has its roots in this - that people are still obliged to provide for themselves. But that is economic egoism! In the case of the ordinary wage-earner we generally fail to notice the fact. For we do not ask ourselves:- what is it that values are really being exchanged for in this case? The thing which the ordinary wage-earner produces has after all nothing to do with the payment for his work - absolutely nothing to do with it. The payment - the value that is assigned to his work - proceeds from altogether different factors. He, therefore, works for his earnings, works "for a living". He works to provide for himself. It is hidden, it is masked, but it is so.

Thus one of the first and most essential economic questions comes before us: How are we to eliminate working for a living from the economic process? Those who to this day are still mere wage-earners, how are they to be placed in the whole economic process, so that they work because of social needs?

Must this really be done? Assuredly it must. For if this is not done, we shall never obtain true prices but always false ones. We must seek to obtain prices and values that depend not on human beings but on the economic process itself - prices that arise out of the fluctuation of values.

The cardinal question is that of price. We must observe prices as we observe the degrees of the thermometer, and then look for the underlying conditions. And, just as to observe a thermometer we need some kind of zero point, from which we go upward and downward, so, too, do we need a kind of zero-level for prices. This does in fact arise in a perfectly natural way. Consider the agrarian economy. Here, on the one side, we have land transformed by labour. (See Sketch 2.) Thus we get the transformed products of nature, and this is one point at which values are created - *V1*. On the other side we have labour itself. It, in turn, is modified by intelligence, giving rise to the other kind of value - $V2$. Price, as already pointed out, originates through the interaction of $V1$ and $V2$.

The values on either hand - $V1$ and $V2$ - are in fact related to one another as pole to pole. We can put it as follows: If a person is working in this sphere, for example (Sketch 2, right-hand side), or mainly so - in an absolute sense it is of course impossible, but I mean mainly in this sphere - if his work is of the type that is organised by intelligence, then it will be to his interest that the products of nature should decrease in value. If on the other hand a man is working directly upon nature, it will be to his interest that the other kind of products should decrease in value. Now when this "interest"[20] becomes an effective process (and so, in fact, it does, for were it not so, the farmers would have very different prices, and *vice versa*; the actual prices on both sides are, of course, very hidden), we may be able to observe a kind of "mean price" midway between the two poles where we have two persons (there must always be two, for any economic dealings) with little interest either in land (nature) or capital (the effect of applied intelligence).

When does this arise in practice? It arises when we observe a pure trader, a pure dealer, buying from and selling to another pure dealer. Here, prices will tend towards a mean. If under normal conditions (in due course we shall have to explain this word "normal" (See Discourse 1, p. 186.).) a dealer trading in shoes buys from a dealer trading in clothes and vice versa, the prices that emerge will tend to assume the mean position. To find the mean price level, we must not refer to the interests of those producers who are on the side of land, nor of those who are on the side of capital. We must go to where dealer trades with dealer, buying and selling. It is here that the mean price will tend to arise. Whether there be one dealer more or less is immaterial.

This does not contradict what we have said before. After all, look at typical modern capitalists. Are they not all of them traders? Economically speaking, the industrialist is a trader and only incidentally a producer. Commerce has developed very largely on the side of production so that in all essentials the industrial capitalist is a trader. This is important. In actual fact, modern conditions amount to this: All that arises here (where in Sketch 2 I have written "price") rays out to the one side and to the other. On the one side you will soon recognise it if you study the typical business undertaking. We shall see how it appears on the other in the course of the next few days.

4: DIVISION OF LABOUR AND CREATION OF VALUES
27 July 1922

Yesterday I chose a somewhat crude example as an illustration. It appears that this drastic illustration has caused some of you a good deal of "brain-racking". I refer to the example of the tailor*, who, I said, works less cheaply if he makes his own suit of clothes for himself than he would if, while making clothes for other people, he bought his own from a clothier in the ordinary way. Now it is only too easy to miss the point of such a crude example. For it is quite natural to reckon that the clothier, since he must make some profit, will buy the suit of clothes from the tailor more cheaply than he will sell it. Hence it goes without saying that if the tailor buys his suit of clothes, he will pay more for it than he would if he made it for himself. He will, in fact, have to pay the clothier's profit in addition. This objection is so obvious that it is bound to occur; nevertheless I purposely chose the example because I wished to illustrate how necessary it is, for present-day economic life, to think not in terms of household economics, but in terms of the economic life as a whole. We must, in fact, reckon with all that arises from the division of labour.

You see, the important thing is not to consider how the tailor will stand directly after he has finished making the suit of clothes. True enough, if he proceeds to sell the suit to a clothier, and then buys another suit back again for himself, he will have made a loss. But that is not the point; the point is, how will he stand when he makes up his accounts after a certain lapse of time? Will he be better off if he made his own suit for himself, or if he refrained from doing so?

The effect of the division of labour is to make products cheaper in the right way. They become cheaper, through their very inclusion in the whole system of economic relationships. If we work against the division of labour, we force down the price of one particular class of products; but this depressing of prices will itself go against the main stream of the economic process. In other words, though the tailor may save something on the one particular suit, he

---

* See also Discourse 3.

will - by a very small figure to begin with - force down the price of clothes. If many tailors do the same, the effect will be multiplied. Clothes will become cheaper and the result will be that the tailor will have to supply other suits also at a lower price. It will only be a question of time before he observes in his balance-sheet how much less income he has derived from the other suits because of his depression of prices.

We must not confuse the issue by thinking in the narrow sense of household economics. I did not mean that the tailor has not a perfect right to make his own clothes for himself, or that he might not prefer to do so. Only he must not imagine that it will save him anything in the long run; on the contrary, it will be more expensive. Taking his total balance after a certain lapse of time, he will find that it is more expensive. I admit that in this crude example the effect will be comparatively slight, for the amount by which the price is forced down will only become evident after a considerable lapse of time. The tailor will have to make a large number of other suits before the very small fraction by which they are cheapened becomes effective. Nevertheless, sooner or later it will appear on his total balance-sheet. For the economic process consists in an infinite number of interdependent factors. The single phenomenon is the outcome of an untold number of factors, all of which work into one another.

To understand this, it simply will not do in economics to think - if I may put it so - so very near at hand. Such thinking will lead to disaster if you let your thoughts be guided only by what lies in the immediate neighbourhood. You must learn to envisage the social organism in its totality. And if you do so, you will also feel impelled to illustrate the facts by such extreme examples, where the effect, though it does not become apparent in a day, may make itself felt very strongly, say, in the course of a decade.

We must indeed take our start from such - if I may say so - half-absurd examples, so as to detach our thinking from familiar habits and ready it for a comprehension of wider issues. Losing its hard-and-fast outlines in the process, it then gains the power to grasp what is for ever fluctuating. We can only grasp in sharp outline that which lies close to us. However, our task is to achieve real insight, yielding mobile ideas, which never correspond to those derived from our immediate neighbourhood. I want to mention this especially today, for, while we take our start from comparatively simple matters, we shall have to realise nevertheless how the economic process is built up little by little of the most manifold factors.

We must come nearer and nearer to the possibility of grasping the problem of price. With this end in view, we shall again today consider the economic process as such from a particular aspect, beginning with land. In the first place, labour must set to work on land, transforming the products of nature, giving them its stamp, and creating an economic value. In economics we are not dealing with the substance, which, as such, has no economic value. Coal, as such, lying in mines under the earth, has no economic value; nor would it have if it walked of its own accord from the mine into the hearth. What turns substance into value is the labour that has been impressed upon it, that is to say, all that had to be done to bring it to the light of day, to prepare the mines themselves, to transport the coal and so forth. It is only labour impressed upon the physical coal which gives the latter economic value. This is the proper content of economic science.

You cannot grasp any phenomenon of economic life if you do not start from such ideas as these. And now we come to the division of labour - an extension of the application of labour to land. The division of labour arises whenever people work together in any task that has significance for economic life.

Take the perfectly simple example of a certain district, in which a number of people have been doing a certain piece of work. From the various places where they live, they have walked to the common scene of their labour - to a place where some particular product of nature is exploited. Suppose we are still in a very primitive period and that there is no other means of arriving at the work-place other than on foot. But now someone conceives the idea of making a cart, and using horses to pull it. Henceforth, what formerly had to be done by each one alone will now be done in conjunction with the provider of the cart. A certain piece of work is thus now divided. It will, of course, be the case, that everyone who makes use of the cart will have to pay a certain quota to the enterprising individual who provided it.

The inventor of the cart, however, thereby enters the category of capitalist. For him, the cart is now genuine capital. Wherever you look, you will always see that this is so: Capital always originates in the division of labour.[21] But now, how was the cart invented? It was invented through intelligence. Indeed, every such process consists in the application of intelligence to labour. In one respect or another, labour is permeated by intelligence. It is this that arises through the division of labour, giving rise to capital. The first phase of capital always consists in labour, hitherto applied to land, becoming modified by intelligence.

It is indeed necessary to see the formation of capital very clearly from this point of view. Only then can we understand the function of capital in the economic process. The forming of capital is always a concomitant of the division - that is to say, the sharing by division - of labour.

In this process something of the direct, immediate intercourse, which the human being has in relation to land, is always loosened. So long as economic life merely consists in the exploitation of nature, we are concerned only with the creation of value by the elaboration of land by labour. But the moment human intelligence organises labour - organises, that is to say, labour as such (for, after all, to the person who creates capital in the shape of his cart, it will matter nothing to what end or for what purpose he transports people from one place to another) - an emancipation from land begins to take place.

Here (Sketch 2, left-hand side), we still see land shining through labour at all points. Although the value is constituted not by the coal as a substance but by the labour which is stamped upon it, nevertheless the product of nature still shines through the labour. This is one side from which economic values originate.

The other side is this. Whatever of labour is organised by intelligence emancipates itself from land, is lifted away from land, until at length we have the capitalist, to whom the relation of the labour which he organises to land may be a matter of complete indifference. This may happen in a very simple way. Suppose the person who has hitherto been driving people from many places, say, to do agricultural work in the fields, suddenly prefers to take the cart away and drive people to quite a different place and quite another kind of work. Wherever intelligence is applied, you will inevitably find the organised division of labour becoming emancipated from land. Here, then, you have the emancipation of capital from land - the foundation of economic life.

From various points of view, the idea has been expressed in economics that capital is stored-up labour-power. But this is no more than a definition, which will only fit the facts at a certain stage, because things are always fluctuating. So long as the organisation due to intelligence is narrowly bound to a certain kind of labour, land will still shine through. But the moment we emancipate ourselves, thinking only of how to make fruitful what we gain by application of intelligence - the moment we do this, the more we shall observe the labour becoming indistinct within the total mass of capital. In its peculiar and specific character, labour vanishes.

Suppose you have been amassing capital for a considerable time and that it continues to work in the economic process. The person who, to begin with, had only a single cart can extend his economic activity by acquiring a second cart, and so on. His capital is working in the economic process; but there is really nothing left in it of the nature of the labour. In a miner, for example, you still see very much of the nature of labour. But in capital you see less and less of it. Moreover, suppose the owner of the cart hands the whole business over to someone else: This will very likely mean that the newcomer will only be concerned in fructifying what has thus been brought about by intelligence. The nature of the labour thus organised will be a matter of indifference to him. He is only concerned in organising labour, no matter what its kind.

In other words, we have here a real process of abstraction. Precisely the same thing that we do inwardly in our abstract logical thinking, is here accomplished outwardly. The specific quality disappears. The specific qualities, both of the physical substance of land and of the different kinds of labour, gradually disappear in the masses of capital. And, as you will presently see, if we follow the economic process still farther, nothing whatever is left of the labour which was originally organised. The further development of the economic process will be somewhat as follows: The maker of the cart did at least stamp his own being upon the whole invention; but now he earns more values than he can manage by himself. Are these values to remain unused in the whole economic life? Of course not. Someone else must come along, able to manage them by means of a different application of intelligence. He will then turn the values to good account - make them valuable - in quite a different way.

After a time, for instance, the values created by the inventor of the cart - the fructification which has thus resulted - may pass over to a skilled smith. The smith has the intelligence to erect a workshop; but with his intelligence alone he can do nothing. The other person has already created certain economic values; these he must now transfer to the smith. Here you have indeed, in the outer world of reality, the completest imaginable process of abstraction. Moreover, it is essential if the thing is to go on at all (for how else could the cartwright transmit his values to the smith?) for something to be there which is related as an abstract element to all the specific elements contained in the economic process. What is this something? It is, of course, in the first place, money. Money is nothing but the externally expressed value which is gained in the economic process through the division of labour and transmitted from one person to another.

Thus, capitalism arises in the process of the division of labour, and in the process of capitalism (already at an early stage) the financial system, money economics. In relation to all the particular economic processes, money is completely abstract. If you have five pounds in your pocket, you can buy a midday meal for it just as well as an article of clothing. To the money itself it is irrelevant what you do, or what it is exchanged for in the economic process. Money is something absolutely indifferent to the single factors in the economic life, in so far as they are still influenced by land. For this very reason money becomes the means of expression, the instrument, the medium for intelligence to enter into the economic organism in the division of labour. Without money, it is absolutely impossible for intelligence to enter in and play its part in the economic organism which depends on the division of labour. We may say then:- What in a primitive economic condition is originally all together - what every single human being in his egoism does for himself - is now divided up among the whole community. Such is the division of labour, and in capital the single parts are gathered up again into a total process. The forming of capital is essentially a synthesis. And now the person who first emerges as a creator of capital, being able to change it into money capital (since money must necessarily appear at this stage), becomes a creditor[22] to another person, who possesses nothing but his intelligence. The latter now receives the money, which is the true and proper representative of economic values created by intelligence.

We must really consider this from the point of view of pure economics. However bad money may be from a religious or ethical point of view, in the economic sense money is very definitely intelligence at work in the economic organism. Once more then: Money must be created in the economic process, if intellgence is to progress at all from the initial point where it applies itself merely to land. Intelligence would remain in an altogether primitive condition if it could do no more than this. To pour back again into the economic process what has been gained by its application, intelligence must be realised as money. Money is intelligence realised. In this way, its concrete quality comes back immediately. In the first place, money is something abstract, for, as we said before, to the money it is a matter of indifference whether, for the £5 in my pocket, I buy an article of clothing or get my hair cut. But the moment money returns to the individual human being, i.e. to the individuality in him, it becomes economically active once more as a concrete and specific fact. For intelligence is economically active in money.

At this point a very special relationship arises. He who acquired the money to begin with becomes the creditor. The other, who receives the money - the one, we will suppose, who only has intelligence - becomes the debtor. You have here a relationship between two human beings. The same relationship will also come about if the creditors are a whole number of people who hand over their superfluous capital to an individual, so that a higher synthesis is brought about by his intelligence. He is then the debtor, and works on a foundation entirely emancipated from land. For what he actually receives from the original capitalists themselves is, in his hands, a nonentity. He will have to give it back again after a time - it does not really belong to him. Actually, it is only from one side that he works economically as a debtor; from the other side he is economically responsible as a creative individual. Truth to tell, and of special importance in relation to the social question, this is perhaps one of the healthiest relationships - that of one whose activity is freed[23] being enabled to work for the community by the community giving him the necessary money (so far as he is concerned, it is the community). How property, possession and the like enter into the matter is a question we shall have to consider another time; our present object is only to trace the econonic process as such. And here it is a matter of indifference whether or not you conceive the creditor as the real owner and whether or not you conceive the debtor as jurisprudence does. For the moment, we are only concerned with this question: How does the economic process take its course?

Here then we have a part of the economic process where the work is founded purely on what applied intelligence has already been able to achieve and acquire. That is to say, the very foundation of the work is already emancipated from land. True, it originated in the organisation of labour; but we are now at a second stage, and if at this second stage - where freed activity works through debt - you were still to describe the capital thus used as "crystallised labour" or the like, you would be talking - economically - sheer nonsense. It is immaterial to the economic process how the capital thus owed originated. The important thing now is: What is the intelligence of the person who receives the money? Will he be able to lead it over into fruitful economic processes? The original labour through which the capital arose no longer has an economic value. The intelligence applied in turning the money to good account (giving it value) - this alone will have economic value at this stage.

For, however much labour you conceive as being stored up in capital, if a fool gets hold of it and scatters it all to the winds, it is an altogether different thing than if a clever person gets hold of it and starts a fruitful economic process with it.

At this second stage, therefore, we have to do with creditor and debtor, and with capital from which labour has already disappeared. What then is the economic significance of this 'capital from which labour has disappeared'? It is twofold: In the first place, it has been possible to raise and collect the capital for lending purposes, and in the second place the capital thus raised can be given value through intelligent use. Therein lies its true economic significance.

The reality which emerges from the process is the relation between the debtor and his creditors. In the economic process to which he now gives rise, the debtor stands in the middle. On the one hand, we have him as a debtor; on the other hand, we have that which proceeds from him as an intelligent and resourceful person. With this transfer[24] capital passes over into the second stage of the economic process.

This is simply the circulation of capital - nothing else. But this circulation is part and parcel of a social organic activity, just as you have the blood in a human or animal organic activity, when it flows through the head and is used for what the head produces. I may put it in this way: What is it that is brought about through this relationship of creditors and debtors? It is something very similar to the "difference of level" we meet with in physics. If you have water up here it will flow down there, simply through the difference of level. In like manner, there is a social difference of level between the first position of capital and the second - the position of the creditor who does not know what to do with it, and the position of the debtor who can make good use of it. This difference works as a difference of level.

But you must pause a moment to consider: What is the active driving force in this difference of level? The active principle is not simply the intelligence which is at work in the whole process: It is the diversity of human talents and dispositions. That is the determining factor in the difference of level. If a dullard possesses capital, then, in a healthy economic organisation, he will be up here, while the clever person will be down there. The result is a "drop", or difference of level and the capital flows downward to the clever person.[25] It is through the difference of level between the talents of individuals that capital is brought into flow. It is not even the positive activity of human beings; it is simply the human qualities of those who, united together in the social organism, produce this "difference of level" and, in doing so, carry the economic process forward.

Look at this economic process quite concretely, and you will say: We start from land, which has as yet no value. Clearly it has no value, for the sparrow, satisfying its needs from nature, pays nothing for it. This is evident from the contrast of sparrow economics and economics proper. Economic value begins where labour unites itself with land. Next, the economic process is continued through the division, the differentiation of labour. Let us take it to begin with in an absolutely general way: Labour applied to land. I will put it down as follows (though the full economic meaning of this will only emerge in the further course of these lectures). Let us designate what arises at this stage by Lw (using "w" (work) to symbolise labour) - 'land taken hold of by labour'. What is it, economically speaking? It is, as we have already seen, a value - 'land taken hold of by labour, and thus made into a value.' LwV. That is one side.

Now comes the division of labour signifying a dividing-up of those processes which were performed in the first place as single completed labour-processes applied to land and which now live a separate life. If I make a whole stove, I shall be performing many, varied labour-processes; if I now introduce division of labour, I peel and part the labour-processes one from another. I divide. If LwV is 'land transformed by labour and made into a value', then what arises by the division of labour (of course, we might denote it in many different ways) will be $LwV1$, $LwV2$, and so on.

Now if all this is a real process, how shall we express what happens when the division of labour makes its appearance? Clearly, by a division, by a fraction. When the value which I have here written down passes over into the division of labour, the thing that is there in the reality must in some way be divided. The only question is: By what? What is the dividing principle? What is it that divides up the process? Well, we must now look to the other side. In pure mathematics we only have to take what is given as number; but when we are to seek such arithmetical processes in the world of reality itself, we must look for the real divisor, the real dividing principle. Now we found, on the other side of the picture, 'labour taken hold of by intelligence'. Over against LwV we may, therefore, place labour taken hold of by intelligence. This becomes a value on the other side: LiV. But we have today reached a certain conclusion concerning this 'labour taken hold of by intelligence'. We have seen what must arise if it is to work on beyond a certain point in the economic process, and if this (LwV) is divided and is to work on in the economic process - we have seen what enters the process for this LiV (labour organised by intelligence and made into a value): It is money.

$$\frac{LwV}{LiV}$$

But money appears at this point not in its fully abstract nature; it is abstract, to begin with, if I may put it so - abstract as the substance to which intelligence first applies itself - but it grows highly individualised, highly specific, when intelligence takes hold of it and uses it for this or that purpose. In this sense, it is intelligence as such which determines the value of money. Here, you see, money begins to gain a concrete and specific value. For whether one is a fool and throws money away on a thing that turns out unfruitful, or whether one applies it in a useful way, this now emerges as a very real value in the economic process. For your denominator, therefore, you will here get something that has to do with money; while your numerator, I need hardly say, will have to do with the fact that you have before you that into which the substance of land has been transformed. What is the substance of land, transformed by labour and present in the economic process? It is a *commodity*. This, then, is the numerator; and for the denominator, corresponding to "labour organised by intelligence", you will have money - thus:

$$\frac{LwV \; = \; \text{Commodity}}{LiV \; = \; \text{Money}}$$

New values come to light: "commodity-value" and "money-value". In the economic process founded on the division of labour, we must recognise this truth: The quotient of the total commodities present in the economic organism and the money present in the economic organism (taking as "money", not what is reckoned up in the cash-books, but what is actually taken hold of by the intelligence of human beings) will represent a real inter-action. Money is the divisor. This interaction, which cannot be represented by a subtraction but only by a division, represents the real health of the economic process:

$$\text{Economic health} = \frac{LwV = \text{Commodity}}{LiV = \text{Money}}$$

To understand wherein this health consists, we must learn to understand what is at work in the numerator here and in the denominator. We must understand more and more wherein the essential nature of a commodity, on the one hand, and of the medium of circulation, money, on the other hand, consists. The most essential economic question cannot be solved at all unless we proceed in this exact way. But we must not forget that whatever appears in the economic life will always be fluctuating. Thus the moment the commodity is taken from one place to another, the numerator here will change. Indeed, I can do no other than point out at every turn, how fluctuating all things are in the economic process. There is a great difference between the purse I have in my pocket which contains £5, and the purse someone else has, also containing £5. It is not a matter of indifference whether the £5 are in the one pocket or the other. This too must be taken as a thing that belongs to the real economic process. Otherwise you will only get a few rigid, abstract, arbitrary concepts of price, value, commodity, production, consumption and so on; you will get nothing to lead you to a true understanding of the economic process.

This is the infinitely sad thing in the present day. For many centuries humanity has grown accustomed to sharply outlined concepts, such as are inapplicable to a living process. Today we are called upon by the facts of life to get movement into our concepts, so as to penetrate the economic processes with conscious understanding. We must attain such mobility of thinking as enables us to think a process through to its end quite inwardly.

True, in ordinary science we also contemplate processes, we "think them through", if you will; but we always see them from outside and that is of no avail in economics. To contemplate the economic process as the chemist contemplates his processes, from outside, you would have to go far up above the earth in a balloon.[26] The economic processes are distinguished by the fact that we ourselves are within them; therefore we must see them from within. We must feel ourselves inside the economic processes, just as a being would do who was inside the chemist's retort where, with a great generation of heat, something is being concocted. The being in the retort, whom I am now comparing with ourselves, cannot of course be the chemist. It would have to be a creature taking part in the heat, boiling with it, as it were. The chemist cannot do this; to him the whole thing is external. In natural science, we stand outside the process. The chemist could not take part in it, with the temperature in the retort far above boiling-point.

But the economic process is different; we ourselves partake in it inwardly at every point. Hence, too, we must inwardly understand it. A mathematician may well object: You have written something like a formula, but we are not used to building up our mathematical formulae in this way. True enough; for as a rule we only build up a mathematical formula as a result of contemplating natural processes from without. We must evolve a faculty of insight to get a numerator and denominator in this way, or to understand that it must be something like a division - that it cannot be a subtraction in this case. We must try to think our way into the economic process. For this very reason I chose that crude example yesterday. I did not introduce to you a tailor and a clothier from outside, as a natural scientist would. The essential could not have been found in that way. But with our thinking accustomed to see things only as the natural scientist does from outside, we feel it strange to get inside a thing. Nevertheless, we must conceive inwardly the countless processes that intervene between the tailor and the effects which follow in the economic process.

I should not be true to the task you have set me if I described these things in any different manner. I am well aware that it makes it somewhat difficult at the outset.

5: THE PRODUCTION AND CONSUMPTION OF VALUES

28 July 1922

We are now going to pursue a little further the sequence of events within the economic process which we considered yesterday. The economic process, as we have seen, is set in motion by labour working upon land, so that from the mere raw material - which has as yet no value in the economic process - we get the product of nature transformed by labour. At the next stage, labour is, as it were, caught up by capital, which divides and organises it, until it eventually disappears in capital. To continue the economic process, therefore, capital itself must labour, that is, work economically. But this labouring of capital is not labour in the old sense; rather the capital is taken up by a purely invisible activity. The economic process now goes forward by intelligence "making good" capital, giving it additional value, as I described in the last lecture.

We must try to understand more and more the formula which was indicated yesterday. To this end, let me now describe diagrammatically - symbolically, as it were - what I explained yesterday. We may say: Land goes under in labour (i, Sketch 3). We have therefore this stream from land into labour. Labour continues to evolve. Then the values evolved stream onward, as it were, until labour vanishes in capital (ii). You can easily continue it for yourselves. The cycle must necessarily be completed in some way. Capital cannot merely be blocked at this point (iii), for otherwise we should be dealing, not with an organic process, but with one that would come to an end in capital. Capital must disappear once more into land (iv). But you must first call to your aid another idea if you wish to understand this rightly.

Consider for a moment the economic process as we have traced it up to the present. First, the elaboration of land by labour, then the organising of labour by intelligence and with it the rise of capital - for capital is a concomitant of the organising of labour by intelligence. Then the existence of capital as such, capital become independent. Labour disappears in its turn, and now intelligence works in capital as inventiveness in connection with the whole social life. The technical aspect of invention need not concern us here; this will only come into question at a later stage.

If you now review all that I have described to you, you will see that I have presented everything from one side only. This was inevitable for, apart from the odd hint, I have been speaking only of production. I have included occasional ideas to do with consumption, especially when touching on the question of price, but otherwise practically nothing else in our discussions so far. I have been speaking of production; and yet, of course, the economic process does not merely consist of production, but also of consumption.

A simple reflection will show you that consumption is exactly the opposite pole to production. We have been endeavouring to trace the values that arise in the economic process within the sphere of production. Consumption, on the other hand, consists in a perpetual elimination of these values, thus fulfilling the other important part of the economic process - the constant devaluation of values. Indeed it is just through this fact that we have a certain right to call the economic process an organic one, an organic process into which intelligence inserts itself. For it is of the essence of a living organism that something is continually being formed and then unformed. In any organism there must be a continual production and consumption, and this must be so in the economic organism too. There must be a constant producing and a constant using-up of what is produced.

At this point we begin to see in a different light, and from a different point of view, the value-creating forces which we have been considering. Hitherto we have only shown how values arise as the process of production takes its course. But now, every time a value approaches its moment of devaluation, the whole movement which we have been witnessing hitherto will change. So far, we have been observing a progressive, forward movement - values arising through the application of labour to land; values arising through the application of intelligence to labour; values arising through the application of intelligence to capital. All this is a forward movement.

In fact, we have been observing the value-creating movement in the economic process. But since the devaluing factor of consumption enters into the process at every point, there will be something else as well. There will be that development of values which arises as between production and consumption themselves. When a value enters the process of consumption it no longer moves forward. It does not attain a higher degree of value; it no

longer moves, for something now stands over against it. This is consumption
- the development of a need. Here the value enters into a very different sphere
from that which we have hitherto been studying. Having considered value in
its progressive, forward movement (Sketch 3), we must now imagine it
reaching a certain point and there being arrested. Every time a value is
arrested, there arises, not a further *value-creating movement*, but a *value-creating tension*.

This is the second element in the economic process, in which process there
are not only value-creating movements, but also value-creating tensions. We
can observe them most conspicuously and simply where a consumer stands
face to face with a producer or trader and in the very next moment the creation
of value comes to an end, passing over into devaluation. Here tension arises,
held in equilibrium by the human need on the other side. This tension is
comparable to a force that is arrested and held in balance, rather than to a force
that is working itself out. There is here a true analogy with the contrast in
physics between kinetic and potential energies - between kinetic energies and
those energies of position where an equilibrium is brought about. If you
overlook these energies of tension in the economic process, you will be
driven to the strangest of misconceptions. On the other hand, ideas such as
those indicated here, lead to an intelligent conception of every economic
relationship, without which we are led into the greatest confusion. If, for
example, you limit yourself to considering only moving economic energies,
you will never understand why the diamond in the Crown of England has
such immense value. For here you are at once obliged to have recourse to the
idea of economic tension-value. Many economists take into account the
rarity of particular products of nature; but we can never understand rarity as
a value-creating factor if we regard movement in the economic process as the
only creator of values. We must also learn to understand how there arises here
and there - most of all through consumption, but through other relationships
as well - what I would call the creation of value by tensions, situations,
equilibria.

Thus you see that devaluation also takes place in the economic process. As
values proceed on their way from land through labour to capital, they will be
accompanied by a continual process of devaluation. What would happen if
this corresponding devaluation could not take place? You can see this from
the diagram. To make it clear, let us consider the question of credit. To place
capital into the service of intelligence in the sense which I explained
yesterday, the one who produces by means of intelligence becomes a debtor.

It is only through his having credit that he becomes or can become a debtor. At this point in our diagram (iii) credit steps in - the thing which may be properly called "personal credit".[27] A person has credit. The credit can be expressed in figures. The capital which many others advance to him is, so to speak, his personal credit. Now, as you know, personal credit has a certain consequence, at any rate when considered within present economic conditions. Its economic effect is connected with the rate of interest.

Assume that the rate of interest is low.[28] If through my creativity in the economic process I become a debtor, that is to say, if I demand credit, I shall only have to pay a small sum for it. Having less interest to pay, I can produce my goods more cheaply. Thus I shall have a cheapening effect on the economic process. We may say, therefore: Personal credit cheapens production when the rate of interest falls. So long as capital continues to be turned to good account or made valuable by intelligent use in the economic process, it is always so. When the rate of interest goes down, creditors (i.e. personal creditors - Ed.) have more freedom of movement. They can play their part far more intensively in the economic process - more intensively, that is to say, for their fellow human beings. For if they cheapen their commodities they are playing a fruitful part in the process - at any rate from the point of view of the consumer.

But now let us take the other side. Assume that credit is given on land, real credit.[29] Then the situation is essentially different. Assume that the rate of interest is 5%. Capitalising this, you will get the capital corresponding to the particular piece of land - that is to say, you will get the amount which would have to be paid to buy the piece of land outright. Assume now that the rate of interest falls to 4%. More capital can then be "credited into" the land - this at any rate is what actually happens.[30] Thus we see everywhere, a fall in the rate of interest, makes land more expensive. When the standard rate of interest goes down, land does not become cheaper but dearer. "Real credit" makes things more expensive, while "personal credit" makes things cheaper. That is to say, real credit makes land more expensive while personal credit makes commodities cheaper. This is of great consequence in the economic process, because when capital returns to land and simply unites with it in the form of real credit, then the economic process will tend more and more in the direction of dearness.

Thus, the only sensible thing will be for capital at this point (iii, Sketch 3.) not to preserve itself in land, but rather to vanish into land. How then can capital vanish into land? So long as it is at all possible to unite capital with land - that is to say, so long as you can make land in its original unelaborated condition more and more expensive through the accumulation of capital - so long as this is possible, capital cannot vanish into land. On the contrary, it penetrates into land and maintains itself there. Thus, in all countries where the law of mortgage makes it possible for capital to unite with land, we shall find a congestion of capital in land. Instead of the capital being expended at this point (iv) - instead of its disappearing, instead of a value-creating tension arising - there is a further value-creating movement, which is harmful to the economic process. There is only one way of preventing this. In a healthy economic process we must not and cannot give "real credit" - credit based on the security of land - not even to a person working on the land. He, too, should only receive personal credit - that is to say, credit which will enable him to turn capital to good account through the land. If we simply unite land with capital, capital will become congested the moment it arrives again at land. If on the other hand we unite it with the intelligence of those who have to administer the land and further the economic process by working upon it, then, you see, capital vanishes. As it reaches land, it will not become congested; it will not be preserved, but will go right on through land, back again into labour, to begin the cycle once more.

At this juncture you may, of course, make a serious objection. In the course of this movement, you may say, capital has come into being. Suppose it now arrives again at land and there is too much of it. (It would be different if we were able to lead it over into labour - if we were able, let us say, to invent new methods so as to improve the exploitation of raw materials. For in such a case we should be uniting not land but labour with capital. If we arrive at this point with our capital and extract or make use of raw materials in a more economical way, for example, or open up new sources, then we are leading capital directly over into labour.) But suppose there is too much capital.[31] The several owners of capital will become painfully aware of the fact; they will not be able to start anything with their capital. This is indeed the case if you look into the matter historically. In actual fact, too much capital did arise, and the only way out which it could find was to conserve itself in land. Thus, we witnessed in the economic process the so-called rise in the value of land.

But, consider the matter in our present, larger context. Land reformers always describe these things in an inadequate way, so that the thing cannot be understood. Consider it in a larger context and you will say: If I unite capital with land, the value of land will of course be enhanced. The more a thing is mortgaged, the more will eventually have to be paid for it. The value is constantly increased. But is this increase in the value of land a reality? Certainly not. By nature, land can never increase in value. Its value can at most be enhanced by its being worked upon in a more rational and scientific way, but in that case it is labour that increases the value. But to imagine land itself, the land as such, increased in value is absurd. It is absolute nonsense. If you do improve the quality of land, you only do so by working upon it. In so far as it is mere nature, land can have no value at all. All you can do is to give it a fictitious value by uniting capital with it. Therefore, what is called the value of land in the sense of present-day economics is in truth none other than capital fixed in land. And this is not a real value but an apparent one - a semblance of a value. That is the point.[32]

In the economic process it is high time that we learnt to understand the difference between real values and apparent values. You see, if you have an error in your system of thought you do not observe its full effect to begin with. For, however many disturbing processes in the organism are in fact connected with the error in thought, the connection is only recognisable if our science expands to include the intangible, but without losing the discipline that observation of the natural world schools us in. The connection escapes the crude natural science of today.[33] People are unaware, for instance, how digestive and similar troubles in our peripheral organs arise as a result of such errors. But in the economic process it is precisely errors and semblances that have obvious effects, which grow real and have real consequences. Economically speaking, it makes no essential difference whether, for example, I issue money which has no foundation in reality but represents a mere increase in the amount of paper money, or whether I assign capital value to land. In both cases I am creating fictitious values. By inflating the currency I increase the prices of things numerically, but in the reality of the economic process I effect absolutely nothing except a redistribution, which may do immense harm to individuals. In like manner, capitalising land harms those involved in the economic process.

It would make a very interesting study to compare, for example, the mortgage laws existing before the War in the Mid-European countries with the English mortgage laws. In the Mid-European countries it was possible to screw the so-called value of land up and up without limit. The law itself made this possible. While in England on the other hand it is true to say, in a certain sense, that this is not so. Compare the effect on the economic process in the one case and in the other. This would make an interesting subject for a dissertation, to compare statistically the working of the English mortgage laws with those of Germany.

I have thus illustrated the essential point in our present context. At this point (v), land simply must not be allowed to tend towards a conservation of capital. Capital must be allowed to work on, unhindered, into labour. But what is to happen if more capital arrives at land than we are able to make use of? The only way to prevent such excess is to see that it is used up along this path (iv), so that in the last resort only so much of it is left at this point (v) as can enter once more into the work to be done upon the land. That is to say, only so much of it is left as is required for this work. The essential and obvious thing is that capital should be used up, consumed along this path. Indeed - assuming for a moment for the sake of hypothesis that it could be so - it would be a most appalling thing if nothing were consumed along this whole path. We should have to take the products with us. The process only becomes organic through the fact that things are used up. Just as the products of nature, transformed by labour, get used up, just as labour which has been organised by capital gets used up, so in its further path capital itself simply must be used up, properly used up. This is something which positively must be brought about.

It can only be brought about, however, if the whole economic process from beginning to end - right up to its return to land - is ordered rightly. There must be something there like the "self-regulator" in the human organism. The human organism, at any rate when it is functioning normally, manages to prevent promiscuous deposits of unused foodstuffs. And if unused foodstuffs are deposited here or there, we are ill. Suppose, for instance, that in the process of digestion in the head, substances are deposited, that is to say, an irregular digestive process arises in the head. The substances are no longer carried away; their consumption is not properly regulated. Then we get migraine conditions. In like manner, you will see the same principle at work in all parts of the human organism; the cause of morbid symptoms lies in the inadequate absorption and removal of what has to be digested. It is just the same in the social organism, when that which ought really to be used up at a certain point becomes accumulated. It is a matter of sheer necessity for capital to be used up along here (iv), in order that it may not unite with land and so become unliving - as if a petrified deposit in the economic process. For capitalised land is indeed an impossible deposit in the economic process.

Let me expressly state that there can be no question here of any sort of political agitation. I simply unfold these matters as they take shape naturally. We are only considering the scientific aspect. Nevertheless, a science that deals with human behaviour cannot possibly be pursued without indicating the kinds of morbid symptoms that can arise; just as we cannot study the human body without indicating its various possible morbid symptoms. There must, therefore, be a proportionate consumption of capital - certainly not a total consumption, for it is necessary that a certain amount should pass on, so that land may be worked upon once more.

This again I can make clear to you by a picture. Consider a farmer in his economic life. He must certainly try to get rid of the yield of his acres; but he must also keep sufficient seed for the next year. Seed must be preserved. This is a very apt comparison, and we may well apply it to the process we are now considering. Capital must be used up, until that alone remains which we may conceive as a kind of seed to kindle the economic process anew - once more from the starting-point of land. That alone must remain which may be necessary for a more effective use of natural resources - of raw materials, or for an improvement of the land, for example, by the creation of better manures and the like. Now in every such case labour must be applied. Thus it is that amount of capital which can work on as labour, which must be withdrawn from consumption. Before this point in the diagram is reached (v), therefore, the surplus capital which would otherwise unite with land in an inorganic way must be used up.

Here you may say: " Well, tell us how it is to be done? How is it to be brought about that only just enough capital arrives at this point for use as a seed for the future?"

In economics we stand on the ground, not of logic, but of reality. We cannot give the kind of answers which are sometimes given, for example, in the theory of ethics. In ethics we can admonish a criminal very soundly and we shall have done all that is required. But the economic process must go on, and we must speak of realities. When we spoke of production, showing how it created economic values, we were indeed speaking of realities. And that consumption is a reality, everyone is well aware. In economic science one must always be speaking of realities. Ideas by themselves have no effect in the real world. That which will rightly regulate the economic process finds expression in what I call "economic associations".[34] If you make the economic life independent;[35] if you bring together, in associations suitably composed, the human beings who are actually taking part in the economic life

- whether as producers, as traders or as consumers - then, through the economic process itself, these human beings will find it possible to arrest the formation of capital if it is too intense and to stimulate it if it is too feeble.

This of course implies a right observation of the economic process. For instance, if at any place a certain kind of commodity becomes too cheap or too dear, those concerned must be able truly to observe the fact. The mere fact in itself is not the point. But when, through experiences which can only grow out of the concerted counsels of the associations, they are able to say, as a result of such experiences: "Five units of money for so and so much salt are too little or too much, the price is too low or too high" - then and only then will they be in a position to take the necessary steps.

If the price of a commodity becomes too cheap, so that those who produce it can no longer receive sufficient remuneration for their excessively cheap services and their excessively cheap products, it will be necessary to assign fewer people to work on this particular commodity. People will therefore have to be diverted to another piece of work. If, on the other hand, a commodity becomes too dear, people will have to be led over into this branch of production. Thus the associations will always be concerned with the proper employment of people in the several branches of economic life. We must be clear on this. A real rise in the price of a given economic article indicates the necessity for an increase in the number of those who are working on this article, while an undue fall in price calls for measures to divert people from this field of labour to another. In reality, we can only speak of prices in relation to the distribution of human beings among the several branches of labour in a given social organism.

The kind of view that sometimes holds sway today, where people always have the tendency to work with notions rather than realities, is illustrated by some advocates of "free money". To them it appears quite simple. If prices anywhere are too high, so that too much money has to be spent in purchasing a certain article, they say: Let us see to it that the amount of money becomes less; then the commodities will be cheaper, and vice versa. But, if you think it through more deeply, you will find that this signifies nothing else for the economic process in reality, than as if by some mischievous device you were to cause the column of mercury to rise when the thermometer indicates that the room is too cold. You are only trying to cure the symptoms. By giving the money a different value you create nothing real.

You create something real if you regulate labour - that is to say, the number of people engaged on a certain kind of work. For the price depends on the numbers engaged in a given field of work. To try to regulate these things bureaucratically, through the State, would be the worst form of tyranny;[36] but to regulate it by free "associations," which arise within the social sphere, where everyone can see what is going on - either as a member, or because his representative sits on the association, or he is told what is going on, or he sees for himself and realises what is required - that is what we must aim at.

Of course this also involves quite another social need. We must see to it that people are not restricted to one solitary activity throughout their lives, but are able to turn their hands to other things. Moreover, as I beg you to consider, this will be necessary, if only for the reason that otherwise too much capital would arrive at point (v) in the diagram. You can use up the surplus capital, which would be excessive at this point, to instruct and educate people in one thing or another, so as to be able to transplant them into other callings. You see, therefore, the moment you think in a rational way, the economic process will correct itself. That is the essential thing. It will never correct itself if you say: "By this or that measure, by inflation or by the issue of such or such official instructions, the thing will be improved." By such means it will never be improved. It will only be improved by enabling the economic process to be clearly and transparently observed at every place, assuming always that those who make the observations are in a position to follow them through to their logical conclusions.

I wanted to reach this point in our argument today, in order to show what follows from a real and true study of the economic process itself.

6: "TRUE PRICE"
29 July 1922

In my book on the threefold social order (see Note 2) I endeavoured to express in a formula how we may arrive at a conception of "true price" (as we will call it to begin with) in the whole economic process. Needless to say, to begin with such a formula is only an abstraction. But it is the object of these lectures (which, I believe, in spite of shortness of the time, will really form a whole) to work the whole science of economics, at least in outline, into this abstraction.

The formula I gave was as follows:-

A 'true price' is forthcoming when a person receives, as counter-value for the product he has made, sufficient to enable him to satisfy the whole of his needs, including of course the needs of his dependants, until he will again have completed a like product.

Abstract as it is, this formula is nonetheless exhaustive. In setting up a formula it is always necessary that it should contain all the concrete details. For the domain of economics, I believe this formula is no less exhaustive than, say, the Theorem of Pythagoras is for all right-angled triangles. The point is that, just as we have to introduce into the Theorem of Pythagoras the varying proportions of the sides, so shall we have to introduce many, very many more variables into this formula. Economic science is precisely an understanding of how the whole economic process can be included in this formula.

Today I intend to start from one essential feature of the formula, namely, that it does not point to what is past but to what is going to happen in the future, for I say in it, of set purpose, 'the counter-value must satisfy the person's needs in the future - that is, until he will have made a like product again.' This is an absolutely essential feature of the formula. If we were to demand a counter-value, literally, for the product which has already been finished - if we expected this to be true to the real economic facts - it might well happen that he would receive a value which would only satisfy his needs for, say, five-sixths of the time which he will take to finish the new product. For the economic facts alter from the past into the future. He who imagines that he can draw up any kind of table from the past, will invariably go wrong in economics. Economic or business life essentially consists in setting future processes in motion with the help of what went before. But where past processes are thus used to set future ones in motion, it inevitably happens in some cases that the values are considerably shifted. Indeed they are constantly shifting. Hence in terms of this formula it is essential to say: "If someone makes a pair of boots, the time he took to make them is not the determining factor in the economic sense. The determining factor is the time he will take to make the next pair of boots." That is the point, and we must now try to understand its fuller implications within the whole economic process.

Yesterday we brought before our minds this cycle: Land, labour, capital - that is, capital endued with value by intelligence. At this point (iii, Sketch 3; but see also Sketch 4) I might just as well write (instead of "capital") "intelligence." To begin with we followed out the economic process in this direction, counter-clockwise, and we found that at this point (v) congestion must not be allowed to occur. On the contrary, only so much must be allowed to go into land as will act as a kind of seed to continue the process. A state of economic congestion must not be allowed to arise through a fixation of capital in ground rents. Now, as I said, fundamentally speaking, the return for land when it is sold - i.e. when land is given a value in the economic process - works in direct opposition to the interests of a person engaged in the manufacture of goods. For if someone wishes to manufacture goods with the help of capital, it is to his interest that the rate of interest should be low. Having less interest to pay, he will be less hampered in his use of the capital he has borrowed. The landowner, on the other hand (I may go fully into these things, as they are of economic significance), or anyone who has an interest in the land becoming more valuable, will be able to make it dearer simply by a reduction in the rate of interest. A low rate of interest to pay, and the value of land rises; commodities, on the other hand, which depend mainly on manufacture, become cheaper. You can easily work it out. It is an economic fact.

It would appear, therefore, to be necessary to arrange for two different rates of interest: A rate of interest as low as possible for manufacture; and a rate of interest as high as possible for everything that falls under the heading of "land". This follows directly from what we said before, but it cannot easily be carried out in practice. A slightly higher rate of interest for capital advanced on land might be practicable, but this would be of little help. A considerably higher rate of interest - for instance, a rate of interest which would keep the land at an ever constant value, namely, 100% - would be extremely difficult to realise in practice without taking additional steps. 100% interest for money borrowed on land would mend matters at once, but it cannot be carried out in practice. In all such cases, the first thing is to see with full clarity into the economic process. When we do so, we soon realise that the life of associations is the only thing that can make it healthy. Rightly to see the economic process will lead to our being able rightly to direct it.

As I indicated yesterday, in regard to the economic process we must speak of production and consumption. This contrast has played a great part recently in various much-canvassed economic theories which in due course have been used for purposes of agitation. There has especially been much discussion about whether the application of intelligence, as such, is in any way value-creating in the economic sphere.

A person who performs freed activity is certainly a consumer. Whether he is also a producer in the economic sense is a question which has been much debated. Extreme Marxists, for example, have again and again cited that luckless fellow, the Indian book-keeper, who has to keep the accounts for his village community. He does not till the fields or do any other productive work; he merely registers the productive work done by others. The Marxists deny him the faculty of producing anything. They declare that he is simply and solely maintained out of the surplus value which the productive workers create. This worthy book-keeper is worked as hard in economics as Caius is in the formal logic which we did at college. Caius's job is proving the mortality of man. You remember: "All men are mortal, Caius is a man, therefore Caius is mortal." His everlasting function of proving the mortality of man has made him immortal in the world of logic. The same thing has happened in Marxist literature to the Indian book-keeper who is maintained simply by the surplus value of the productive workers. He has become a classic.

This question is, if I may say so, extraordinarily full of snags, on which we very easily get caught when we try to work it out economically. I mean the question: How far (if at all) freed activity[37] is economically productive? Now here it is especially important to distinguish between the past and the future. For if you consider, if you reflect statistically on the past only, with respect to the past and to all that is only the unbroken continuation of the past, you will be able to prove that freed activity is unproductive. From the past into the future within the material sphere, only purely material work and its effects can be held to be productive in the economic process. It is quite a different matter, however, when you turn your eye to the future. And, as we said, to be engaged in economics is to be working from the past into the future. You need only think of this simple instance. Assume that in some village a person, who manufactures this or that, falls ill. Under certain given circumstances - let us say, if he falls into the hands of an unskilful doctor - he will have to lie in bed for three weeks, during which time he will be able to do nothing, disturbing the economic process to no small extent. If he is a cobbler, for example, for a period of three weeks boots and shoes will not be brought to market - taking the word "market" in the widest sense. But now suppose he gets a very skilful doctor who makes him well sooner, so that he can go back to work again in a week. In all seriousness you can now decide the question: Who made the boots for the remaining fortnight, the cobbler or the doctor? In reality it was the doctor. And now the thing is altogether clear. As soon as you take into account the future from any given moment onward - towards the future - you can no longer call intelligence unproductive. In relation to the past, those human beings whose work is freed activity are consumers only. In relation to the future they are decidedly productive, indeed they are the producers, for they transform the whole process of production and make it pronouncedly different for the economic life. You can see this from the example of the tunnel. What happens when tunnels are built nowadays? They could not be built unless the differential calculus had been discovered. To this day, therefore, Leibnitz is helping to build all tunnels. The way prices work out in this case has really been determined by that application of his intelligence. You can never answer these questions in economics if you consider the past in the same way as the future. Life, however, does not move towards the past, nor does it even prolong the past; it goes on into the future.

Hence no economic thought is real which does not reckon with what results from freed activity, that is to say, fundamentally by thinking. But freed activity is not an easy thing to get hold of. It has its own peculiar properties which are by no means readily grasped in economic terms. Freed activity begins the moment work itself - that is to say, labour - is organised. The organising work of thinking begins the very moment labour itself is organised and divided. Thenceforward, it grows more and more independent. Consider the freed activity of one who directs some undertaking within the material sphere. For all his immense amount of freed activity, he is still dependent on the resources with which the economic process provides him from out of the past. And yet, even on quite practical grounds, you cannot get round the fact of freed activity - even, one might say, completely freed activity. When someone invents the differential calculus, for example, and even more so when he paints a picture, there we have a case of completely freed activity. At any rate, relatively speaking, we can call it freed. For whatever materials are derived from the past - the paints and the like - they no longer have the same significance in relation to the eventual products they will become as do the raw materials, for example, purchased for manufacture.

We have, therefore, the region of freed activity. (see Sketch 4.) In this sphere we find, above all things, teaching and education. From the point of view of the purely material economic process, it is especially people such as teachers who are, in relation to the past, absolutely and exclusively consumers. Of course, you may say, they produce something, and, if they are painters, for example, they are even paid something for what they have produced. In appearance, therefore, the economic process is the same as when I manufacture a table and sell it. And yet the process is essentially different as soon as we cease to consider the buying and selling of the individual and turn our attention to the economic organism as a whole, which is what we must do in the present advanced stage of division of labour.

There are also pure consumers of another kind within a social organism, namely, the young and the very old. Up to a certain age, the young are pure consumers, while those who have become pensioners are again pure consumers. A very little reflection will suffice to convince you that if there were no pure consumers in the economic process - mere consumers who are not producers at all - the thing could not go forward at all. For if everyone were producing, all that was produced could not be consumed. This is the case for human life, at any rate, which is not purely economics, but must be taken as a whole. The economic process can only really go forward if it includes pure consumers.

Let me throw light on this fact from a different angle. You see, this circle (see Sketch 4) can be made very instructive - we can endow it with all manner of properties. The question will always be, how to bring the several economic processes and facts into this circle, which represents for us the cycle of the economic process. Something very important happens when, in buying and selling in the market, I pay on the spot for what I get. The point is not that I pay for it with money; I might equally well barter it for a corresponding commodity which the other person was willing to accept. The point is that I pay at once. Indeed it is this that constitutes "paying" in the proper sense of the word. Now here once more we must pass from the ordinary, everyday conception of payment to the true economic one. For in economic life the various concepts constantly play into one another; the total phenomenon, the total fact, results from the interplay of the most diverse factors. You may say: "It is conceivable that some regulation should be made, so that no one need ever pay cash down; then there would be no such thing as 'paying at once'; one would only pay after a month or after some other interval of time." (Credit cards without the credit element! - Ed.) But the point is this: We are forming our concepts altogether wrongly when we say: "Someone hands me a suit of clothes and I pay for it after a month." The fact is that after a month I no longer pay for this suit of clothes alone. In that moment I am paying for something quite different. I am paying for something which circumstances, by raising or lowering prices, may have made quite different. I am paying for an ideal element in addition. In fact, we cannot do without the concept of "immediate payment" - it is the essence of simple purchase. More than this, a thing becomes a commodity on the market through the very fact that it is paid for at once. This is generally the case with those commodities which represent "land transformed by labour." (Food, clothing - "consumables". - Ed.) For such commodities, their value is determined in the very moment at which I give away my money, or exchange my commodity for another. That is payment. That is one thing there must be in the economic process.

The second thing, which plays a similar part to payment, is lending. This does not interfere with the concept of payment as such. Lending is an altogether different fact which simply exists. If I have money lent me, I can apply my intelligence to this loaned capital. I become a debtor; but I also become a producer. In this way, lending plays a real economic part. If I have intellectual or creative capacities in some direction, it must be possible for me to obtain loaned capital. No matter where I get it from, I must have it. Thus, in addition to payment there must be loan (see Sketch 4).[38] Here then we have two very important factors in the economic process:- Payment and loan.

And now by a simple deduction you can find the third. You will not doubt for a moment what the third thing is - gift. Payment, loan and gift - this is a real trinity of concepts, essential to a healthy economy. There is a prevailing disinclination to include "free gift" in the economic process as such, but, if there is not a giving somewhere, the economic process cannot go on at all.

Imagine for a moment what we should make of our children if we gave them nothing. We are constantly making free gifts to children. If we consider the economic process as a whole - as a process that goes on and on continuously - giving is part of it. There is no escaping the fact. It is wrong to regard the transfer of values from hand to hand, representing a process of free gift, as something inadmissible in the economic process as such. Precisely this one of the three is found where values are to be transferred. The transfer of the means of production, for instance, to one who has the faculties necessary for managing them further, should be effected by a process really identical with giving. Care must, of course, be taken that such giving is not done in a haphazard way. But in the economic sense such transfers are free gifts, and such gifts are absolutely necessary. You will find this more and more to be an economic necessity.

The trinity of payment, loan and gift is there in the economic process. Consider the matter thoroughly and you will recognise that it must be contained in every economic process, otherwise it would be no economic process, but would lead to absurdities at every point. People may rebel against these things for a time; but we must remember that economic wisdom today is not all it might be. Those especially who want to teach it should be under no illusions on this point. Modern economic knowledge is by no means great. People are little inclined to go into the reality of economic relationships. This is an obvious fact, so obvious that if you look in today's *Basler Nachrichten* you will find curiously enough a reflection on this very fact. Neither governments nor private people nowadays, it says, are inclined to evolve real economic thinking. I think we may take it that anything expounded in the *Basler Nachrichten* is likely to be obvious. It is indeed a palpable fact and it is interesting to find it discussed in this way. The article is interesting, inasmuch as it endeavours to set in a glaring light the absolute impotence which prevails in the economic sphere; interesting, too, because it says that these things must be changed - it is time governments and individuals began to think differently. But there the matter ends. How they are to think differently - on this you will, of course, find nothing in the *Basler Nachrichten* - which is also interesting!

Now it is possible to interfere in the economic process so as to disturb it, if one does not rightly relate the one thing with the other in this trinity. Many people today are enthusiastically demanding the taxation of legacies (which, of course, are also gifts). Such proposals have no deep economic significance. For we do not lessen the value of an inheritance if, say, it has a value n and we divide the value n into two parts, $n1$ and $n2$, giving $n2$ to some other party and leaving the legatee with $n1$ alone. All it means is that the two together will now do business with the original value n, and the question will be whether he who receives $n2$ will husband it as advantageously for the economic life as would the original legatee who would otherwise have received the two together. Everyone, of course, may settle this question for himself according to his taste - whether a single clever person, receiving the whole legacy, will husband it better, or whether it will be better for one to receive only part while the State receives the other part, so that the individual is obliged to do business in conjunction with the State.

This sort of thing definitely leads us away from pure economic thinking. It is a thinking based on resentment, on feeling. People envy the rich heir; there may be reason for it, but we cannot look at it only from this point of view if we claim to be thinking in an economic sense. The point is, how must the thing be conceived in the economic sense, for whatever else has to be done must take its start from this. You can, of course, conceive a social organism becoming diseased through the fact that payment is not working together in an organic way with loan and gift, since one or the other is being obstructed and one or the other fostered. But they will still go on working together in some way. If you abolish giving on one side, you merely effect a redistribution, and the question to be decided is not whether this ought to be done, but whether it is necessarily advantageous. Whether the individual heir alone should receive the inheritance, or whether he must share it with the State, is a question which must first be settled on economic grounds. The point is:- which is more advantageous?

The important thing is this:- the realm of freed activity arises almost of necessity out of the entry of intelligence into economic life. As a result, there will be pure consumers so far as the past is concerned, but what of this in relation to the future? Here freed activity is productive - indirectly it is true - but nonetheless extraordinarily productive. Imagine a society in which the individual's faculties were always able to evolve to the full; the consequence would be an extremely fertilising influence on that which enters into the processes of material production. Considered in this light, the thing takes on a decidedly economic complexion.

It is by no means a matter of indifference whether in a given region all those whose activity is freed are exterminated (for instance, if they got nothing to consume; the right to live being admitted only for those who work directly in material production) or whether really free beings are allowed to exist within the social organism. For the latter have the peculiar property of loosening and liberating the mother wit of the others. They make their thinking more mobile, and these others are thus able to work into the material process more effectively. You must not try to refute me by pointing to Italy and saying: There is a great deal of culture there, yet the economic processes which proceed from intelligence have not been stimulated to any unusual degree. Granted, it has a great deal of culture; but it is a culture handed down from the past. There are statues, museums and the like; but they do not have the economic effect I am referring to. Only what is living is effectual - that is to say, what proceeds from one free being to another. This is what works as a productive factor into the future, exerting a healing influence on the economic process by giving the individual a free field of action.

Suppose now a society with a healthy associative life. The task of the associations will be to arrange production in such a way that when too many people are working in any sphere they can be transferred to some other work. It is this vital dealing with people, this allowing the whole social order to originate from the insight of the associations that matters. And when one day the associations begin to understand something of the influence of freed activity on the economic process, we can give them a very good means of regulating the economic circuit. The associations will find that when freed activity declines, too little is being given; they will see the connection.

There is, then, a very definite possibility of driving the rate of interest on land-property right up to 100% by transferring as much land-property as possible in the shape of gifts to those whose activity is freed. In this way you can bring the land question into direct connection with what works particularly into the future. In other words, capital which presses to be invested, capital which tends to march into mortgages and stay there, must be placed at the disposal of those who produce culture, in the wide sense of the word, those, such as teachers, who work in cultural institutions - schools, theatres and the like.[39]

That is the practical aspect. Let the associations see to it that the money which tends to get tied up in mortgages find its way into free cultural institutions. There you have the connection of the associative life with the general social life. Only when you try to penetrate the realities of economic life does it begin to dawn on you what must be done in the one case or in the other. I do not by any means wish to agitate that this or that must be done. I only wish to point out what is. And this is undoubtedly true: Something we can never attain by legislative measures - namely, keeping excess capital away from land - we can attain by the life and system of associations, diverting capital into free cultural institutions. I only say: If the one thing happens, the other will happen too. Science, after all, has only to indicate the conditions under which things are connected.

7: **THE FACTORS OF PRICE FORMATION**
30 July 1922

We have now seen how the economic system as a whole takes its course; we have seen how purchase, loan and gift act as impelling factors, motive factors, within this system. Let us realise at once that there can be no economic system without this interplay of loan, gift and purchase. The influences - of which we have already spoken from one aspect - which create economic values and lead to the forming of price, therefore proceed from these three factors. Only by understanding how these three factors work in the forming of price, shall we succeed in any degree in formulating the price problem.

It is very necessary that we should have a distinct view of the real nature of separate economic problems. In this respect our present economic science is full of unclear ideas - ideas which become confused mainly because they try to grasp at rest what is in constant movement.

Granting, then, that gift, purchase and loan are inherent in economic movement, let us consider what in our present-day economy are - if I may so call them - the principal factors of rest. Let us turn for a moment to what is perhaps one of the commonest topics nowadays and a principal source of the errors that find their way into economics. People talk of "wages", and they talk of them in such a way as to make them look like the price of labour. If the so-called wage-earner has to be paid more, they say, "the price of labour has gone up." If he has to be paid less, "labour is cheaper." Thus they actually speak as though a kind of sale and purchase took place between the wage-earner who sells his labour and the person who buys it from him. However this sale and purchase is fictitious; it does not in reality take place. That is the trouble in our present economic conditions. On all hands we have hidden or masked relationships, which develop in contradiction to their deeper reality.

As we have already seen, value in the economic system can only arise through the exchange of products through the exchange of commodities. It cannot arise in any other way. But what follows? If value can only arise in this way, and if moreover the price of the value is to be arrived at along the lines laid down yesterday (that is, by seeing that the producer of a given product receives, as its counter-value, what he will require to satisfy his needs during the production of another like product), if this is to be possible, the various products must, as it were, reciprocally determine one another's value. It is not difficult to see that this is what actually happens in the economic process, only it is masked by the fact that money steps in between the objects exchanged. Yet the money is not the important thing; we should not take the slightest interest in it if it did not facilitate the exchange of products, making the process not only more convenient, but less expensive. We should have no need of money, were it not for the fact that when a person brings a product to the market - under the influence of the division of labour - he cannot be bothered to fetch what he needs from wherever it may happen to be; instead, he takes money for it, so that he may supply his needs later on at his own convenience. Thus, we may say that it is the mutual tension, arising between the various products in the economic process, which must be concerned in the forming of prices.

Let us consider from this point of view the so-called wage-nexus, that is, the labour-nexus. We cannot really exchange labour for anything since, as between labour and anything else, there is no possibility of reciprocal determination of value. We may fancy that we are paying for labour, we may even actualise this fancy by letting in the wage-nexus. But we do not really do anything of the sort. In reality, even in the labour-nexus, it is values which are exchanged. The worker produces something directly - he delivers a product - and it is this product which the entrepreneur really buys from him. In actual fact, down to the last penny, the entrepreneur pays for the products which the workers deliver to him. It is time we began to see these things in their right light. The entrepreneur buys products from the worker; and after he has bought them it is his business to impart to them a higher value, by making use of the conditions present in the social organism and by his own enterprising spirit. It is really this which gives him his profit. He gains on the transaction because, having bought the commodities from his workers, he is able by his knowledge of the market to enhance their value.

Thus, in the labour-nexus we are dealing with a true purchase. Nor can we speak of a surplus value arising through the labour-nexus as such. All we can say is that in such and such circumstances the price which the entrepreneur pays is not according to the true price, of which we spoke yesterday; and this is a thing we shall often find in the economic process - that, although the products reciprocally determine one another's value, although they have their real values, these values are not actually paid for in the course of commercial dealing. It is easy enough to see that all values are not really paid for. Take the case of a manufacturer on a small scale, who suddenly inherits a large legacy. Tired of the whole factory business, he decides to sell his stock-in-trade, and does so at an absurdly low price. That does not mean that the commodities decrease in value; it only means that the true price is not paid. Thus, in actual economic intercourse prices are constantly being falsified. We must not forget this. In the course of commercial dealing prices may often be falsified. There is, nevertheless, a true price. The commodities sold in the above example are worth just as much as the same commodities produced by someone else.

Let us now consider what is involved by rent - by the price of land. You see, the conditions under which the price of land originates are not those of a mature economy. To take an extreme instance, we may consider how a piece of land may have come under the control of particular people by conquest, that is, by the exercise of force. Even here, no doubt, the element of exchange will enter in to some extent; the invader will have granted certain portions of the conquered territory to those who helped him to victory. Here, then, at the starting-point of an economic process, we have something that is not properly economic - something to which we can only apply the word "might" or "right". By means of power, rights are gained - rights, in this case, over land. Thus we have the economic domain bordering on the one hand on relationships of right and power.

What is it that takes place under the influence of such relationships of right and power? It happens continually that the person who has the free right of disposal over land looks after himself better than those others whom he attaches to himself as labourers - who deliver the products to him by their labour. I am speaking now not of labour, but of the products of labour; it is the products of labour with which we are concerned. The others have to deliver more to him than he delivers to them. This, indeed, is only the extension of his relationship to them of conquest or right. Now, what is this excess of what they give him over what he gives them? What is it, in other words, that falsifies the price relationship in this case? It is none other than compulsory gift! Here, then, the relation of giving comes in, with the sole difference that the one who is to make the gift does not do so of his own free will, but by compulsion. It is in fact a compulsory gift. That is what happens in relation to land; through compulsory gift, the price which farm-products really ought to have in terms of other products is actually raised.

Thus, the price of all things capable of subjection to such relationships of "right" has an inherent tendency to rise above its true level. So, for instance, if foresters or hunters are living with farmers, the foresters and hunters will come off better than the farmers. Farmers, among forest people, have to pay higher prices to the foresters for what they give them - higher prices, that is to say, than the true exchange prices as between their respective products - for the simple reason that in forestry, more than anywhere else, it is a pure matter of right that the owner has the thing at his disposal and determines prices. Farming entails some real labour; but in forestry, hunting and the like, we come very near to the pure "labour-less" valuation - a valuation proceeding solely from relationships of right and power. And, if manufacturers[40] are living among farmers, prices once again will tend to rise above their true level on the farmer's side; while on the other hand they will sink beneath the true level as against manufacture. Life is dearer for manufacturers among farmers, comparatively cheaper for farmers among manufacturers (assuming there are enough of them to make any appreciable difference). Thus, the sequence governing this tendency for prices to rise above or to sink below their true level is as follows: First forestry, then farming, then manufacture and, lastly, entirely freed activity. These are the lines along which we should approach the problem of price-formation in the economic process.

There is an inherent tendency in the economic process to create rent. The economic process tends, as it were, of its own accord, to submit itself to this necessity of paying more dearly for farm products than for other things. This tendency obtains where there is division of labour (and all our remarks have reference to a social organism in which there is division of labour) and is brought about by the fact that what I had to repeat twice over a few days ago, to the bewilderment of a large number of the audience (namely, that the person who provides for himself lives more expensively and for that reason must take more for his products, must estimate them at a higher value than one who gets his products in free commercial dealing from others), simply does not come in in the case of farming, although it does in trading.

In relation to the various branches of manufacture, this has a very real meaning, albeit you may have to think a very long time to find your way to that meaning. But in respect to agriculture and forestry it has no meaning. We must never forget that, when we are dealing with realities, the various concepts only hold good for certain regions; they change for other regions. This is equally true in other walks of life. What is a means of healing for the head, is pernicious - is a means to disease - for the stomach; and *vice versa*. So it is in the economic organism. For example, if it were at all possible for the farmer not to provide for himself, the rules we apply for the general circulation of commodities would be right in his case, too. But the fact is, he can do no other than provide for himself; for within the economic process the entire agriculture of a social organism forms of its own nature a single entity, however many individual land-owners there may be. Accordingly, the farmer must in every case keep back, from the totality of his products, what he has to provide for himself. Even if he gets it from another farmer, in reality he is still keeping it back. The farmer is essentially someone who provides for himself. Hence he is obliged to value his goods more expensively. The consequence is that prices must rise on his side. It follows that there is an inherent tendency to create rents in the economic process. The only question will now be: How to make these rents harmless in the economic life? But in the first place we must know that this tendency to create rent exists. If you abolish rents, in one form or another they will be created again, for the simple reason which I have just explained.

For the same reason which underlies the creation of rent, there arises, on the other hand, the tendency of manufacturers to devalue capital, to make capital cheaper and cheaper. We shall best understand this tendency if we get it clear to begin with that capital cannot really be bought. True, there are dealings in capital; people "buy" capital. But every such purchase of capital is once again merely a masked relationship; in reality we do not buy capital, we only borrow it.[41] Yet, in the end, even if the relationship is apparently other, you will always be able to unmask it and expose the loan character of industrial capital (i.e. capital used for manufacture in its widest sense. - Ed.). I say expressly, of industrial capital, for if you extend the principle to rents it is no longer the case. But it is certainly the case with industrial capital, for the simple reason that there is a constant tendency to undervalue, as compared with other things, that which depends on human will[42] - that is to say, manufacture and entirely freed activity. Industrial capital is altogether implicated in the freed activity of intelligence; hence it is constantly being devalued. So we may say: Capital has a permanent tendency to go down in its economic value, or rather in its economic price; rents have a permanent tendency to rise in price.

There is another reason from which you will see that industrial capital must inevitably devalue. We said just now that in farming one cannot help providing for oneself. It is just by this self-provision that the rise in the value of farm-products is brought about. At the same time you will see that in the case of industrial capital, where the loan principle predominates, one cannot provide for oneself. One cannot provide for oneself with capital. What one does provide for oneself must be included in the balance sheet nowadays in precisely the same way as what one borrows - if the balance sheet is to be correct. Here, therefore, the opposite tendency obtains - the tendency towards lower prices.

Everything depends on our seeing clearly into these relationships in the economic process. For then we shall see that it is by no means easy to establish true prices. True prices are constantly being upset by the fact that, on the one hand, there are things appearing on the market which tend to be too high in price, while, on the other hand, there are things appearing which tend to be too low. And since price is settled by exchange, being in the middle, it is continually exposed to these influences. You can observe this very clearly in the economic process. In the same measure in which the products of forestry and agriculture become more expensive, those produced by freed activity grow cheaper. Thus, there arise those relationships of tension which lead to social unrest and discontent. The most important question in relation to the formation of price is, therefore: How can we deal with the natural tension which exists in the creation of prices, as between the values accruing to goods arising out of freed activity, and the values accruing to those goods belonging to production derived from land? How can we get at this tension? How can we equate the one, the downward, tendency with the other, upward tendency?

Through division of labour, more and more highly differentiated products arise. You need only remember how simple are the products arising, let us say, among a hunting or forest community. Here the price difficulty scarcely comes into question; but as soon as agriculture is added to forestry, the difficulty begins. In effect, the difficulty lies in the differentiation; the further the division of labour extends, and new needs arise in the process, the more does the differentiation of products increase, and the difficulties connected with price-formation accumulate. The more varied are the products, the more difficult does it become to bring about their reciprocal valuation - and the valuation can only be reciprocal. This may be seen from the following comparison: There is a reciprocal valuation even in the case of products only slightly differentiated one from another - say, for instance, wheat and rye and other agricultural products. But follow the thing out over a long period of time and you will find the reciprocity of value as between wheat, rye and other cereals remains fairly stable. If wheat goes up, the other cereals go up; if wheat goes down, the other cereals go down with it. This is due to the fact that there is comparatively little differentiation between these products; as soon as the differentiation becomes greater, this constancy no longer obtains. For it may well happen, through various events in the social organism, that some product which someone has been accustomed to exchange for another suddenly shoots up in price, while the other may go down at the same time. Think what revolutions are thus brought about in economic relationships. Indeed, events in the economic world depend far more on the relative risings and fallings in price than on any other circumstance. It is by the relative rise and fall in prices that the difficulties of life itself are introduced into the economic sphere. As to whether products as a whole rise or fall - if they all rose or fell uniformly, it would concern us very little. What interests people is that the price of products rise or fall to a different extent. This fact is emerging in a very tragic way just now, under present economic conditions.[43] Products rise and fall in varying measure. Money-values especially are rising and falling, but in the money-values we simply have stored up what were once real values. By this rising and falling, an entire mingling and confusion is now being brought about in society.

From this we can see that there is another way, too, in which we must look at the factors operative in the economic organism. We took our start from the several factors which are enumerated by classical economics, but we saw that the mere enumeration of land, labour and capital leads us no farther. By adding what we have said today to what has been said before, you will see that the pricing or valuing of the products of nature does not come about through purely economic relationships, but also through relationships of right or title; while, on the other hand, the valuing of industrial capital is influenced by free will, with all that it unfolds when it is active in public life. Consider all that is necessary in order to collect a sum of capital for a given purpose. Here free will comes in. Where lending is concerned, free will has a very great part to play - indirectly perhaps, for the person who wants to keep savings is naturally going to invest those savings; but whether he ever saves at all, or not, is an expression of his will. Here, then, free will plays a real part. Now, if we take this into account, we shall find yet another classification of the economic factors besides the one which we have been considering so far.

Up to now I have given you a diagrammatic classification. I showed: There is land, but value only arises through its elaboration, that is to say, it only arises when land moves in the direction of labour - *V1*; and again, value will only arise through labour when it moves on towards capital, i.e. towards intelligence - V2. In this way the tendency arises to return again to land. This, as we saw, can be prevented by leading over excess capital, not into land, where it would become fixed, but into independent cultural undertakings where it vanishes, save for the remnant which must continue as a kind of seed, by which the economic process may be fertilised and maintained.

Now, in addition to this movement which moves anti-clockwise (see Sketch 4), there is another movement. The former movement, as we have seen, gives rise to elaborated land, organised or articulated labour, and emancipated capital - capital, that is to say, which figures only within undertakings dependent on intelligence - active capital. The other movement does not lead to the creation of values in this way, the preceding element always being taken on by the next, but goes in the opposite direction. The first movement runs counter-clockwise, the second clockwise. In the first movement, something arises through the former member always working on into the next; in the second something arises through the fact that that which flows in one direction receives, as it were, what is flowing in the other direction and embraces it. You will see what I mean directly. Remember that capital is, properly speaking, intelligence realised in the economic process; so that where I have written "capital", I can also write "intelligence" - which gives us land, labour and intelligence. Now when intelligence absorbs and receives the elaborated land (land transformed by labour) - when it does not merely lead it on into the economic process in the continued counter-clockwise movement, but absorbs it - means of production arise. (See Sketch 5.) Means of production is something different - it is in quite an opposite process of movement - from a product of nature which has been elaborated for consumption. Means of production is a product of nature taken hold of by intelligence - a product of nature which intelligence needs. From the pen of the writer to the most complicated machinery in a factory, the means of production are, as it were, land taken hold of by intelligence. Land can be elaborated and sent on in this direction, in which case it becomes capital; or it can be sent in the other direction, in which case it becomes means of production.

And now, what arises at this point with the help of means of production can move on and be taken in charge in turn by labour. Just as land is here received by intelligence, so can the means of production (in the widest sense of the term) be received in turn by labour, giving rise to industrial capital, for in effect industrial capital consists in this very union. Thus if you follow the process through, you get a movement whereby means of production and industrial capital coalesce. (Sketch 5, outer circle.)

And if this movement be now continued, so that land (albeit another portion of land) from time to time receives what has been produced with the help of means of production and industrial capital, then and then only does there arise in the economic process what we may call commodity in the proper sense. For the commodity is at once taken over by the processes of nature. Either it is eaten, in which case it is taken up very decidedly by nature, or it is used or otherwise destroyed. In short, a thing becomes a commodity by the very fact that it returns to nature.

We have now traced out the movement inherent in the whole economic process and which contains the three factors:- means of production, industrial capital and commodity. Here, at this third point in the diagram, the distinction becomes unusually difficult; for when the thing we are seeking is shifting to and fro in the process of exchange proper - that is, in purchase and sale - it is extraordinarily difficult to distinguish whether it is moving in this direction or in that - whether it is a commodity, or something that cannot be called a commodity in the true sense of the word. How does a good become a "commodity"? In describing this counter-clockwise movement, to make the nomenclature quite exact, I ought really to write "goods" instead of "commodities" and in the opposite movement I ought to write "commodity"; for "commodities" may be defined as goods in the hands of merchants who offer them for sale and do not use them themselves.

Today my main purpose was that we should acquire such concepts as point to the true relationships in the economic process. These true relationships are again and again being diverted, by falsified processes, into a mode of operation which introduces constant disturbances into the economic process. Continually to smooth out and compensate for these disturbances is one of the essential tasks of economics. People keep on saying that we ought to get rid of the evils of economic life; and they are inclined to have at the back of their minds the notion: "Then everything will be all right and earthly paradise will begin." But that is just as though you were to say: "I should like, once and for all, to eat so much that I need never eat any more." I cannot do that; for I am a living organism wherein ascending and descending processes must constantly be taking place. Such ascending and descending processes must equally be present in the economic life; there must be the tendency on the one hand to falsify prices by the formation of rent, and on the other hand the

tendency to lower prices on the side of industrial capital. These tendencies
are present all the time, and we must understand them in order to obtain, as
far as possible, those prices which represent a minimum of falsification.

To this end it is necessary, by direct human experience, to take hold of the
economic process, as it were, in its nascent state - to be within it all the time.
However, the individual alone can never do this; nor can a society above a
certain size, such as the State. It can only be done by associations growing out
of the economic life itself, and able therefore to work out of the immediate
reality of economic life. The greater the technical accuracy with which we
study the economic process, the more we are led to recognise that the required
institutions must grow out of the economic life itself. Then, they will be able
to observe the kind of tendencies that are at work and how these can be
counter-acted.

8: **ON SUPPLY AND DEMAND**
31 July 1922

Today we shall have to correct certain current misconceptions which merely hinder anyone who wishes to think in accordance with economic realities, or to enter with such thinking into the actual course of economic life. For an economic science which cannot fertilise our practical life is of no real value; its concepts must always prove rather inadequate.

We have already seen that the most important question in economics is that of price. The point will now be to observe prices in the sense which I have indicated. The rise or fall, or stability of prices - the fact that the prices of certain products are too high or too low (for one can have a feeling for these things) - indicates whether or not the economic organism is in good order. It must be for the associations to discover, from the barometer of prices, what is to be done in the economic life as a whole.[44]

You are familiar with the point of view, still widely prevalent, that nothing can be done in practice with the price problem except to allow the so-called law of supply and demand to take its course.[45] It is true that under the pressure, not so much of economic facts as of the increasingly urgent demands of the social movement, this theory has been shaken - the theory (maintained by many others besides Adam Smith) that prices regulate themselves of their own accord through the working of supply and demand. The theory simply says: If the supply is too great, this will of itself lead to its reduction. In this way a regulation of prices will automatically ensue. Similarly, if the demand is too great (or too small) it will inevitably follow that the producers will regulate matters so as not to produce too little (or too much). Under the influence of supply and demand it is thus imagined that prices on the market will, automatically, as it were, approach a certain stable level.

It is important to know whether with such an idea as this we are merely moving in a theoretical notional world, or whether we are truly entering into realities, which we certainly are not. For as soon as you really tackle these concepts of "supply" and "demand" you will see that it is quite impossible, economically speaking, even to establish them. As contemplative students of economics you can do so, no doubt - you can send people into the market to observe how supply and demand are working. But the question is: With such observations, are you entering deeply enough into the working of economic processes? Can you make any use of these concepts? In reality you cannot, because you are leaving out in every case what lies behind the processes which you are trying to grasp. You look at the market; you see the working of "supply" and what is called "demand". But that does not include what lies behind the phenomenon of "supply"; nor will it comprise all that precedes the appearance of "demand". Yet it is there that you will find the real economic processes, processes which are only summarised, so to speak, in the market itself. The best evidence of this is the extraordinary fragility of these concepts.

If we wish to form proper, useful concepts, they can and must be mobile in relation to life. We must be able, as it were, to carry such a concept about from one domain of reality to another, and as we do so the concept itself must change. It must not simply go up in smoke. That, however, is just what happens with the concepts of "supply" and "demand". Take "supply": It is "supply" when someone brings commodities to market and offers them for a price. That is "supply", you say. But I say, no, it is "demand". For if someone brings commodities to market to sell them, his is unquestionably a demand for money. In effect, if we do not enter further into the economic process, it makes no difference at all whether I have a supply of commodities and a demand for money, or whether I come forward with a "demand" in the cruder sense. If I wish to develop a demand, I must have a supply of money.

Supply of commodities is demand for money, and supply of money is demand for commodities. The economic process (insofar as it consists in trade or barter) cannot take place at all, unless there are *both* supply and demand in the case of *both* buyer and seller. For what the buyer has for supply - namely, money - must also first have been evolved in the economic process somewhere behind his back, as it were, or behind the back of the demand, just as the commodity which appears as a supply must also first have been evolved or produced. Our concepts are quite unreal if we imagine that price arises from the inter-action of what is ordinarily called "supply and demand". Price does not evolve at all as defined by this line of thought. Not only must there be a certain number of commodities available as supply, but also there must be a certain number of people able to develop a supply of money for these particular commodities; and *vice versa*. This will show you at once that we cannot simply speak of an inter-action of supply and demand.

If we look not to the concepts (which may always be wrongly formed) but to the real facts - the facts of the market or even of the pure, "marketless" exchange of commodities and money - it is unquestionable that prices evolve as between supply and demand, but between supply and demand on both sides. This is undoubtedly the case, as a pure matter of fact.

The important thing is this:- supply, demand and price are three factors, every one of which is primary. We cannot merely write: "Price is a function of supply and demand," or - to speak mathematically - treat S and D as variables, and P, the price, as a third magnitude resulting from the other two, i.e. $P = f(S, D)$. No; we must regard all of them, S and D (supply and demand) and P (price), as mutually independent variables and by that means arrive at another magnitude, X. You see, we are coming to a formula. We must not merely suppose that S and D are independent variables and that price is a function of the two. All three are mutually independent variables, and their mutual interplay gives rise to something new: $X = f(S, D, P)$. The price is there between the supply and demand, but in a particular way.

The fact is, we must approach this whole line of thought from another angle. If we do see supply and demand, at any given point in the market, in the relationship in which Adam Smith saw them - if it really is so in any particular domain - then it is so only for the circulation of commodities as seen from the standpoint of the trader, although even here, it is not entirely the case. And it is absolutely not the case from the standpoint of the consumer, nor from that of the producer. For the consumer something quite different is true. The standpoint of the consumer is conditioned by what he has. Between what the consumer has and what he gives, a relationship arises, similar to that which arises for the trader as between supply and demand. The consumer has to consider the mutual inter-action between price and demand. He demands less when for his pocket the price is too high; he demands more when it is sufficiently low. As a consumer he confines his gaze altogether to price and demand.

We may say, therefore, that in the consumer's case we must observe rather the inter-action of *price and demand*; in the trader's case, the inter-action of *supply and demand*. Lastly, in the producer's case, between *supply and price*, for he will seek to arrange his supply of commodities according to the prices that are possible in the whole economic process. Thus, we may call our first equation the trader's equation: $P = f(S, D)$. It is this that Adam Smith applied it to the economic system as a whole. But thus applied, it is incorrect. For we can also form a second equation, that of the consumer, with supply, S, as a function of price and demand: S = f(P,D). And thirdly, we can indicate demand as a function of supply and price. In this last equation we shall have: D = f(S, P) - that is to say, demand is a function of supply and price. This is the producer's equation.

P = f(S, D)   Trader's equation.

S = f(P, D)   Consumer's equation.

D = f(S, P)   Producer's equation.

Please note, these equations are also qualitatively different, inasmuch as here (in the consumer's case) the supply is a supply of money, in the producer's case it is a supply of commodities,[46] and in the case of the trader something between the two. (Namely, price. - Ed.)

You see how far more complicated our thoughts about economic life must be. It is just because we try to get at the ideas so easily and quickly, that we have no proper science of economics today. If we wish to enter into the realities, we must ask ourselves: What really lives in the economic life? We may say: In the first place that is where I get my own needs met (I will speak of "property" and "ownership" at a later stage; at present I will express myself as indefinitely as possible - even so, it will suffice to cover the facts), for which I give money or something that I have produced instead of money. That is how things happen as a rule. But think, have we thus explained the full reality of economic life? After all, I may acquire things otherwise than by exchanging a commodity for money or money for a commodity. Suppose I steal them. Then, too, I shall have acquired something. And if I should carry on the stealing on a large enough scale - as the old robber barons sometimes did for decades at a time - then, to describe such conditions, a quite different science of economics would have to be evolved from that which has, generally speaking, to be evolved for our own code of ethics! Well, it may seem a grotesque example, but what is stealing in reality? To steal is to take something away from someone else without his being in a position to defend himself, or without the stealer finding it convenient to make a fair exchange. Compare, for example, this now disreputable concept of "stealing" with the concept which we (in the German language) signify with a foreign word, when we speak of "requisitioning" or "commandeering". Under certain circumstances one commandeers things - that is to say, one takes something away from people and gives them nothing in return. In other cases, too, it happens in the economic process that something is taken away from people and they receive nothing in return. I mention these things, not in order to agitate, but in pursuit of economic science and clarity. Assume for a moment that somewhere or other - within a comparatively small region - I establish a social order wherein money is abolished. In its stead, I organise a system of armed raids, so that those who possess anything are knocked down or killed and their things taken away. Well, what is there against that happening? There is this: That the others may perhaps defend themselves, in which case they must have the means to do so. Or again, it might not be worth while, for example, if my territory were too small.

This shows that something else has to play over into the economic process at this point. I cannot without more ado take something away from someone else because such behaviour has first to be recognised by my fellow human beings, who will by no means do so. What is it then that plays into the economic life at this point? It is the life of rights. You cannot really consider the economic process without observing how law plays into it at every point. You cannot think out the economic life, nor can you bring to pass whatever it may be that you intend, without considering this interplay of rights and economics. The moment you pass from mere barter to money-based trade, you see directly how the principle of law plays into economics. For how otherwise could it be possible, in return for a pair of boots, to get, not a hat, say, but money or whatever it may be. I have saved myself the trouble of giving the trader a hat; I have given him money instead. I have my boots; he has the money. How otherwise should this be possible? If money (even if it were gold) were not recognised by everyone as having real value - a value for which something could be received again in return - if it were not rightly placed in the whole economic process, the cobbler might have collected ever so much money; it would be of no use to him. Thus the moment money makes its appearance in economic intercourse we see quite palpably the element of law. It is extremely important to bear this in mind. We can only look at the social organism as a whole, if we pass from purely economic events to events which take place under the influence of the life of rights.

Let us now assume that I have got my pair of boots from the cobbler and have given him money. Now it might happen that the cobbler, just after having sold me the pair of boots, suddenly remembered that cobblers have at times in the world's history been something else besides cobblers (witness Hans Sachs and Jacob Boehme) and having got money he might think of doing something quite different with it instead of making another pair of boots. He might do anything with it, into which he put his ingenuity, his genius. So that money would suddenly have quite a different value for him than the value of a pair of boots. Thus, the moment we have transformed the commodity into money, that is to say into a lawful right (i.e. a universally recognised right - Ed.), the right can either be kept (using the money to buy something equal in value to boots), or through my ingenuity I can do something with the money to produce an altogether new value in the economic process. It is here that human faculties come in. The individual faculties, which grow quite freely among human beings, enter in and incorporate themselves in the rights which people acquire with money, just as money, which may be regarded - in this sense - as rights realised, incorporates itself outwardly in the commodity. Thus we have now placed into the organic process - which we described provisionally when we spoke of land, elaborated land, and labour divided and organised by intelligence - the factors of rights and of individual human faculties. We have found, within the economic process itself, a division which is in truth a threefold order - a threefolding. It is necessary, however, that we think of this in the right way.

If we observe the economic process, we perceive that just because the things I have now been describing are real facts, certain impossibilities are actually realised in the economic life. For, you see, one can also acquire a right by conquest or the like; by having the power to take it. One does not always acquire a right by mere exchange. Here we have an element, which, insofar as it is present, is quite incapable of comparison with commodities. There is no point of contact between commodities and rights. Nevertheless, in the actual economic process, commodities (or the money-values representing them) are perpetually being exchanged for rights. Precisely when we pay for land, even when we merely help with our rent to pay for the value of the land, we are paying for a right with a commodity, or with the money which we have received for a commodity. In the same way, when we appoint a school teacher and give him a certain salary, we are (sometimes, at any rate) paying for his faculties with the value of a commodity or its corresponding money-value. Thus, there perpetually occur in the economic process exchanges between rights and commodities, between faculties and commodities, and between faculties and rights.

Mutually incommensurable things are exchanged for each other in the economic process. Consider what happens when someone gets paid for an invention, which he has patented. To begin with he accepts payment for a purely intangible value that is being paid for in commodity-values. There is absolutely nothing that could figure as a standard of comparison in such a case. Here we are touching on an element where life enters into the economic process with a vengeance! It becomes still more complicated when we introduce the concept of labour.

I have already pointed out how the wage-labourer does not in reality receive what is generally understood by the idea of "wages", but that he really sells the product of his labour to the entrepreneur and thus receives payment. It is only through his expert knowledge of the market that the entrepreneur gives the proper value - or at any rate a higher value - to that which he buys from the labourer. Economically considered, the profit is not extracted from labour as a surplus value. By economic thinking we cannot possibly arrive at such a view. We can at most arrive at it by a moral judgement. The profit is due to the fact that the labourer is in a less favourable social situation. The products which he sells have less value at the point where he sells them than at the point where the entrepreneur sells them. For the entrepreneur is in a different position - knowing the market better, he can sell at a greater advantage. The worker's relation to the entrepreneur resembles the case of someone who goes to the market and buys a commodity for a given price. He must buy it there, for the simple reason that his circumstances will not allow him, let us say, to buy it anywhere else. Another person may perhaps be able to buy it more cheaply somewhere else. The two cases are exactly the same. Economically speaking, that which obtains as between the entrepreneur and the labourer is simply a kind of market.

It makes a great difference whether I am fully conscious that this is the case or whether I imagine that I am paying the labourer for his labour. You may think the difference merely theoretical, but let such views become real, and you will see how the economic relationships change under the influence of the one or the other. For what happens between human beings is, among other things, the result of the ideas they entertain. As our outlook changes, it changes the course of events. Today the whole proletariat bases its agitation on the idea that labour must be properly paid for. But in fact labour is nowhere paid for; only the products of labour are paid for; and this - if it were truly understood - would also come to expression in the actuality of price. We cannot say that it makes no difference whether we call something a wage or the price of a commodity. For the moment we speak of wages, we imagine that we are paying for labour, and then we go on to all the secondary concepts which confuse labour as such with other economic processes which are value-creating. Then social conflicts arise in a false way. They arise in a true way, in so far as they arise out of sentiments and feelings, which are always in some way right; but we can never correct what ought to be corrected if we have not the right concepts. This is the fatal thing in social life: Grievances often arise in a way which is right, but are remedied under the influence of false concepts. In every detail people evolve these false ideas and carry them over into their whole conception of the economic process, resulting in havoc.

Take a very simple example. A gentleman (this is a true story) once said to me, "I am very fond of sending picture postcards to my friends. I send lots of them." I said, "I am not at all fond of sending picture postcards - and that," I said, "for economic reasons." "Why?" he asked. I said, "Every time I send a picture postcard, 1 cannot help thinking: Perhaps someone will have to run right up to the fourth floor with it. In short, I cause a change, a redistribution, in the economic process. It is not the labour that matters, but when it comes to delivering post you cannot easily distinguish the 'service' - the thing done - from the labour. It is the service that we must estimate. If I keep sending picture postcards to my friends, I increase in an uneconomic way the services people must render." "That is an economic fallacy," said the other man; "for on the assumption that one person need only do a limited amount, an increase in the number of picture postcards will mean that more people will have to be employed and they will get paid. So you see," he said, "I am really a benefactor to the people who get these jobs." I could only answer: "Yes, and do you also produce all that they eat? You do not increase the available means of consumption in the very least. You merely bring about a redistribution. To employ more people is not to increase the available means of consumption."

Just such an idea often brings about the very crudest of errors in individual cases. For suppose that there is a town or city council consisting of people like my friend - as may well happen; indeed, such men may even become cabinet ministers and then it will be a cabinet. Then they will say: "There are so and so many unemployed. Let us put up new buildings or the like, then the people will be provided for."[47] Yes, for the next five steps ahead you have rid yourselves of the problem, but you have still produced nothing new. The workers as a whole have no more to eat than they had before. If I let one side of the scale sink, the other side must rise. Thus if you give such instructions, not as part of a whole coherent economic process but as a mere isolated measure, an economic calamity must necessarily have arisen on the other side. If we knew how to observe these things, we should be able to reckon it up. By making social reforms in this way, merely giving means of subsistence to the destitute or unemployed, by having new buildings erected, we shall have increased the price of this or that article for a number of other people. In the economic sphere, above all, we must not think short-sightedly. We must think all things in connection with one another, as a totality.

But that is not at all easy to do, for the simple reason that the economic process is very different from a scientific system. A scientific system in its totality can be grasped by a single human being - albeit only in outline. But the economic process can never be encompassed in its totality by a single human being. The economic process can only find its reflection where judgements, proceeding from people who stand in the most varied spheres, work together.

The only possibility of arriving at a real judgement on these things - not merely a theoretical one - is by way of association. Going back to the three equations (p. 106.): A trader will always have the first equation in mind. Traders under the influence of this equation will know the influence it exerts. Likewise a consumer who intelligently follows and observes the process of consumption will understand the influence of the second equation; and a producer will know all that is subject to the influence of the third. At this point you may say: But surely, human beings are not so unintelligent as not to be able to think beyond their own narrow horizon? Yes, that is perfectly right, where one general world outlook is concerned. But in practical economic life there is no other effective way of knowing what is going on in trade, for example, except to be engaged in trade oneself. You must be in the midst of it, you must be trading. There is no other way. You cannot theorise about it. Theories may be interesting, but theories are natural science. The point is not that you should know how trade goes on in general, but that you should know how the products circulate in your immediate neighbourhood. And if you know that, you do not thereby know how they circulate elsewhere. The point is not that we should know about things in general, but that we should know something in a particular region. Likewise if you can form an effective judgement as to the higher or lower prices at which scythes or other agricultural implements can be manufactured, you do not thereby know the prices at which screws can be manufactured or the like. And so on.

The judgements that have to be formed in the economic life must be formed out of immediate, concrete situations. And that is only possible in this way: For definite domains or regions (whose magnitude, as we have seen, will be determined by the economic process itself) associations must be formed, in which all three types of representatives will be present - those of production, consumption and distribution.

It is really tragic that no understanding should be found in our time for what is after all so simple and so sensible. For, the moment there is a real understanding, the thing can be done, not even by the day after tomorrow, but by tomorrow. It is not a question of radical changes, but of seeking for the proper associative union and co-operation in each case. You need only summon the will and the intelligence to do it. This is the thing that touches one so painfully, for at this point, after all, economic thinking does to some extent coincide with moral and religious thinking. To me, for instance, it is quite unintelligible how this way of tackling the economic problem could have been entirely neglected by those who are officially in charge of the spiritual needs of the world. For there can be no doubt, during recent times it has clearly emerged that the economic facts are no longer being mastered. The facts have gone beyond the mastery of human beings. And we shall not regain this mastery otherwise than by human beings in association.

I do not wish to make a play on words at the end of a very solemn line of thought, but I would say: Economics has not kept pace, in its conceptions, with the transition which has actually taken place from the economics of barter to the economics of money and of human faculties. In its essential concepts, economic science still fumbles about within the economics of barter. It continues to regard money as though it were just a symbol for barter. I know that this will not be readily admitted. But it is implicit, nonetheless, in the prevailing theories. And so we have this situation: In the older economic systems (though these may no longer appeal to us today) people bartered or exchanged (German ta*uschen*, to barter). Then money came in. (As I said, I do not wish to make a pun, but the genius of language itself is working here.) "*Tauschen*" (barter) became "*täuschen*" (illusion or deceit) and everything became unclear. Today we deceive ourselves in almost all our economic processes. The "*tauschen*" has become a "*täuschen*" - the exchange (or barter) an illusion. I do not mean that there is deliberate deceit, but that the whole process becomes confused and deceptive. That is why we must first get to the root of things once more and see how economic processes inwardly take place.

9: THE FORMS OF CAPITAL
1 August 1992

The equations I gave yesterday are not, of course, mere mathematical formulae; like the ones given earlier in this course, they must be verified in life itself. Moreover, they must be conceived in such a way that they actually live within the economic process.

How are we to understand that this is so? In the first place, everything that circulates within the total economic process must have a certain value. On the other hand, we must also realise that many things can occur in the economic organism, the value of which is not immediately expressed in the economic processes themselves.

Let me give you an example that will serve as an introduction to some further economic ideas. In his book on economics,[48] Unruh has described very well such things as the following, revealing as it were the more hidden connections. I give only one example which I have verified; although Unruh himself, being completely wrapped up in state economics and thinking politically rather than economically, is unable to bring these things into their right relationship.

I am referring to the price of rye in certain districts of Central Europe. It is a striking example of the complicated way in which things take their course in the economic process. If one hears big farmers or estate owners speaking of their work, one often hears them say: "We make nothing on the price of rye; on the contrary, we lose on it." What does this really mean? To begin with, it means that these people cannot sell their rye as other things are sold, where the price is composed of the costs of raw materials, the costs of production and a certain margin of profit. Taking the actual prices of rye in this way, we should find that they do not correspond to the costs of production plus a certain profit. On the contrary, they fall far short. And if, in balancing his accounts, a farmer were merely to include the actual market prices of rye he would undoubtedly underestimate its value. As I said, we can follow the matter up and it is absolutely correct; the rye is sold below cost price. And yet it impossible for this to go on in reality. What happens is this: Rye yields not only grain but also straw; and farmers who sell the grain below cost price scarcely sell any of the straw at all. They use it on their own farms, thereby striking a balance. What they lose on the rye is made up for by the manure they get from the animals. For this is the very best manure, being extremely rich in bacteria. Thus from the standpoint of his accounts the farmer gets the manure thrown in as a free gift and in this way, in the long run, a proper balance is struck.

We are thus obliged to posit an economic concept which, though it is most important, is comparatively little considered in the ordinary literature of economics. The concept is that of "internal economies" within the general economic life. You have an "internal economy" whenever an economic organism, a business, does business within itself - exchanges products within itself. That is to say, it does not sell such products outwardly or buy them from outside, but lets them circulate within the business itself. This I would call an internal economy as against the general social economy. Wherever such an internal economy is in force, it is quite possible for products to be delivered below the price which would otherwise be economically necessary. Needless to say, this implies that the forming of price within any economic domain is an extremely complicated chain of events.

Such connections, as I said, have been observed as matters of pure fact by economists. There is another chain of events which I have touched upon from a certain point of view and which must now be regarded also from a different aspect. I mentioned a few days ago that we do not take in at a glance all the links in the economic chain. Imagine, for instance, that a cobbler falls ill and has an unskilful doctor to attend him. He remains ill and for three weeks cannot make any boots; and so his products - the boots which he would have made during the time of his illness - are withdrawn from economic circulation. And now, I said, suppose he gets a skilful doctor who makes him well within a week, so that he gets an extra fortnight in which to go on making boots as before. Economically speaking we can now ask: Who made the boots? Economically speaking, undoubtedly - at this moment of the economic process - the doctor did; there can be no doubt about it.

Yet here again we come to another point. For you may ask: Did the doctor also get paid for them? No, in reality he did not; for you can make the following calculation. Reckon it up according to the market: What did the boots the doctor made amount to? And now if you draw up a rather full statement of account (it would have to be a very full one), you can set this off against what had to be spent on his training. And you will find, in all probability, that what was spent on his training was not so very different from the value of all the boots he made and all the stags he shot; for it is not regarded as universally characteristic of doctors that they withdraw from economic life, on one week only, patients who would otherwise be withdrawn for three. Be that as it may, however the final balance emerged, we should not make a true calculation in the wider economic sense if we did not strike the balance in this way, setting off against the cost of his training the boots he makes, the stags he shoots (assuming that he cures the hunter quicker than would otherwise have been the case), the corn he harvests, and so forth. Only, of course, the economic process is very complicated, and so the payment also proves extremely complicated.

From all this you can see: It can by no means be said with certainty, at any given place, what is the true source of payment for a given thing within the economic process. We must sometimes go far afield to discover this. People who look for mere simplicity in the economic process will never arrive at economic concepts coinciding with reality. They will not get far enough. They will not get behind the formulae of price, supply, demand, etc., which is what we need to do. The reason it is so difficult to estimate the economic process rightly is because outlay and return are often so widely separated. That is why it is difficult to see clearly within the economic process as a whole what it is that is paid for, what it is that is bought, what is lent and borrowed, and what is freely given. For example, assume for a moment that what I advocated a few days ago is realised. Assume that capital is withdrawn from the tendency to get congested in land and given to the cultural life - in the form of foundations, scholarships or the like. These are free gifts. And now you will begin to see what happens on the one side of your gigantic ledger, for it must be a ledger that comprises the real economic life in its totality. The boots the doctor makes during the extra fortnight may actually contain an item which you must look for on the other side under the heading of "free gifts". For it may well be that he had a scholarship to help him in his training, or that he benefited from some foundation. In short, from this point of view you can raise the weighty question: What are the most productive of all transformations of capital in the economic process? Follow out such connections as I have just described, especially those amounts of capital which go into foundations, scholarships and so on, which in due course fertilise inner creativity and enterprise of every kind - and you will perceive that free gifts are the most fruitful thing of all in the whole economic process. We cannot arrive at a healthy economic process unless, in the first place, it is made possible for people to have something to give and, in the second place, unless they have the goodwill and intelligence to give what they have. Here, then, we have something which enters into the economic process in a very specific way.

Remarkably, this is something which we cannot extract from theoretical notions, but only from a wide range of experience. Indeed, I would recommend you to keep this question in mind when you are choosing subjects for dissertations: What becomes of free gifts in the whole economic process? You will find that capital freely given, gift capital, is the most productive; loaned and borrowed capital is less productive, in the economic process; and the least productive is that which stands directly under purchase and sale. That which is paid for immediately on a transaction of purchase and sale is the least fruitful in the economic process; that which depends on lending and comes into the economic process through functions of invested capital is of medium productivity; while that which enters into the economic process through free gifts is of the very greatest productivity - if only for the reason that the work which would otherwise have to be done to earn what is here given freely, or rather the product of that work, is actually saved. We freely give the available proceeds of the economic process, which would only do harm if they were left to congest in land.

We see, therefore, that at any given moment of its evolution the economic process gives no real information of itself. The "before and after" must always be taken into account, but the "before and after" cannot be taken into account unless it is based on the judgement of human beings who join together in association and who gain a corresponding insight into both past and future. We have to build the economic process on the insight of those whose feet are planted within the economic process. Once more, we come to the same conclusion: It is, generally speaking, a difficult and lengthy business to estimate how the several factors in the economic process play their part in the whole of human life - I mean the material life.

We have spoken of trade capital, loan capital and industrial capital within the economic process; circulating capital is more or less covered by these three categories, which are contained in the economic process in the most varied of ways. You remember that such "internal economies" as were referred to at the beginning of this lecture are scattered everywhere throughout the economic process. And where you have an economic process taking place within a larger whole, it is really extremely difficult to say what are the respective contributions, quantitatively speaking, of loan capital, industrial capital and trade capital to general economic welfare. Yet it is possible to arrive at reliable concepts, if we give our survey a wide enough horizon.

Let us, to begin with, turn our attention to the economic life of entire nations, or state-economies as we must call them, according to the economic life of recent times. Take France, for instance. The world-economic connections of France, especially as they were before the War, and as they revealed themselves in their effects during the War, are a good example of how loan capital works in the economic process on a larger scale. France always had a certain inclination to invest capital in loans - that is, in effect, to treat "loan capital" (investment capital) literally as loaned capital. You are probably aware how these things penetrated into the political sphere, clearly illustrating the harmful effects of the coupling together of the economic life and the life of rights, how it came out in the extensive loans made by France to Russia and Turkey. France exported a very large amount of loan capital to Russia and to Turkey. Even in Germany, though Germany was not exactly in her good books, French capital found a home - for instance, when the construction of the Baghdad Railway was begun. England withdrew, but France did not withhold her capital from those who stood at the head of the undertaking - Siemens & Gwinner, for example.[49] France, therefore, was in the main a lending country, so that in France one could see how loan capital becomes involved in the whole economic process.

Further - and I am not defending or attacking anything, but simply describing things objectively - there is one historical phenomenon in which you can truly recognise the interests of loan capital. When we turn our attention, say, to "private" economies or businesses, we shall always find, as any banker will tell you, that the private business person is peace-loving. For he knows very well that his interests and dividends will be upset if, just as his capital is nicely invested, a war begins to sweep through the economic connections of the world. Economists always reckon with the fact that lenders are peace-loving people. That is the reason why it is always possible to say that France was innocent of the War. For, the moment we want to prove that the War was not sought by the French people, we need only point to the interests of the numerous small investors there, and not to the interests of those who urged it on. Such a fact of history may show us on a larger scale what is equally true on a small scale. A person who lends - being the happy possessor of capital available for investment - is essentially someone who would like to see the economic life protected, if possible, from disturbance either by events

outside it or by catastrophic upheavals within it. And the investor is all the
fonder of tranquility because it saves him the trouble of having to form an
independent judgement. He likes to be able to rely on the assurance of
someone else that such and such is "a good thing". In our age, though public
opinion has a high regard of itself, it is, indeed, more opinion than judgement.
Such investment is generally connected to a very strong faith in authority,
both in economic matters and in other respects. This clouds economic
judgement to no small extent. Those, for example, who are in any way titled
or officially labelled very easily get money lent them. This is often the
decisive factor, the consequences of which are plain to see. For, in the one
case, those who are really better cut-out for it will be enabled to enter
productively into the economic process, while in the other case it will be
simply people with handles to their names - members of Chambers of
Commerce and so forth - and often people who have got the name, not by
reason of genuine ability but for some quite extraneous reason. It is one thing
if people of this kind are helped to work into the economic life, and quite
another if a human being has to depend on the recognition of his genuine
faculties by an untainted public judgement. Here, once again, something
elusive enters into the economic life. (In certain circles it has recently become
far too common a practice to use a certain word whenever one fails to keep
pace with things with one's clear thinking. In many places recently, I have
frequently heard this word, the *imponderables*. I wish to emphasise that I
desire to avoid this word. All that I wish to point out is how these things,
which we would like to be simple, are in fact complicated, leading us along
paths that may be more curved and winding than is our wont. It is
unnecessary, as soon as this begins to happen, to have recourse to so
convenient a term as "the imponderables", which we have heard *ad nauseam*
in certain quarters.) So much, at the moment, for loan capital.

Moving on to industrial capital, if we wish to study the essence and function
of industrial capital we shall be able to do so especially well by observing the
rapid rise of industry in Germany in the decades before the War - though its
history here is hardly an edifying one. We can study it here especially well,
because, under the influence of entrepreneurship, industrial capital then
arose by direct transformation out of loan capital to a greater extent in
Germany than in any other part of the world. What I said in the first lecture
is most decidedly true. In England, for example, trade capital was
transformed gradually into industrial capital, because in England
industrialism evolved out of trade, and did so far more slowly than in
Germany, where it shot up with immense rapidity. Industrialism exists in its

pure form where it transforms not trade capital, but loan capital into industrial capital. Hence, it is best studied in the life of Germany.

Now the point is that industrial capital is really placed between two buffers. The one buffer is raw materials; the other is markets. Industrial capital is obliged, on the one hand, to look around as far as possible for its sources of raw materials and, on the other, to arrange for markets. This is not quite so easy to study in the example of Germany industry, where you can better study how industrial capital functions in itself. Still, the emergence of industrialism is evident in all countries during the nineteenth century and on into the twentieth, and so you observe this standing "between two buffers" everywhere. Only you must search out the true facts. As I have said, it is a good thing to order one's ideas, by taking things that can be surveyed as a whole - something that is not easy to do in the case of smaller economic territories, and leading to extraordinarily difficult paths being traced out. It is better to get your orientation and to derive your calculations from wide comprehensive regions, the paths growing easier through observing large scale economic organisms. Then, for example, you will perceive how as a rule the concepts of force or might (which often appear masked under the guise of right or justice) come about most strongly where it is a question of opening up new sources of raw materials. We can study this, for instance, in the Boer War, where it was mainly a question of opening up the sources of precious metals. The Boer War was a real war for raw materials. Of course it always showed itself in a kind of mask; nevertheless it was a war for raw materials. To take another example of how the economic life unfolds in a political way, playing over into the domain of political power - consider Belgium's military enterprises which had the ivory and rubber of the Congo as their object. Or again, take the case of North America, which annexed the Spanish possessions in the West Indies, because it was looking for sources of raw materials - sugar in this instance. In every case we can see how the search for raw materials very easily drives the purely economic life into the political, towards the development of might or force. This is the one side - the one buffer, if I may describe it so.

With the search for markets it is different; it is easy to demonstrate from history that the search for markets does not lead into the political life in the same way. In this case the plain fact is that human nature does not tend so much to the use of force. We can see this in a rather glaring example from the nineteenth century - the so-called "Opium War", whereby England conquered for herself the Chinese opium market. Even there things did not proceed purely by military means, peaceful persuasion, peaceful politics, having had not a little to say. For when things began to grow uncomfortably hot, a hundred and forty-one doctors were found to pronounce an expert judgement to the effect that opium is no more harmful than tobacco or tea. Here, then, politics - peaceful-politics - played a certain part. Politics in any case is always difficult to keep out. You know the saying of Clausewitz: "War is the continuation of politics by other means." Such definitions are all very well, but by the same method we could establish the proposition: 'Divorce is the continuation of marriage by other means.' The relationships of life can always be represented in a particular light by using this kind of logic, and people admire it! Curiously enough, everyone sees through it at once if I say: Divorce is the continuation of marriage by other means, but when it is everywhere proclaimed that "War is the continuation of politics by other means," they do not notice the absurdity, but on the contrary they admire it. In terms of method, I should like to say that if we employ this sort of logic in economics, we shall not advance one step. Speaking of the second buffer, of the hunt for markets, we must undoubtedly admit that a far greater part is played by human cleverness, which fluctuates between the extremes of slyness, astuteness, and wise economic guidance. In the arranging of markets a great deal could be seen at work of all three - particularly in the way they were arranged in those large economic domains which the states themselves had become as politics and economics coalesced. Very much was done in this direction by way of wise guidance, but also by way of deceit, cleverness, slyness and the like. Thus, the concepts which we need to form in respect of smaller economic domains, concerning the relations, say, between a single industrial undertaking and its source of raw materials and its markets, can only be made clear and tangible by considering such things on a large scale.

If we want to study the functions of trade capital, we should take England, especially in the period when she made her great economic progress. This she did by means of trade; consequently her trade capital continued to increase in such a way that England entered quite gently and imperceptibly into the new industrialism. At the time when industrialism was transforming the world. England already had her trade capital. In this early period, therefore, we can study trade capital most readily in England. In more recent times England has been chosen by Marx as a means of studying the economic functions of industrialism ; but in the earlier period - the period immediately preceding the creation of modern industrialism - going back, that is to say, to the last decades of the eighteenth century, it is the functions of trade capital which we can best study in the light of England's economic destiny. Now it cannot be denied that here, either in the open or behind the scenes, the essential thing is always competition. Whether on the large scale - in the economic life of the nation as a whole, where it is mainly based on trade - or within trade or commerce itself, competition is the essential thing. Of course by the introduction of various ideas of what is decent and proper conduct, competition may become very fair, but it is competition nonetheless. Productivity in trade - such productivity as to enable trade capital to become like industrial capital - such productivity depends in the last resort on the tendency of trade capital to accumulate, something that is impossible without competition. Thus, the functions of trade capital afford the best means of studying the functioning of competition in economic life.

At the same time these things are connected with historical changes. Right up to the first third of the nineteenth century - if we are considering the world economy which was gradually coming into being as a single whole (such as it was in a high degree before the War) - the economic processes of trade and industry still played the most important part in economic life. The blossomtime - the classical age, if I may put it so - of loan capital only began in the nineteenth century - indeed only towards the second third of the nineteenth century. And it is at this point that we notice the rise of those institutions which more especially serve the process of lending - I mean the banks and the banking system. The classical age of loan capital, and with it the evolution of the banking system, falls into the last two-thirds of the nineteenth century and the first decades of the twentieth. With the evolution of the banking system, borrowing and lending develop on an ever larger scale, entering more and more as a prime factor into the economic process. But, at the same time, precisely in connection with lending, a remarkable phenomenon appears: Through the instrumentality of large scale lending, and the accompanying expansion of the banking system, the control of the circulation of money is withdrawn from the human being as such, until it becomes a process taking place - I can find no other word to express it - impersonally.

The time has actually come when money does business on its own account, while human beings fluctuate up and down according as they are drawn into this whole stream of money economics, money business. They are drawn in far more than they imagine. Precisely during the last decades of the nineteenth century, the circulation of money became objectified, impersonal. This brings me to a peculiar phenomenon of that time. In economics, everything depends on an open-minded consideration of life as a whole; we must gain a clear vision of the whole of life. The phenomenon to which I refer appears, to begin with, in the psychological sphere, but afterwards plays a great part in the economic life. It is this: Conditions which were brought about in the first place by very real forces, afterwards continue rolling on by a kind of social inertia, just as a ball will do when you have given it a certain momentum. They go rolling on and on, even after the original impulses have ceased to be active in them. Up to the first third of the nineteenth century, there were true economic impulses present in the whole system of loan and investment. Then, through the instrumentality of the banking system, these economic impulses began to change into purely financial ones; and in this process the whole thing became not only impersonal, but also unnatural. Everything was drawn into the stream of money, as it moved itself along. Pure money business, without any natural or personal subject - that is the end towards which, as the nineteenth century drew to a close, everything which had originally been upheld by a personal and natural subject was gravitating.

Strangely enough, this "subjectless" economic life, this "subjectless" circulation of money was accompanied by another phenomenon: States themselves began to do business out of economic impulses. It was out of such impulses, for example, that they began to colonise. We shall see later what influence colonising has; de-colonising, too, will have to be considered in this connection. We can observe very well, as a real economic process, the significance of colonisation in the case of England. Fundamentally speaking, England scarcely ever went beyond the kind of colonisation, which we may perhaps describe as "imperialism with an objective content". Such imperialism, I mean, as contains real economic substance; real economic meaning. But if, on the other hand, you take the case of Germany, you need only look at the colonial accounts and you will see that German colonisation was burdened from the start with an adverse balance. There were at most tiny areas which showed a favourable balance. And in other countries too the tendency crept in, merely to enlarge themselves by acquiring colonies. Isolated commentators - Hilferding, for instance, in his book *Finanzkapital*, published in Vienna in 1910 - actually called this process "objectless imperialism", imperialism without an object.[50]

These two modern phenomena are particularly instructive: On the one hand, the subjectless circulation of money, impersonal and unnatural; and, on the other hand, objectless imperialism. Characteristic as they both are of large-scale economy, their appearance together suggests that the one depends upon the other.

Such a thing is purely psychological, to begin with, though in its further course it becomes economic; for if we have unproductive colonies we must pay for them - and that means that they at once affect the economic life.

So much for what we had to discuss today.

10: ON ASSOCIATIONS
2 August 1922

We have now to consider the relation between labour and that which happens when land is transformed and elaborated into an object of economic value. In the further course, as we saw, organised labour - divided labour - is caught up by capital; and capital eventually emancipates itself and passes over completely into freed activity, if we may so describe it. From all this you will observe that while labour has no direct economic value (as has already been explained), nevertheless, it is labour which sets economic value in motion. The product of nature as such comes into economic circulation by its being worked upon and thereby brought into movement. It is so at least within a certain sphere. Subsequently it is intelligence working in capital which keeps the movement going. For as soon as we enter the sphere of capital, we have to reckon with the movement that takes place through trade capital, loan capital and eventually through production capital proper, industrial capital.

Speaking of this movement, we must be aware of one thing above all, namely that there must be something to bring values into economic circulation. To get the right idea in this respect, we must today concern ourselves with the somewhat ticklish question of profit, economic profit.

The question of profit is extremely difficult. Let us imagine, for instance, that a purchase is taking place: A buys from B. In ordinary lay thinking, we generally apply the concept of profit to the seller only. The human being who sells is supposed to make a profit. It is, of course, really an exchange between what the buyer gives and what the seller gives; and if you think the matter through exactly, you can by no means admit that the seller alone makes a profit. For if the seller alone were to profit, then in the total economic life the buyer would always be placed at a disadvantage; and you will readily admit that this cannot be so, otherwise every purchase would be an exploitation of the buyer and that is obviously not the case. When we buy something we seek to do so advantageously. Thus, the buyer too can buy in such a way as to make a profit. We have, therefore, this peculiar phenomenon: Two people make an exchange, and - at any rate in the normal process of purchase and sale - each one of them must make a profit. For practical economics it is far more important to consider this than is generally realised.

Let us therefore suppose that I sell something and receive money for it. I must gain by giving my commodity away and getting money for it. I must desire the money more than I do the commodity. The buyer on the other hand must desire the commodity more than he desires the money. This, then, is what takes place in the reciprocity of exchange. Both objects passing in exchange - one in one direction and the other in the other - increase in value. By the bare process of exchange, the things exchanged on both sides become of greater value. How can this be?

Only in this way: When I sell something and receive money for it, I am enabled to do more with the money than he who gives it can. Conversely, the other person, who receives the commodity, must be able to do more with it than I can. The two of us, buyer and seller, stand in different economic situations. Increases in value only come about through what lies behind the actual process of purchase and sale. Thus, when I sell something, I must be so placed, economically speaking, that the money I receive has a greater value in my hands than it has in those of the seller; while in his case, by virtue of his particular connection with the economic system as a whole, the commodity I am selling has greater value in his hands than in mine.

We cannot merely consider the fact of buying or selling in the abstract. The essential question is: What are the respective economic relationships in which the buyer and the seller stand? If we look at things precisely, we are led, as so often, from what takes place immediately before our eyes at any given place to the whole inter-connected economic system. This can also be seen by taking another illustration.

Consider barter: Fundamentally, the line of thought I have just opened out can tell you, what is quite true, that barter is not entirely transcended even by the introduction of money into an economic community. In effect, we still barter commodities for money. Precisely inasmuch as both parties make a profit in the transaction, we shall see that the important point is not the mere fact that the one possesses a commodity while the other possesses money. The real point is this: What can each party make of that which he receives? What can he do with it by virtue of his particular economic situation?

To understand it more exactly, let us turn back to the most primitive form of barter in order to throw light on more complicated economic circumstances. Suppose that I buy peas. I can do many different things with these peas. I can eat them. And so, assuming that barter is the order of the day and that I have exchanged some other things which I have produced - that is, some commodity - for peas, I get the peas by means of barter and I can, if I like, eat them. But suppose I have acquired a very, very large number of peas, so many that I cannot eat them all - not even if I have a large family - then I shall find someone who may be needing peas, and I shall exchange them with him for something which I in my turn require. I give him peas in return for something which I for my part can use. Substantially, the peas have remained the same; but economically they have not remained the same at all. Economically they have changed through the very fact that I, instead of consuming them myself, have passed them into circulation. Economically speaking, what have the peas become by this process? Given the necessary conditions, including a statute enacting that everything shall be exchangeable for peas (a sufficient number of peas would have to be produced and it would have to be the law that everything can be exchanged for peas) - the peas would be money. In such a case, peas would have become money in the true sense of the word. A thing does not become money by being essentially different from other things existing in the economic process, but by undergoing - at a particular point in this process - a transformation from commodity to money. This has been the case with all forms of money. They have all at one time or another been turned from a commodity into money.

Hence we see once more that with the economic process we always come to the human being: We can do no other than place him into the process. The human being is there in any case as a consumer from the very outset. But if he has an economic role other than as consumer, he enters into quite another relationship with economic life than that of a pure consumer. Such things must be taken into account if we would work towards the formation of true economic judgements, the kind of judgement, in fact, which must above all be formed in what I have called associations. Within the associations there must be people who by their practical experience can form their judgements on the basis of such points of view.

The point is : If we have any kind of elaborated land or divided labour in the economic process, we must investigate what it is that brings these economic elements into movement, into circulation. Yesterday, in another circle (see Discourse 2), I said that we ought to bring into our economic thinking the work or labour which is active in the economic process, in precisely the same way that the physicist, for example, brings the concept of "work" into his thinking about physics. He does this by developing a formula, that includes mass and velocity. Mass is a thing which we determine by the balance, without which there would be nothing to move forward in the process of "work" in the sense of physics. The question arises: Is there anything similar in the economic process, so that here, too, labour or work can be seen to give value to objects, and then at a later stage the active entry of intelligence? Is there anything in the economic process comparable, as it were, to the weight of an object in the process of "work" in the sense of physics? If I describe diagrammatically the progression of the several economic processes, I see at once that something must be there to bring the whole thing into movement - to push or press the economic element, so to speak, from here to here (see Sketch 6). Moreover, the thing would be still more pronounced if there were not only a pressure working from here to here, but in addition a suction from the other side, so that the whole thing were driven forward by a real force present in the economic process. The economic process would, in fact, have to contain something that drives it forward.

What is it then that drives it forward? I showed you a little while ago how certain forces constantly arise, in the case of both buyer and seller. With everyone who has something to do with any other human being in the economic process - not at all in the moral but in the purely economic sense - advantage or profit arises. There is no place within the economic process where we cannot speak of profit. Nor is this profit anything merely abstract; the immediate economic desire of the human being attaches to it, and it must needs be so. Whether he is a buyer or a seller, his economic craving attaches to the profit, to the advantage to be had from the transaction. It is really this attachment to profit which generates the economic process, corresponding to mass in the process of "work" in the sense of physics.

We have thus revealed something very weighty in economics - literally weighty. Weight is a most prominent thing in purely material products - those products for which the stomach craves. It is the stomach which tells the purchaser that fruit is more advantageous than money, in the moment at which he makes the exchange. Here, then, we find the driving motor in the human being himself. And in other cases, too - not only in the case of material goods - there must be such a driving force. You need but consider that the mood or feeling of making an advantageous deal is also present in me when I sell a thing and receive money for it. I know that I shall be able to do more

with the money than with the commodities which I possess, my faculties tell
me so.

Transfer this idea to the sum-total of loan capital in any economic organism
and you will see: Those who desire to undertake something have precisely
the same motive force in their need for capital as is inherent in the striving
for profit. Only, the loan capital works as a kind of suction. If we regard profit
as an impelling, pushing force, the effect of loan capital is one of suction.
Moreover, it sucks in the same direction in which profit pushes. Thus, in
profit and in loan capital respectively, we have the forces of pressure and of
suction in the economic process. (Sketch 7.)

We thus gain a clear picture of the fact that, inasmuch as the economic process
consists in movement and everything must be brought about in it by
movement, we must place the human being in it everywhere. For an objective
science of economics this may be uncomfortable because the human being
is an unknown quantity and changeable. We have to reckon with him in so
many different ways. This is a fact from which we cannot escape.

We have now seen that in the process of lending a kind of suction takes place
in the economic process. You know there were times when it was considered
immoral to take an interest on loans: It was only considered moral to lend free
of interest. Under such conditions there could be no profit in lending. This is
indeed the fact. Originally, lending did not arise from the profit derived from
it, that is to say, from the interest; it arose from the following presumption.
If I lend someone something, he can do something with it which I cannot do.
Take the simplest instance: Suppose that someone is in dire need and that he
can alleviate his need if I am in the position to lend him something. Under
conditions more primitive than those of today, he would not pay me interest,
but the presumption would be that if I, too, were ever in need, he in his turn
would help me out. Wherever you trace the matter back in history, you will
see that this is the pre-supposition of lending: The other human being will
lend to me in turn when the need arises. It even applies to more complicated
social conditions, for the same thing happens when someone borrows money
from a money-lending firm and requires guarantors. It has always been the
experience of money-lenders that mutual aid plays a great part even in this
service. A comes to a money-lender, bringing B and C with him to stand
sureties; they enter their names as guarantors. In such a case, money-lending
firms always reckon on the probability that if B ever comes to borrow money,
he will bring with him A and C ; or again, B having paid his debt, C will arrive

one day and will bring with him *A* and *B* as guarantors. In certain circles this is taken as a matter of course. Economists declare that such a law can be assessed just as well as any that can be clothed in a mathematical formula. Of course these things are to be taken with the well-known grain of salt which we must always take into account. Our power to do so is part of the mobility of the economic process.

To sum up, therefore, we must say: Originally, there is no return for the service of lending, save the presumption that the borrower will lend to us again; or, if not, that at least he will help us in borrowing, as we helped him. Notably where it is a question of lending and borrowing, human mutuality or "give and take" enters the economic process in a striking way.

If this be so, what is interest? Interest - as has already been remarked by some economists - interest is what I receive if I renounce this "mutuality", that is to say, if I lend someone something and we agree that he shall be under no obligation to lend to me. If I renounce this mutual right, he pays me interest for it. Interest, therefore, resolves something which takes place between two human beings; it is a compensation for the human mutuality which otherwise plays into the economic process.

This is, however, something which we must set in its right context in the whole economic process. In doing so we must, of course, remember that there is no sense nowadays in studying economic processes other than those which stand entirely under the sign of the division of labour; for it is these with which we are in fact concerned. When labour is divided and distributed, human beings grow dependent on the principle of mutuality to a far greater extent than is the case when every human being not only grows his own cabbages but also makes his own hats and boots. It is with the division of labour that the dependence on mutuality comes. In the division of labour we have a process working in such a way that the several currents diverge. Yet in the economic process as a whole these different streams tend to unite again, only in a different way, through exchange, which, in the case of a more complicated economic process, takes place with the help of money. Thus, at a certain stage the division of labour makes mutuality a necessity. In other words, it involves the same element in human intercourse which we find in the case of lending and borrowing. Where much is lent, this principle of mutuality is inherently involved, but in this case it can be redeemed by interest. For interest is mutuality realised - monetised - transformed into the abstract form of money. The forces of mutuality behind the interest have undergone a metamorphosis. Moreover, what we see quite plainly here in the payment of interest takes place throughout the economic process.

This is the great difficulty which besets economics and makes the academic world so uneasy: You cannot form economic ideas otherwise than by conceiving things pictorially. No abstract concept can enable you to grasp the economic process; you must grasp it in pictures, passing from merely abstract concepts to ideation of an imaginative kind. We can never found a real science of economics without developing pictorial ideas, even as reagrds the details. And these pictures must contain a dynamic quality; we must become aware how such a process works under each new form that it assumes.

You will understand me rightly if you will acknowledge to yourselves that there are actually people in the economic process - no doubt at its more primitive stages - who are quite unable to think in the way you have learned - or are supposed to have learned - to think in the course of your studies. Nevertheless, they are often excellent husbandmen, excellent economists. They feel precisely whether a given object can be bought or not be brought at such and such a price - whether there is any profit in it. Sometimes a peasant, for example, has not the remotest notion of economic concepts; yet, having attained a certain age, having simply observed the conditions of the market here or there in his district, he knows with precision - without relying on any theoretical concepts - what the picture signifies, when he gives a certain sum of money for a horse or plough. Of course he may make a mistake, but you may do that even if you have studied the logic of economics! - but the mistake will not be the most important thing. The picture that is composed before his mind - the picture of a certain sum of money and a plough - calls forth in him the immediate feeling that he can still afford to give so and so much more money, or else that he cannot. He has it directly out of his feeling-experience. Even in the most complicated economic process, this feeling-experience is not to be eliminated. It is this that thinking in pictures entails.

Merely abstract ideas would only be fruitful if we could say definitely, that one thing is a commodity and another thing is money and that we are trading the commodity for money, the money for the commodity. If that were all, matters would be simple; but as I showed you just now, even peas may become money. It is simply not possible to grasp the economic process by working abstract concepts into it. For instance, we may have the picture of peas on their way from the market-stall to the mouths of people only. That is one definite picture. Or we imagine peas being used as money. That is another picture. Even in economics we must work towards such pictures, pictures built out of immediate perception. In other words, to act rightly in the economic sense, we must enter into the events of production, trade and consumption, with a picture-thinking. Even so our concepts will only be approximate ones, but they will be of real use to us when we wish to take an actual part in the economic life. Above all, such conceptions will be of use to us when what we have not sensed for ourselves is supplemented or corrected by others associated with us. There is no other possibility. Economic judgements cannot be built on theory; they must be built on living association. The value of any given thing must be determined out of the association - the immediate experiences - of those concerned with it.

Strange as it may sound, it is not possible to determine theoretically wherein the value of a product may consist. We can only say: A product enters into the economic life as a whole through the several parts of the economic process; and its value at a given place must be judged and estimated by association.

How can such judgement be formed - judgements which arrive at the truth? You can understand it best by analogy with any human or animal organism. For example, the human being absorbs food, permeates it with ptyalin and pepsin, then passes it through the stomach and intestines. No matter whether the food is meat or vegetable, the first thing necessary is for it to be killed; its life must be quelled. Thereupon, it is sucked up by the lymphatic glands and called to life again within ourselves. That which passes from the lymphatic glands through the lymphatic vessels into the blood consists of nature-products (plant or animal) which have died and have been called to life again. Now if you wanted to determine theoretically how much a certain lymphatic gland should receive and call to life again, you simply could not do so: for in one human being a lymphatic gland must absorb more, and in another less. Not only so; in one and the same human being a lymphatic gland at one place must absorb more and a lymphatic gland at another place less. Digestion is a most complicated process; no human science could keep pace with this wisdom of the lymphatic glands, with all their beautiful division of labour.

In such a case we are not dealing with judgements propounded, but judgements working in reality. In very truth, between our intestinal organs and our arteries, such a sum total of intelligence is working that nothing comparable to it is to be found in all our human science.

So it is with the economic process. The economic process can only be sound when such a wise self-active intelligence is working within it. This can only happen if human beings are united together - human beings who have the economic process within them as pictures, piece by piece; and, being united in associations, they complement and correct one another, so that the right circulation can take place in the whole economic process. Of course, the right mentality is needed for such a thing as this, but the mentality alone is not enough. You may even found associations, whose members may have a great deal of economic insight; yet if something else is not contained within the associations, all their insight will be of little avail. Something else must be there, and will be there, once their necessity is seen. There must be a kind of public-spiritedness, concern for the other, the sense for the economic process as a whole. The individual who immediately uses what he buys can do no other than satisfy his own egoistic sense. Indeed he would come off very badly if he did not. As a single human being in the economic life, he cannot say, if someone offers him a coat for 40 francs: "Oh, no, that price does not suit me; I will give you 60 francs for it!" That will not do. But the moment associative working enters the economic process, it is no longer a question of immediate personal interest. The wide overview of the economic process will be active, and the interests of others will be actually there in the economic judgement that is formed. In no other way can a true economic judgement come about. Thus, we are impelled to rise from the economic processes to the mutuality, the give and take between human beings, and furthermore to that which will arise from this, namely working in associations. Such a sense of and concern for the other, however, will not proceed from any "moralic acid" but from a realisation of the necessities inherent in the economic process itself.

There is no lack of people nowadays who say: "Our economic life will be good - ever so good - if once human beings are good; they must become good." Think of the people like Professor Förster[51] and his kind, who go about preaching: "If human beings will only become selfless, if they will only fulfil the categorical imperative of selflessness, the economic life will become good." Such judgements are really of no more worth than this one: If my mother-in-law had four wheels and a handle in front, she would be a bus! Truly, the premiss and the conclusion stand in no better connection, except that I have expressed it rather more radically.

There can be none of this moralic acid. Rather the purpose is to show, simply out of the economic facts, how selflessness cannot help being inherent in the very circulation of the elements of economic life. This is the case, even in the detailed instances. Take, for example, the case where someone is in a position to receive loan capital on credit and is thus enabled to establish an undertaking or an institution and to produce by means of it. He goes on producing so long as his own personal faculties are united with the institution. Afterwards, the thing he has worked up will be handed on in the most intelligent way to some other individual who has the necessary faculties. It will be transferred by a gift - a gift, not from one human being to another, but one that takes place through the whole course of economic life. We need only consider how such gifts will be able to be made in an intelligent way by the threefold social organism. Here the domain of economics borders on the social element in the human being, in the most comprehensive meaning of the term. It touches on that which needs to be conceived for the social organism as a whole.

And you can see it also from the other side. I pointed out how in the simple case of exchange - where money becomes more and more important, or indeed where exchange is recognised at all - the economic life enters directly into the region of law and rights. Moreover the moment Intelligence is to enter the economic life, we must allow to flow into the economic domain that which prevails in a free cultural life. The three members of the social organism must stand in the right relation to one another, so that they may work on one another in the right way.

This was the real meaning of the threefold social order - not the splitting into parts of the three members; the splitting apart is always there. The point is rather to find how the three members can be brought together, so that they may really work in the social organism out of their inherent wisdom, just as the nerves-and-senses system, the heart-and-lungs system, and the metabolic system, for example, work together in the human organism.[52] That is the point, and of this we shall have more to say in the near future.

11: THE CONDITIONS AND CONSEQUENCES OF A WORLD ECONOMY
3 August 1992

In the opinion of a number of economists it was quite impossible for the War to last as long as it actually did last. From their knowledge of economic relationships, these economists declared that the economic life of the time would not permit such an extensive war to last more than a few months. Yet, as you know, the facts of life refuted this idea. If people thought objectively, this in itself would convince them of the need to revise their science of economics. For if you took the trouble at this moment to follow up the reasons which some economists, at any rate, adduced for their assertion, you would by no means be able to conclude that they were mere fools. Quite the contrary; their arguments were not at all bad and carried some conviction. Nevertheless, life refuted them and the War went on far longer than was theoretically possible. Obviously, therefore, economic science did not embrace the reality.

We can only understand such a thing as this if we see clearly the nature of the evolution of economic life on earth. Its earlier stages continue to exist side by side with the later. Similarly we may say that the lowest organic forms now living are somewhat like the earliest living creatures. Thus in a sense the most primitive creatures are still here, existing side by side with the highest creatures yet evolved. There is a difference, but there is also a marked resemblance in the forms. So it is in the economic life. The phenomena of primitive phases of economic life are still here today, side by side with those which have attained a higher stage. But in the economic life there is another peculiarity. While in the animal kingdom, for example, the more primitive forms can live literally side by side with the more highly evolved, in the economic life the more primitive processes are constantly inter-penetrating with the more highly evolved ones. We might very well compare it with those cases where bacteria penetrate inside higher organisms. Only, in the economic life it is infinitely more complicated. Nevertheless, we can detect certain underlying structures, and from these we can take useful examples which will help us to bring our line of thought to its conclusion.

The more primitive forms of economic life must be conceived as private argicultural economies on a larger scale. Their magnitude is relative, of course; but we must understand that if the private agricultural economy is self-contained, it includes within it other aspects of the social organism. It has its own administration, possibly even its own defence force, its own police, and moreover its own cultural life. Such a private economy - grown to gigantic proportions, it is true, but still preserving in all essentials the character of a simple agricultural concern, a gigantic farm - was the so-called kingdom of the Merovingians.[53] It was a kingdom in a quite external sense, but it was certainly no State. It was in fact no more than an immense farming estate, comprehending a huge area. The entire social structure of the Merovingian kingdom was really no different from this: The economic life underlay everything. On this was built an administrative system which accorded with the prevailing ideas of right and justice: And into this was placed a cultural life - an extraordinarily free one for that time. For it is only in more modern times and notably under the influence of "Liberalism"[54] that we have seen the rise of the maximum of unfreedom in cultural life. Not until Liberalism came did cultural life begin to grow more and more unfree; and it reaches the zenith of unfreedom in that embodiment of all political bliss, the Soviet Republic of Russia. Only books approved by the Soviet Government can be sold at all. The Pope does at least content himself with proscribing books; but under the Soviet Government proscription is automatic, inasmuch as no books are printed and published save those which the Government permits.

Now if we trace the further course of evolution, we see how private economies gradually passed over into national economies, which again at a certain time - at the beginning of the modern period - tended to become state-economies. The way it happens is characteristic. Private economy - initiative in private business - gradually passes over into the hands of government departments, and thus the fiscal administration grows increasingly into industrial organisation. We see economies passing over into the life of the State, absorbing cultural life in the process. Thus, we witness the rise of the modern economic and cultural organism of the State, now grown increasingly powerful.

In the main, private economies gradually joined together on a pretty large scale. They grew into what could be called economy on a larger scale - national economy; and in this way a new social structure was created. Yet, within the new, the element of private economy was still preserved. The more primitive phase of evolution was still there as an insertion in the new. Now something arises at this stage in the true sense of national economy, namely, mutual exchange between the several private economies. Regulated in many different ways - the regulation hovering like a cloud over it all - commerce between private economies is the essential thing that arises with their welding into a national economy. But with what outcome?

We saw yesterday that in the process of economic exchange each of the parties makes or can make a profit. Therefore, when single economies join together for the sake of mutual exchange (the essential thing in all economic life) they profit by doing so. Single economies, single businesses, gain an advantage by joining together. They profit by it simply because they can now exchange one with another. We can draw up a statement. We can calculate how much the one private economy or business will gain by means of the other private economies with which it is now connected. Each party gains an advantage, and the gain of each and all becomes significant for the entire national economy.

When today's economics was founded, that particular stage had already been reached. National economies had developed out of the private economies. This must be borne in mind if we wish to understand the economic ideas of Ricardo or Smith, for then we can understand the thoughts they evolved about "political economy", as they called it. It was this working together of private economies which they actually saw and upon which they based their views. In Adam Smith you can see it again and again - how he thinks from the point of view of private economy or business and thence draws his conclusions. At the same time he has before him the picture of their joining together into a national economy. Yet even in their ideas about this latter process the older economists retained to a large extent a way of thinking based on private business. They treated national economy on the analogy of private economy. Thus the fertility, the prosperity of a national economy, as they conceived it, lay in this - one national economy would exchange with another, would come into mutual intercourse with another and would thus derive profit and advantage. The "Mercantilist" school[55], for example, was based on the advantages arising from such exchange between national economies.

Now already at this early stage there is sure to arise a kind of leadership. In effect, the most powerful of the private economies which have merged into a larger complex will naturally assume the leadership; and this would undoubtedly have happened at the transition from the stage of private economy into that of national economy. But it was masked and hidden; it did not come fully to expression, because the State undertook the leadership. If this had not happened, one private economy - the most powerful of them - would naturally have been the leader. So in effect it happened that the single private economies actually passed imperceptibly into the form, not of national, but of state-economy.

It was different, however, at the next stage, when in the further course of modern history the mutual exchange between national economies - world trade, in other words - became more and more comprehensive. Then, indeed, such a leadership emerged quite obviously. It happened, as an absolute matter of course, in the further progress of economic life, that England's national economy became the dominating one. From another point of view, I have already drawn your attention to the fact that England evolved directly from trade into industrialism. Let us think what happened while England was acquiring her colonies. She set the standard for currencies. Her colonies, in the manner of private economies, joined together into a larger complex. In the first place this gave rise to those internal advantages which are always the result of mutual exchange. But, not only that: It also gave rise to that powerful economic hegemony which, with the further evolution of world trade, subsequently exerted a dominant influence on the economic life of the world. England set the standard for currencies, because it was precisely through England that gold was forced on those countries which adopted it throughout the world. For, as you may easily compute, in economic intercourse with a rich country having a gold currency, any country which did not posses it would be at a disadvantage. Thus it was that, under the influence of world trade, England became the leading economic power.

And yet, while this was going on, it was still possible to develop concepts of national economy in a straight line - with whatever modifications and improvements - from Hume[56], Adam Smith and Ricardo, and, we may add, Karl Marx[57] - for fundamentally, though he turned their ideas pretty well upside down, Karl Marx only continued along the same lines. The ideas of these economists are only to be understood if we have before us the picture of that economic life, which arose under the dominating influence of England's economic power.

Now with the last third of the nineteenth century, there was a transition from world trade to world economy - a very remarkable process. Definitions are of course inexact, for these transitions tend to take place in successive stages;

but if we want a definition we must say: At the stage of world trade the economic life of the world is characterised by single national economies exchanging with one another. This traffic quickens the whole process of exchange and thus essentially alters prices - alters the whole structure of economic life. But in all other respects economic life is carried on within the several territories. As against this it may be called "world economy" when the single economic units not only exchange their products one with another, but when they actually work together industrially: When, for example, half-manufactured products are sent from one country to another, for their manufacture to be continued there. That is a radical example of what I mean by their working together industrially.[58] So long as it is merely a question of raw products, the account will continue to show a condition of pure trade. This cannot yet be described as an actual working-together in the industrial life. But when all factors in human life (in so far as they are affected by economics), that is to say, when all production, all distribution, all consumption - not merely production alone or consumption alone - are fed from the entire world; when all things are intricately interwoven and fed from the entire world - then we have world economy. And through the rise of this world economy, certain advantages which existed formerly for the national economies are lost.

Let us look back once more. When private economies join into a national economy they gain on the whole; every single one derives advantages. But, apart from this, what is it that impels them? It is of course not always conscious insight, for in most cases the feeling for liberty is too great; the private entrepreneur is not as concerned as all that with the piling up of the profits which arise in this way. Economically, these profits certainly arise; but the process is more complicated than that. The fact is that the single private economies or businesses have the same characteristic as every living organism, namely, their life tends in the course of time to become weaker and weaker. This is a universal law, applicable equally to economic life. An economic life which is not being constantly improved always deteriorates. Thus, as a rule, the merging into larger entities did not take place with the object of making private businesses profitable beyond their original level, but with the object of protecting them from imminent decline.[59]

When once they join together, they gain the corresponding advantage, though of course it varies from one case to another. And whatever the single economies have lost in course of time is amply made up for by their joining into national economies. Indeed, as a rule, it is more than compensated. By the same token, whatever the national economies have lost in course of time is amply made up for by world trade and the transition into world economy. But when world economy is once achieved, what then? With whom can it exchange? This, in effect, is what has happened. We have seen the economic life of the entire earth gradually merging into world economy, at which point the possibility of reaping further advantages by merger is at an end.

The economists who declared that the War could not last as long as in fact it did last were thinking in terms of national economies, and not of world economy. If world economy had been national economy, their declarations would have been quite true. But from the very beginning the War was a world war. It had the tendency to spread and spread, and by this very fact it had a longer life. If in the state of world economy we continue to think in the spirit of national economies world economy itself will at a certain point break up.

You see how there play into the economic domain circumstances which are clearly perceptible, but which cannot in the nature of things be easily taken hold of with figures and statistics. Thus it is quite impossible to prolong in a straight line the old economic ideas. We are obliged to admit that a science of economics is now needed which will express the realities of the immediate present. The economic categories formed about a century ago no longer hold good today. What we need is an economic science capable of thinking in the spirit of world economy. Herein you see one of our greatest historical problems.

Observe the leading statesmen of today coming together at Versailles, Genoa or the Hague. Science has only provided them with a way of thinking in terms of national economy. Whatever results they arrive at, unless and until they are permeated with world-economic thinking, they must lead downhill. Can they deny that they are tearing the economic life still more to pieces, erecting fresh artificial barriers and thus hindering the transition into a pure world economy? We see this tendency in the immediate past - the tendency to break the world asunder as far as possible even in the economic life, and at the same time to conceal the tendency under the cloak of political and national pleas. Yet we shall have to pass into a real world economy and a corresponding economics, or we shall create an economically impossible state of affairs over the earth. Such a condition of affairs can only continue in being for a time through one part of the earth stealing advantages at the expense of another by means of differences in currency, or the rates of exchange. This is precisely what is happening in economic life at the present moment.[60]

To conceive what world-economics really means, we must see clearly, to begin with, that at the frontiers of the domain of world economy the conditions will be quite different from those of economic domains bordering on one another. Relatively speaking, world economy exists today; and becauseits domain borders on nothing else, it is necessary for us to observe still more precisely those economic processes which emerge within a closed economic domain, independently of its external frontiers. This, then, is the cardinal problem for modern economics to solve: The problem of the closed economics domain - a self-contained domain of one giant economy. For today the very smallest question - even the price of coffee - is influenced by the economic life of the entire earth. If it is not so, it only means that progress is partial. This state of affairs is actually on the way and our thinking will have to follow suit.

To understand the economic conditions in a closed economic domain, we must see clearly that within the economic domain - in the mutual interplay of production, consumption and commerce (that is, in effect, circulation) - we have on the one hand consumable commodities, some of them relatively lasting, no doubt; while on the other hand we have the thing we call "money". Now as regards the form of economy to which these things are subject, it makes an essential difference how we envisage the class of foodstuffs for example (short-lived products), or of clothing (more long-lived), or, let us say, of furniture or houses (more long-lived still). With respect to their use and consumption we have these important differences of duration as between different kinds of economic products. As an instance of a really lasting economic product, we might point once more to the diamond in the Crown of England, or any other crown. Or, again, we might think of the Sistine Madonna. Such things may be to some extent regarded as a kind of product that will keep; we find them especially among works of art. Now in a social organism subject to division of labour, having therefore an extensive process of circulation, there must be some equivalent of every product. There must be the money-value, representing the price. But a very little observation of the economic realm will convince you that this equivalent between commodity-value and money-value is fluctuating. A product is worth so much at one place and so much at another. A product can be worth more if it is worked-up in one way, or less if worked-up in another. Be that as it may, in the total economic life you will perceive that, apart from a few exceptional goods of very long duration, we always have to do with goods which pass away in time. They lose their value, and after a certain lapse of time are no longer there.

The one exception, strange to say, in our whole economic life is money. Although it occupies a position of perfect equivalence to the other elements of economic life, money does not wear out. You can get to the root of the matter in this way: If I have £20 worth of potatoes, I must see to it that I get rid of them. I must do something to get rid of them. After a time they are no longer there; they are used up, they are gone. Now if it were in true relation of equivalence to the goods that are produced, money, too, would have to wear out, like other goods. That is to say, if the body economic contains money which is incapable of being used up - money which does not wear out - we may well be giving money the advantage over goods, which do wear out. This is a most important point and it becomes all the more so when we take the following into account. Think of all that I must do, if - let us say - through my activity and labour I want to thrive so well that as a result of having a certain amount of potatoes today I shall have double the amount in 15 years' time. Then think, on the other hand, how little an individual person has to do if he possesses £20 in money today and wishes to possess double the amount in 15 years' time. He need do nothing at all; he can withdraw his entire labour-power from the social organism and let other people work. All he need do is to lend his money and let other people do the work. Unless he himself in the meantime sees to it that the money is spent, the money need not be used up.

This is the very thing which brings into the body social so much of what is afterwards felt - shall we say - as a social anomaly, as an injustice. Indeed, gigantic changes are brought about in the body social, even economically speaking, by this reshuffling - not of the relationships of property, but of work and activity. And we may ask: How are these changes related to another factor, by which it is perhaps more easy to apprehend them? For there is still something rather vague about it if I merely describe empirically, as I did just now, this existing discrepancy as between money and the real objects in the economic organism. How can we get a pictorial idea of some particular instance?

Consider, to begin with, how absolutely fundamental for the whole economy of a closed domain is the consumption by all the human beings contained in it. This is the very premiss: The total consumption by all the human beings who live in the economic domain. That is something which is simply there; it is presupposed, a given.

But there is also another thing which is of fundamental significance; and that is the land as such. Though this was badly misunderstood by the Physiocrats,[61] for example, nevertheless the land is of fundamental significance, in spite of the fact, which has emerged from these lectures, that it must be constantly devalued. Indeed, it is just because of its fundamental significance that it might again be devalued. The Physiocrats made the following mistake. They lived in a time when land (as is of course still the case) had capital value. They conceived their ideas under the influence of this fact. They traced the economic relationships, indeed, in a very clear and graphic way. Of all the economists, they are the most rational. And from their standpoint they came to the conclusion that the intrinsic worth of an economic realm lies in the cultivation of the land, i.e. in the production of food. So long as we remain within this field, we must in fact regard the land as the more or less fixed and given foundation of the economic realm, constituting its intrinsic worth. You need only reflect how those who work upon the land to produce food, in effect - so far as food is concerned - feed everyone else along with themselves. All others are dependent on them; all others must be fed by them. The others, it is true, can somehow get the means to pay for it, and pay more or less dearly. But we may think it out in simple terms in order to grasp the essential point. Let us suppose that there is a certain number, A, of eaters. This number A will include all the farm workers, all the industrial workers, all the investors, all the traders, and all the teachers and such like - in effect everybody. All require feeding. There will be another number, B, comprising those who have food to offer, those who provide that part of the sum-total of consumption represented by the food consumed. Now if A is increased to $A1$, while B remains constant, B's product will have to be further divided; and, unless B can also be increased in value somehow, people will have to be brought into the country in order to increase the yield from the land.

In other words, you cannot arbitrarily increase the number of those engaged in freed activity, for example, within a given economic domain, without increasing on the other side the number of those who are responsible for the production of foodstuffs. Alternatively you can increase the fertility of the soil. The latter may, of course, be the result of freed activity, but in that case it follows that those so contributing in a period when fertility is higher must be wiser; they must have higher faculties than those who went before them.

Thus, the increased yield of farm labour is in a certain sense equivalent to the enhancement of the insight with which we elaborate the products we receive from land. This may be done in many different ways. A person may enhance the forestry of a whole country by improving the bird-life of the country. It may be done in countless ways; we are only concerned with the principle.

So long as we are only thinking in terms of national economy, it is clear enough that such things can happen. Into a country endowed with a lesser degree of insight cleverer people may immigrate from another country, and they may then improve the cultivation of the land. Or, on the other hand, if more people move up into the classes which are not actually producing food, fresh workers may be called into the country. All these things actually happen within and across the frontiers of national economies which border upon other national economies.[62]

All that we can think upon this matter may now be expressed in the question: What is to be done if, on the side of A, consumption is in excess of what B can produce? Whatever we may think at this point in terms of purely national economy, it ceases to be thinkable when world economy arises, and when the conditions of the world are already in a certain sense disposed as for world economy. What we have to do is to form an idea of the changes entailed by the existence of a self-contained economic domain.

We can study it empirically by observing some small economy wherein exports and imports can be more or less disregarded. After all, there have been such economies. Empirically, we can study the condition within a self-contained economic realm. And we find it true: The foundation is the land. What the land yields is subjected to labour - elaborated - and thus receives an economic value. Thereafter labour itself is organised. We come to the class of human beings who are no longer actual producers of food, who are consumers but not producers so far as food is concerned. Especially is this so with people such as preachers and artists. In a self-contained economic realm we must therefore distinguish, with respect to food, a certain number of producers who indeed - if I may say so - are very much aware of the fact that they are the producers; and over against them the consumers.[63]

These things, of course, are relative; the transition is gradual. But if we consider the whole of human life within a self-contained economic realm of this kind, we must bring about what I explained a few days ago: Capital must not be allowed to become congested in land. Hence, at the place where cultural life is most highly involved in the forming of capital (this "place" is, of course, spread out throughout the entire economic realm) the excess of capital which has been acquired must not be allowed to flow into the land, where it would become dammed up. Provision must be made for its elimination. This is to say, at an earlier stage in the process, the congestion must be prevented by the free gift to the cultural institutions, of the excess which has been acquired. Only what I described as a kind of "seed" must be allowed to pass on. It is here that the concept of "free gift" confronts us inevitably; there must be free gifts.

Study any of the self-contained economic realms which have arisen in the course of history, and you will see that the free gift is always there. In all essentials, the cultural life is dependent on what, in the economic sense of the word, are free gifts, pure and simple.

From the simple case where Charles the Bald, out of what he had to give away, maintained his Court Philosopher (which some may regard as a rather superfluous article of furniture!) - Scotus Erigena - to Peter's Pence, whereby Roman Catholics the world over give their free gifts to the Church in tiny doses, such gifts are always there. Wheresoever an economic life, no matter how gigantic it may become, represents an economic domain more or less self-contained, you have the transformation of accumulated capital into gift capital for the maintenance of cultural institutions.[64]

In other words, now that humanity as a whole has come to a closed economic realm - namely that of the entire world - we should reflect that one thing is inevitable in a truly economic sense: What would otherwise become dammed up in the land must vanish into cultural institutions. I say once more, it must somehow vanish into the cultural institutions. It must take effect as a free gift.

For a truly modern economic science, we must seek an answer to this question: In the sense of economics, how must we buy and sell, so that the values, primarily represented by food within the purely material realm, may vanish within the cultural domain? That is the great question. I will formulate it once more: What form of payment must we strive for in our economic intercourse, so that that which is created by the elaboration of land, where the productive process primarily works to feed humanity, eventually vanishes in cultural institutions? This is the great economic question, to the answering of which we shall proceed in the next lecture.

12: MONEY
4 August 1922

Yesterday we formulated a very important question which came to the fore with the transition from national economy to world economy. With this transition the question of price begins to acquire a very different significance from what it had before. But there are other things to consider before we can gain a conception of the factors which really determine price. For the prices - the public prices so to speak - which eventually emerge are really of far less economic importance than that which lies behind their forming, of which price-formation and price-fluctuation are merely effects.

These factors, both on the buying and the selling side, are connected with the social relationships in the midst of which the buyer and seller stand; relationships which determine whether one attaches a greater or lesser value to a certain sum of money. I mean value not only in the subjective sense, but economically speaking; the subjective is only important to the extent that it is properly grounded in the objective - i.e. to the extent that it rests on a true judgement of objective processes. The economic question nowadays cannot be isolated from the social question. Only by observing the interplay of the two can one reach a valid judgement. We must recognise that the social discontent underlying the present social disturbances is connected above all with that which precedes the forming of prices. As I have shown already, even in the payment of wages - i.e. in that aspect of price-formation which, under the existing economic system, ultimately finds expression in the rate of wages - we really have an instance of purchase and sale. Thus everything that leads to wage disputes really depends on social relationships in which both the worker and the entrepreneur are involved, relationships which give rise to the payment of wages. Accordingly, the first thing to investigate is: How does money itself influence the forming of price? For money plays the chief part nowadays both in ordinary purchase and sale and in the payment of wages, as well as in all the rest of economic life. We must distinguish between that which eventually emerges as price in terms of money, and that which constitutes the essential value of the money in the hand of one human being or another - in the hand of the seller or of the buyer. Today, therefore, we must pause for a moment to consider money as such.

In the current treatises on economics you will find various elegant statements on the nature of money. For instance, you will find a list of the qualities which money must have in order to enable it to be used as money. Let us consider critically some of the qualities which are thus enumerated, for this will show you how necessary it is to get away from many of these current ideas into a rather different way of thinking. For instance, it is said: In the first place money must have a universally recognised value. But the question is: Who is to be the recogniser? When you have said that money must have a universally recognised value you have said nothing. You have simply asserted that it ought to have a certain property, but you have not explained how it is to get it.

The second property enumerated is still more remarkable. It is said, for instance, that money must be small in volume and yet, being rare, in spite of its small volume it must be possible for it to have a high value. For this property makes money especially easy to store up and, if only for this reason, will constitute a fairly strong inducement to the amassing of wealth. If sovereigns were as big as tables it would be far more difficult to hoard them. Lycurgus saw this long ago and introduced a bulky currency to discourage excessive enrichment. If sovereigns were as big as tables it would indeed be less comfortable to get rich than it is now. People would notice it more, and so on. The reason, therefore, appears to be a rather superficial one.

The next thing they say is this: Money must be divisible at will. But this again can only be brought about by some act of recognition. Something must first be done to make it so. It is, therefore, once more a rather empty statement. Then they say: Money must be easy to preserve. Well, this property of being "easy to preserve" will be brought home to us in its full significance in the course of today's lecture.

You see, we must not only be clear on this, that land as such only receives economic value when it enters into the general economic circulation - when it is taken up by labour - and again, that labour only receives economic value through the way it is organised or divided, and finally, that capital only receives a value through the fact it is taken over by human intelligence and so worked into the economic process. We must also be clear that money as such receives its value by the free process of circulation. And now we must consider the changes which money undergoes in the course of circulation; the premises are given to us by what we have said already in these lectures.

Speaking of money, the first thing we have to deal with is ordinary purchase money - the money we use to buy anything which serves us for consumption. But we must also consider what we have called loan money. The question now is: Bearing in mind its connection with the whole economic process, is loan money the same as purchase money? If you are considering purchase money you will have to ask: How does purhase money come into existence among all the other elements of buying and selling? It comes about by this means: He who makes use of money, in giving his money, has not only given something which effects an immediate exchange, but he has also given something which mediates an exchange. He gives something which inserts itself into the exchange. As I have shown already in these lectures, everything that enters as a mediator into the process of exchange is money. Suppose I am not content with acquiring as many peas as I can eat myself. Suppose I acquire peas with the object of using them - trading with them - in order to obtain some other things which I require. In that case, simply through this mediating function I am already transforming what would otherwise be an article of consumption into money.

Spengler makes a very shrewd observation on this point.[65] Spengler exploits his ideas along a general line of thought which is unfruitful, but he often makes very sound observations. He says: At a certain period of Roman history human beings, economically speaking, became money. The slaves became money. So long as I used the slaves for myself - that is to say, if as an Ancient Roman I only acquired as many slaves as I could use in my own household - the slave was, of course, a means of production. But it is different the moment the slave is hired out or lent. At a certain period of the Roman Empire this being the case; people had so great an army of slaves that they were able to lend them out. They could apply them to all manner of profitable purposes by trading with them. When this took place the slaves became money, so that for that time, we may say, human beings became money. This is a perfectly correct observation of Spengler's, from which you can see once more how that which acts as purchase money gradually emerges out of what is at first only an article of exchange. It follows from this: That whatever we use as money - to be a really useful form of money - it must not merely oscillate, like peas, between the function of being consumed and the function of being passed from hand to hand. For this would involve constant fluctuations of value in the process of circulation. We want something which is used for no other purpose than for mediating an exchange; and to this end there must be a certain - albeit only a tacit - agreement among those who use the money. This, then, is an essential point: The money must only be used for exchange, as a medium; it must not be used for consumption.

In the case of purchase money you have no other foundation on which to estimate its value - indeed, no other need - than this: How much will you get for it? And as to that, time makes no essential difference. For whether you buy a pound of meat today or after a certain lapse of time, you must estimate the pound of meat according to its consumption-value. Your money may in the meantime have acquired a different value in relation to the pound of meat. But for the human being who eats it, the value of the pound of meat cannot, properly speaking, change in course of time. This, however, is essential: The given pound of meat can only be eaten during a certain period of time. That is to say, it can only have a value for a certain period of time. For it goes bad. And this is a very pertinent economic fact. Everything that is a genuine object of use or consumption is subject to decay.

Now, when for the purposes of pure exchange we use money as an equivalent, we must admit that, as against articles which decay, money is an unfair competitor. For, in normal circumstances, nowadays, money does not seem to decay. I say advisedly, it does not *seem* to decay. Here you can see what an unhealthy element is introduced into the economic life when we bring into it different relationships from those which obtain in reality. For today we give money a fixed numerical value under all conditions, regardless of its relation to the social life, money has its face value and is supposed to keep it permanently. But in reality it does not do so. Everything else is honest. Meat after a period, which varies with its quality, begins to smell. Money does not do this, no matter what its quality may be. Money does not openly "smell". And yet, when we see circumstances bring it about that an article grows cheaper or dearer after a certain time, we are obliged to admit the following: While the article itself, by virtue of the use it will be put to, must retain the same value (for general conditions will ensure its being consumed at the right moment and a new one submitted for it), the same is not true of money. Consequently money, as such, as a pure medium of exchange, is an unfair competitor because it does not reveal in any way the fact that it also is actually subject to change. If I have to pay a certain sum of money for a pound of meat today and a different sum of money a fortnight hence, the difference (the increase, for example) in the money I must pay cannot be due to the pound of meat. It must therefore be due to the money. It is indeed due to the money. And if the money still bears the same face value, then the money is beginning to tell a lie, for its real value has decreased. If I must give more in exchange for a pound of meat, the value of the money has decreased. That is quite obvious. In this way, the very circulation of money, brings into the process something which is not really there economically. Economically the situation is that money itself, simply through the economic process, undergoes changes.

We must now investigate the occasions upon which money undergoes changes. In addition to exchange or purchase money, we have loan money. Take for instance the loan money which a human being obtains in order to set up an enterprise. This is not purchase money; for him it is working capital. Now you must see that this working capital, this loan money, has an essentially different value - an essentially different property. Except for the fact that it still consists of gold, silver and paper, not many of its original properties are left when purchase money is transferred to the sphere of loan money. It acquires its value in quite a different way. The moment loan money comes into circulation it is taken hold of by intelligence. Human thinking sets to work and it is through this entry of human thinking into the process that loan money receives its actual value. When a bank-note is lent to someone who is about to undertake some business - at the moment he begins to use it, it would be far more important to write on the note whether the person is a genius or a fool in business. For the value of the loan money in the whole economic process will henceforth depend upon the uses he makes of it.

Lastly, we must pass from loan money to the third kind of money which I mentioned a few days ago - gift money. As a general rule these days, gift money is not taken into account and yet it plays the greatest imaginable part in the economic process. Fundamentally speaking, gift money is all that is spent on education, all that is spent on endowments and the like - all that has the effect of preventing the damming up of capital in land, which is so ruinous for the economic life. At this point we must say: For the human being whose livelihood depends on purchase money, gift money simply becomes valueless. It loses its value. Gift money is the opposite of purchase money, as we can see from the simple fact that only he who has received the gift can purchase with it.

Thus there are three kinds of money, qualitatively different from one another; purchase money, loan money and gift money. Now to comprehend the relation between the three, we must consider economic systems such, for instance, as the private economies which we assumed hypothetically in the last lecture - economies representing a kind of closed domain. There we shall find that after a certain time all that is loan money passes over into gift money - a fact that holds good also in the case of that closed economic domain which is world economy. Loan money gradually passes over entirely into gift money.

Loan money must not be allowed to be dammed back into purchase money, so as to disturb the latter. Loan money, therefore, passes over into gift money. In a self-contained economic system things cannot be otherwise. And what does it do in the domain where gift money is working? It loses its value. Thus, if we take the domain of purchase money, money will here represent a certain value. In the domain of gift on the other hand, as regards purchase money it has a negative value. It lets the purchase-value vanish into nothing. Finally, between the two, the transition is brought about through loan money, which gradually vanishes into gift money. Perhaps you will say that this is hard to follow. It is! I am only sorry that we cannot go on for months detailing instances where we can see that the facts are as I have stated, with regard to the envaluation and devaluation of money. This, however, should really be our task. All that can be said in the present lectures should be taken as a basis for further researches in economics. In the brief period of a fortnight, only hints and suggestions can be given; but you will find that all the economic statements which have here been made will be transformed by detailed investigation into valuable economic truths - valuable both in science and in practice.

It actually happens that in the economic process money undergoes metamorphoses, acquiring different qualities as it becomes loan money or gift money. We mask this fact if we simply let money be money, and use the number inscribed on it as the unit of measurement and so forth. Then reality takes its revenge, revealing itself in fluctuations of price, with which (though they are actual enough in the economic process) our reasoning faculty cannot keep pace.

We ought not to let money merely flow into circulation and give it freedom to do what it likes. For we thereby do something very peculiar in economic life. If we require animals for some kind of labour, the first thing we do is to tame them. Think how long a horse has to be tamed before it can be used. Think what would happen if we did not tame our animals, but used them wild. Yet we let money circulate quite wildly in the economic process. If and when it chooses to do so - so to speak - we let it acquire the value it has as loan money or as gift money. And we do not foresee, when somebody who is an industrialist possesses money, from whatever source, which has been wrongly transformed from loan money into gift money and pays his workmen with it, that the result will be quite different from what it would be if he paid them, say, out of pure purchase money.

In effect, the more someone is obliged to pay his workers with pure purchase money, the less will he be able to give them - that is to say, the cheaper they will have to deliver their products. On the other hand, the more he is able to pay them with money that has already been transformed in the direction of loan or gift, the higher the wages he will be able to give them, that is to say, the dearer they can sell him their products. The point is to grasp the matter with our reason.

As things are today, the function of money has constantly to be corrected. Take the case, for example, of a national economy bordering on other national economies. By letting money function in a wild unguided way, without bringing any intelligence into the process, a national economy may easily find itself in a disastrous position with regard to the price of some or other thing that is required. So long as the national economy is one among others (and no repressive measures are adopted), people will simply import the article in question. Imports will increase. Things are constantly being corrected in this way. For world economy, on the other hand, no such correction is possible. We cannot import things from the moon. If we could import from, or export to, the moon and Venus and the rest, world economy would also be like a mere national economy. This is precisely the great question: What becomes of economics through the fact that the world itself is now a single closed economic domain?

Now let us suppose that we really make up our minds to allow money to grow old. Suppose you have a certain piece of money, no matter what its substance, or what the date inscribed on it. Say it is 1910. And now you take another piece of money with the date 1915. The 1915 money begins to exist, as money, economically, in that year. And now suppose that by some reasoned treatment it undergoes the process which is undergone by all other exchangeable products, namely, that it loses its value after a certain time. The precise figures I mention are not important; they are merely illustrations. The actual figures required would have to be the subject of infinitely numerous - but perfectly possible - calculations, as we shall presently perceive. Suppose, therefore, for the sake of example, that the piece of money would have lost its value by the year 1940. Now if money loses its value in the

economic process, after twenty-five years a piece of money bearing the date
1910 will have lost its value in the year 1935. Thus to the money which I carry
about on me I should assign a peculiar property - a kind of age. This 1910
money is older; it will die earlier than the 1915 money.[66] Now you may say:
"That is just a scheme." But, it is nothing of the sort. What I have just
explained to you is the actual reality. That is how the economic process
actually wills it. The economic process of its own accord makes money grow
old. The fact that it does not appear to grow old - the fact that we still buy
things with 1910 money after 1935 is only a mask. In doing so we do not really
buy with this money; but with a fictitious money-value.

If therefore the money in my purse grows old in this way, if its date of origin
has a real meaning (and by "grow old" I mean get nearer and nearer to its
death), if this be so, then money, like the human being and every other living
thing, has a certain value impressed upon it by the fact that it is growing older.
The money comes to life and a value is impressed upon it. Suppose you have
1922 money - this 1922 money will be good purchase money, needless to say.
But now suppose that you are an entrepreneur and you ask yourself: "How
shall I supply myself with money for my undertaking? Suppose, according
to my calculations, my undertaking must be planned for a period of twenty
years. Shall I provide myself with old money or with young money?" Then
you will say to yourself: "If I take old money, it will have lost its value in five
years or in two. Therefore it will not do for me to use old money. If, according
to my calculations, I must provide for a long period, I must have young
money." Thus, under the influence of long-term undertakings young money
receives its peculiar economic value - a value far greater than that of old
money. This economic value really exists - and it is there now. On the other
hand, suppose I have to embark on an undertaking which involves
calculations covering a period of only three years; in that case I should be a
bad economist if I used very young money. For the young money, by virtue
of its youth, is the most valuable and accordingly the most expensive. Thus,
if I require the money for a shorter period, I shall provide myself with cheaper
money. Anyone who has to apply his intelligence to money, realises how the
age of money plays a part.

Please note, that this is not an invention. It already exists, but in a wild
untamed way, which results in mutual disturbance and unhealthy economic
conditions. On the other hand, if you tame money, if you really assign to it
a certain age, letting young money - as loan money - be more valuable than
old, then you will be impressing the money with its true value, the value it

derives from its position in the economic process. This value really only inheres in the money *qua* loan money, for even if money is loan money, yet as purchase money it still retains its former value. Nor need you consider too carefully whether you ought to provide yourself with other money in addition for what you, as entrepreneur, are going to consume. These things will correct themselves of their own accord.

And now remember that free gifts also play a part in the process, wherein they have a very real significance. All that we put into the educational system is a gift - notably when it is a question of a really free cultural life. This, too, is happening already, only people fail to notice it. When you give directly, your intelligence is in the process. As things are now people give, of course, but the gift is absorbed into the general pool of taxation. It vanishes into a vague economic fog and you do not observe what happens. So the thing runs wild. In the other case, conscious intelligence would come into it. Consider, for a moment, what kind of money you will use where it is a question of free gifts. If you are thinking in a true economic sense, then, for free gifts, you will use old money - money that loses its value as soon as possible after the gift is made; provided that the person who enjoys the benefit of the gift has just enough time to make his purchases with it.

At this point, needless to say, there must be some rejuvenating process. The money, in fact, must have a successor. The important thing is, as you will readily perceive, that things must not be allowed to happen arbitrarily through the general chaos which the economic State spreads everywhere. The State brings about a hopeless confusion of values by failing to distinguish loan money, purchase money and gift money, though in reality these three are separated all the time. You will readily perceive that if you do not wish to leave the thing to chance - if you wish to bring reason into it - you simply must interpose the necessary associative bodies at the transition points between purchase money, loan money, gift money and the renewal of money. Take the case of one who has money to lend. You will not let him lend it in a senseless way. You will bring him into connection with his association, which will act as a mediator. The association will provide him with the most sensible way in which to lend, or give. When a gift takes place (and every individual is free to give or not to give) the money, if it is date-stamped, as explained above, will not undergo the same process. But the important thing is to bring about sensibly and in accordance with reason the things which happen any way in the economic process, but behind a mask. Money, when it has served its purpose, must be collected. And then once more, at the beginning of the process of purchase and sale, it must receive its original value. That is to say, it receives its new date stamp and passes into the hands of those who are dealing once more with those products of nature which are just beginning to pass into the sphere of labour. For here it is pure purchase and sale that are going on. This is the associative method of economic management.

The three kinds of money must be treated in different ways. In the first place, gift money, which is the oldest, must be handed over to an association which will bring the valueless money back again into the whole economic process, by uniting it with labour at the point where the land-related process begins. There can be no economic difficulty in this. What then will be the essential difference from the existing practice? It will be this: In a self-contained economic realm - which, as we saw, is not like a national economy bordering on others, where exports and imports can be carried on[67] - three distinct domains arise, so far as money is concerned, those of loan money, purchase money and gift money. And when anything occurs which would otherwise have had to be corrected by export and import from another country, it will be corrected by the three domains. If purchase money sets up a disturbance, there will be a corresponding flow between the spheres of purchase money, loan money or gift money. These things will adjust themselves of their own accord. Irregularities will undoubtedly arise, and having arisen they must correct themselves. Life cannot go on without irregularities coming in. It is an irregularity when the stomach is full. Accordingly digestion has to follow. In the same way circumstances must continually arise under which, for certain commodities, purchase money is too cheap or dear - and then the cheap money will flow into the other domain, so that on the other side it becomes dearer again as purchase money. What would otherwise have been corrected by export and import will now correct itself within the self-contained economy. All that is required is actual human intelligence, brought into the process through associations, which will be there observing things with their collective experience and taking the proper corresponding measures.

It is necessary above all to grasp the essential nature of money. People fail to grasp it precisely because it is always there before them without their being able to see what it really is. In the social organism "money as such" does not exist; there are only the three kinds of money. Moreover, each kind of money only becomes what it is at the moment when it is actually entering into the economic process or passing over from one form of economic process to another. In this way, it is constantly being changed. The point is that we must learn to know money properly, before we can pronounce what part it plays when it becomes an expression of the price of something else. To penetrate the economic process clearly, we must not remain at the surface, merely observing how things appear superficially. Seen on the surface a 10 franc coin of yesterday is of course a 10 franc coin today, no matter whether 1910 or 1915 or 1920 is inscribed on it. Outwardly considered it is always the same 10 francs, and of course in ordinary sale and purchase it behaves accordingly. I do not observe that a difference has taken place, until I have less of it or things have become dearer. But in this very "having less" or "becoming dearer",[68] there lies inherent what I expounded to you today as the greater or lesser age of the money. To perceive the economic process clearly, we cannot merely speak of cheap or dear money, or of cheap or dear commodities. We must find out what money is in its real essence; this must first be recognised and known. For it is with money that we master the economic process nowadays.

This is the important thing. We must not fight shy of penetrating beneath the surface, into the depths, to see the real underlying facts. We must not speak merely of cheap or dear money in relation to commodities. We must realise that in the living economic process, we have to speak of money being "old" and "young."

13: THE ECONOMICS OF INTELLIGENCE
5 August 1922

To understand how the sort of thing we discussed yesterday can be maintained, we must now turn our attention to certain features in the economic process which also play a role in the determination of economic values and which at the same time show how very difficult it is to value in the economic sense that which comes into the process through the human mind and intelligence. I will give you an example, not exactly fictitious, but put in such a way that its value as an example does not depend on the specific facts on which it is based.

The following may happen. At a given time there lives a great poet, recognised as such during his lifetime and increasingly so after his death. Now one of those who concern themselves with this poet, being perhaps particularly fond of his poetry, may hit upon the following idea. "In the near future," he says to himself, "they will make more and more of him. I know for certain - at any rate I can afford to take the risk - that in the near future, say within 20 years, they will make still more fuss about him than now. Indeed, they are sure to set up an institution to collect his manuscripts." From various things which he has picked up and turned over in his astute mind, this person says to himself: "These things are quite sure to happen. Very well, I will begin at once to purchase autographed manuscripts of this poet while they are still cheap." Then one day, when he is sitting in the company of others, one of them says: "Personally I am not very keen on speculation: All I desire is to have a reasonable interest on my savings." Another says: "That is not good enough for me. I am buying shares in such-and-such a mining concern. He is more of a speculator; he is buying "paper" (industrial shares). But the third, namely our man, says: "I am buying up the best paper on the market. It is very cheap indeed. But I shall not tell you what it is (for it is part of the venture that he does not give his game away). The paper I am buying will rise in value more than any other in the near future." So he buys nothing but autographed manuscripts of the said poet. And after 20 years he sells them to the archives, or to others who will sell them to the archives in their turn. He sells them for many times the amount he gave. So that he was the biggest speculator of the three!

It is a perfectly real case, only I will not give any further details now. It occurred in fact. And, you perceive, it brought about a very significant reshuffling of economic values. In the first place, simply the prudent exploitation of the fact that the poet's reputation was growing - a growth which in the end found expression in the establishment of archives. But you must add - at any rate as to the reshuffling of values, the bringing of it all into the hands of a single person - the fact that he kept his own counsel and did not draw others' attention to it; nor did they hit on the idea themselves. So he was able to make an enormous profit.

I mention this case only to illustrate how complicated the question can become, how many factors converge in the nature of value and how difficult it is to grasp them all. Thus the question arises: Can they really be grasped at all? Well, for a considerable part of life it will be perfectly possible for human beings of sound intelligence, in the right associations, to estimate the factors, even to the extent of giving them numerical expression. But there will still be many things - things of decisive importance for a true estimate of values - which it will not be possible to grasp with ordinary common sense, unless we look for some fresh aids to understanding.

We saw how land, to acquire an economic value, must be transformed by labour - must, as it were, be combined - with labour. There is the product of nature, which in an economic organisation based on division of labour, has, properly speaking, no value to begin with. Now let us try to find our way into this picture. Values arise by the joining together of the substance of land, if we may call it so, with labour. Thus, if only in a kind of algebraic formula, we may begin to approach the real "function" of value-formation. For instance, we can see at once that it cannot be a question of simply superimposing labour upon the land-element because labour changes the land-element. It cannot be a merely additive function. It will be more complicated than this. Even so, we can hold to what we have already said - economic value arises where the products of nature are first taken over by labour.

Obviously the first stage in this process is direct work on the land. Therefore, we must always look upon the cultivation of land, in the widest sense of the term, as the starting point of the whole of economic life. But what of the other side of the economic process? I need not enlarge on it any more at this stage; it is quite evident from the preceding lectures that even such a thing as the redistribution of values plays a considerable part in the movement of economic values. How shall we find anything comparable in all these different factors? If we regard "land times labour" ($V = L \times W$) as the value which comes up from the one side (or, as I said, whatever the right function is), then we must look for something comparable on the other side. We cannot simply compare land with intelligence, for we shall find no point of comparison - least of all by way of purely economic considerations - if only for the reason that a highly subjective element enters in here.

Think of a simple village economy - a self-contained one, if you will. Imagine the market and the town out of the picture, and it will consist in, to begin with, the things produced. It will consist in the peasants, the workers on the land, the workers in the different trades (those who clothe the population, for instance, and a few others) but no special proletarians; such a thing will not yet exist, nor need we, on our present lines of thought, turn our attention, in that direction. Whatever is relevant to the proletariat will appear in due course. But our village economy will also include the schoolteacher and the parson, or one or two schoolteachers and parsons. They will have to live on what the others give them. Whatever develops there in the manner of free cultural life, will in the main have to develop among the teachers and the parsons - with possibly a parish clerk added. Now let us ask ourselves: How does a proper valuation come about in this simple economic circuit?

There will be very little else of a cultural nature. We can scarcely imagine the schoolteacher or the parson blossoming out into a novelist, for if the village economy is a closed one he would not be able to sell very much. In this community a novelist would only be able to earn if he were able to instil into the peasants, tailors and cobblers a passion for his novels. In that case no doubt he might be able to call into being quite a little industry, although it would cost a great deal to do so. In fact, any wider cultural development must await certain conditions. But from the simple fact that the parson, the teacher and the parish clerk are there, we can conceive how the achievements of their freed activity - for such it is - will come to be valued economically.

What is the requisite condition for such people to be able to live in the village at all? It is that their neighbours send their children to school and that they have religious needs. Cultural needs, therefore, are the fundamental premiss. Failing such needs, they could not be there. And now we shall have to ask ourselves: How will the parson and the teacher give their products value - their sermons, for example (for even these must be conceived in an economic sense), and their school lessons? How will these things be valued in the whole economic circulation?

This is a fundamental question. We shall only gain an answer if we begin by imagining quite vividly what the others must be doing; they must be doing physical work. By bodily labour they call forth economic values, and if there were no need for sermons or school lessons, the parsons and teachers would have to do physical work, too. Everyone would be working with his hands and cultural life would drop out of the picture. We should no longer be concerned with the economic valuation of cultural products. Thus, we arrive at the required valuation precisely by observing that parsons and teachers are spared physical labour. To do their kind of work they must be relieved from bodily work.

Now we can introduce into the line of thought something capable, at least, of a more general treatment. Suppose, for example, that there is only need for half as many sermons and school lessons. What then? You cannot appoint half a parson or half a teacher. So the parson and the teacher will have to spend part of their time doing physical labour. Therefore, the valuation on their side will depend on the amount of physical labour of which they are relieved. This gives us the measure for such work. One human being contributes physical labour, another saves it. Freed activity (see Note 17.) has a value corresponding to the amount of physical labour saved by virtue of it. Take these two economic fields and think the thing through economically, and you will see that even a sermon must have an economic value, and moreover how it acquires this value. It acquires it inasmuch as it saves or spares labour, whereas on the other side labour has to be applied.[69]

The same thing runs through the entire cultural life. What does it signify, in the economic sense, if a human being paints a picture - works at it, shall we say, for ten whole years? It means that the picture acquires a value for him inasmuch as it will enable him once more to spend ten years painting another picture. He can only do so if he can save himself physical labour for a period of ten years. Therefore, the picture will have to become worth as much as would be made by him out of other products by physical labour during ten years. Even if you take such a complex case as I explained at the beginning of this lecture, the same result will emerge. In all cases of cutural production, if you try to find the concept of value you will arrive at this other concept - that of labour saved.

It is the cardinal error of Marxists that they look at it all exclusively from the physical side. They say that capital is to be looked upon as crystallised labour - as a product with which labour has been combined. Now if an artist paints a picture, all he has painted into it in the way of imagination and so on during ten years is certainly combined with it, but this could at most be computed by those who believe that such things are the inner "work" of the human organism transmuted; which is sheer nonsense. The cultural cannot be assimilated to the natural in that facile way. If I complete a cultural product, the point is not that labour is in some way stored up in the product. The work stored up in it is economically irrelevant. *Qua* bodily work it may be very little. Moreover what little there was falls, in any case, under the other heading - that of physical work. What gives value to such products is in truth the labour which they save. Thus, on the one side of the economic process the actual doing of work, the application of labour to the product, is the value-creating factor; the product absorbs labour, as it were, attracts it. While on the other side the product rays out labour, begets labour; the value is the original thing which calls labour into being.

We have now therefore a means of comparison, namely, labour on the one side and labour on the other, and we are therefore in a position to relate them. For we may say: If the value in the one case equals "land times labour" ($V = L \times W$.), in the other we must call it "intelligence minus labour". ($V = I - W$.) The direction is exactly opposite. Physical labour only has meaning inasmuch as the one who wants to contribute it to the economic process actually does it himself. While what is related to the product on the cultural side is the labour which one human being does for another. It must therefore be entered as a negative in the economic process.

It is a remarkable thing. Study the history of economics, and you will always find that what is said is right, but only in a limited sphere. There are economists who believe that it is labour which gives things value - the school of Adam Smith, the school of Marx, for example. But other schools give another definition, which again is right in a certain sphere. According to them, a thing becomes capital - i.e. a source of value - inasmuch as it saves labour. Both points of view are true. Only, the one is true when the economic process is related to land, to the soil; while the other is related to intelligence. Between these two there is a third. For, in effect, neither of the two extremes is ever there in its pure form; they are only there in an approximately absolute sense. After all, even the picking of blackberries (which acquires economic value only inasmuch as people actually go there and do it) - even here there is some freed activity. Of two blackberry-pickers, if one is stupid and makes extra work for himself by picking where berries are scarce, while the other finds a place where they are plentiful and obtains a better yield for his labour, the blackberries of the first are of less value, relatively speaking; he will not get more money for the same amount of berries. Thus, in effect, neither extreme is ever realised absolutely. Even the gathering of blackberries entails freed activity (although we might not call it so). The work of using one's wits creates values, just as it did with the collector of autographs; at least it creates values by hoarding them.

Once more, then, we have labour in both directions, and this alone enables us to compare economic values. However, this comparing is done by the economic process of its own accord. We can at most become aware of it. Indeed, all that I have sought to give in these lectures amounts to this: That we lift certain instinctive processes into consciousness.

As said before, neither of the two extremes exists in any absolute sense. For on the other side $(V = I - W)$, however much a painter uses his intelligence he must still do some bodily work if he wishes to create anything of economic value. Even if he has an idea, or pictures something to himself, even then he must still do some bodily work. Relying on his genius, it may be, he can afford to be dreadfully lazy; still, now and then he must take up the brush. Some bodily work has to be done even in this case, just as some little force of thought must go even into the picking of blackberries. (Things that take place in real life cannot be grasped merely quantitatively. They have to be grasped while they are actually happening. Therefore, we can only grasp them with concepts, if we realise that the concepts themselves need to be kept in constant movement).

Between these two extremes we can perceive more clearly how in real economic life bodily work and freed activity play into one another, moving to and fro. Just as in a machine, there is a regulated backward and forward movement, so in industry bodily work from the one side and freed activity from the other are passing to and fro. It is in this mutual interplay from two directions that we have, as a third factor, that which plays into the economic process between the other two - where a human being has to do physical labour, yet by using his wits he is spared some of it. This is always actually the case, only it sometimes approximates more to the one formula - $V = L x$ W - and sometimes more to the other - $V = I - W$.

In this way we can look into the economic process from this aspect of valuation, valuing what comes from land on the one hand and from intelligence on the other. And at this point we can say: Where positive and negative work into one another, somehow an intermediate condition will emerge. The positive may predominate, for example. In our little village economy it certainly will do so, for in such a community there will be no widespread interest in cultural work, beyond what is absolutely necessary. But the more life grows complicated (or, as we are apt to say sentimentally, the more "civilisation advances"), the more highly freed activity is valued. That is to say, the more labour is saved - a negative element comes in as against the positive. I beg you to consider well: By characterising it in this way we are taking hold of a real process. It is not that physical labour is done on the one side and annulled again on the other (reminiscent of people digging holes, only to fill them up again? - Ed.); that would be no real process in the economic sense; it would at most be a process of nature. Economically seen, all physical labour helps to create values. None of it is destroyed. That which counteracts it - the saving of labour from the other side - does so only in a numerical sense. In the one case, labour is brought about, while in the other it is saved. Only by this means is an effectual valuation brought about.

In this way, things are divested of their particularity and it becomes possible to grasp the process in terms of numbers, inasmuch as it is the same thing which emerges on either side and only the valuation is altered. With the advance of civilisation, then, freed activity increases in importance, and this implies that bodily work has a less powerful effect on the valuing process. Physical strength is of course applied, and it must be so more and more as we go forward. Even the cultivation of the soil must be made more fruitful as civilisation advances. More work must be done, in a positive sense. The point is that the physical labour is divested, to some extent, of its value-creating power. Yet this again can only be so if those who labour evince a growing need for that which has to be achieved from the cultural side. Here, once again, a human factor comes into the economic process. You cannot get round it; indeed, with the advance of cultural life, this particular human factor makes itself felt as an objective necessity.

It is quite true that, to begin with, when there are only the parson and the teacher, there is not much of cultural life in our village. But suppose there are two villages. In one village the parson and the teacher are mediocre people: Things will go on as they are. In the other village the parson or the teacher, or both of them, are first-rate people. They will be able to stimulate all manner of cultural interests in the next generation and, in all probability - by the time the next generation arises, some colleague will be brought into the village. Now there are three of them. In this regard the cultural life has a very fertile power, which in its turn works back into economic life.

What, in the last resort, does this process signify? It signifies that precisely labour, or rather the value-creating power of labour, which in the purely material phase of economic life has an infinitely great value, is more and more reduced in course of time by that which comes to meet it from the other side. One cannot exactly say it is "devalued"; it is reduced numerically. In the working-together as between all that is represented by work on the land[70] - the tilling of the soil, etc.- and that which is cultural, we have a kind of mutual compensation. Rightly so.

Here, again, complex conditions arise. For it may well turn out that in a given place there are too many people engaged in freed activity - i.e. the counteracting labour-saving power may be too strong. Then the resultant value is negative, and the people cannot all live together except by consuming one another. Thus, there is a limit somewhere to this compensation process. In the very nature of the case, for every economic realm there is a certain balance as between land-derived production on the one side and freed activity on the other.

Until this is understood in economics - how the production from the soil, taken in the widest sense, of course, is related to cultural production - until this problem, which has hitherto hardly been considered, is very seriously dealt with, economics shall never prove able to cope with current realities.

The first thing necessary is that we should begin working on definite data, in order to see, in an atmosphere unclouded by prejudice and agitation, how some particular area gets into an unhealthy economic condition, because it contains too much freed activity - and again what power of further development of culture and civilisation an area has, where that limit, of which I have just spoken, has not been reached. Progress is only possible within a given area so long as this limit, determined by the necessary compensation, has not yet been reached. The task then will be to investigate those elements which still survive today from closed economies - such survivals are to be found everywhere, because we are only passing slowly into a world economy - we must investigate those elements as to which the economy of some area is still closed. We must study the aggregate welfare of those areas in which there are comparatively few poets and painters or sophisticated industrialists, etc., and where there is still much agriculture or other activity connected immediately with the land; and then we shall have to study other areas where the opposite is the case.

From the data produced, we must work out empirically such general laws as will emerge for a true theory of balance as between agriculture, or the working of the land in the widest sense, on the one hand and freed activity on the other. For any region, take what we may call the average of those engaged in freed activity (do not choose such as would falsify the whole balance) and on the other hand the average of those engaged in physical labour. Balance the one against the other; you will perceive how they compensate each other.

This point is of cardinal importance for anyone who wishes to contribute to the further progress of economics today. The fact is that this problem, which should really underlie our thinking about price and value, is scarcely anywhere correctly seen as yet. As I said yesterday to a few of those present (see Discourse 5): In economics people are always allowing themselves to be misled into a partial instead of a comprehensive way of thinking. There is no doubt that Spengler makes some very shrewd economic observations at the close of the second volume of his *Decline of the West*. But he ruins these brilliant observations because he does not succeed in translating into terms of present-day economic realities what he perceives historically. He points out very justly how, in the ancient economies, the economic life which comes directly from the soil was predominant; whereas today that economic life predominates which thinks in money - and consists, therefore, properly speaking, in freed activity. But he fails to see that these two stages of economic life, which he records historically, continue side by side to this day. The one has not replaced the other in history; the most primitive abides within the most advanced. Do we not find the amoebae crawling about free in nature and do we not find the same thing in our own blood, in the white blood corpuscles? The different historical stages even in nature live side by side to this day. And so it is in economic life; the most varied conditions co-exist. Sometimes indeed, in the most highly cultivated economic life - if we may call it so - it is precisely the most highly cultivated elements which return to the most primitive. Values created by our living in a sophisticated culture hark back, in a certain sense, to the state of primitive barter. Those who create their labour savings, as it were, will sometimes barter one of these for another, to satisfy certain needs among themselves.

I wanted to add this remark to the present lecture, so that tomorrow I may be able, as best I can, to bring these lectures to a conclusion.

14: KEY CONCEPTS FOR WORLD ECONOMICS
6 August 1922

The main object of these studies was to find concepts, or rather pictures, of economic life, such as would help us actually to get inside it. Critical as I am of much that I regard as unscientific in economics, I in no way mean to disparage science as such. On the contrary, there is a wide range of very useful results in the existing sciences. Only, the method of treatment, both in natural science and in the other branches of knowledge, needs to be developed in some essential respects. Thus, in the main, I have tried to give you pictorial concepts, ideal pictures, to aid you in making proper use of the wide range of valuable material. For this reason I have given you such pictures as could really live. A living thing, however, is always many-sided and contains many meanings. Many of you may go away from these lectures, therefore, with the feeling that various objections can be made to what has been said. In a sense I shall be rather glad if you do have this feeling, provided it is combined with real earnestness and a genuine scientific spirit. Such a feeling is inevitable, for life will not endure dogmatic theories; and it is in this sense that the ideal pictures I have given you need to be conceived.

The picture of money growing old or getting used up is a particularly pregnant one. You must relate yourself to such an image as you would do, let us say, to a growing human being. You have a general feeling that he will prove a very able person in one direction or another. You may have fairly definite ideas of what he will accomplish. But these ideas will very likely turn out to have been mistaken. He may accomplish what he has to do in quite other ways. So, too, for the concept of money getting used up in the course of time, you may find various ways in which this can be brought about. The one I have tried to present is conceived as little as possible along bureaucratic lines, resulting naturally from economic life itself.

Many objections may no doubt be made. Here is a very easy one: How will it be arranged that a given entrepreneur puts young money and no other into his business? After a short time the age of money may no longer be recognisable, for his business will be going on. In answer to this, you must bear in mind that he does not simply get the money from the sky; he borrows it from someone. Moreover, I do not think that interest on money should be abolished, provided the money has real value; on the contrary I believe that up to a point interest is actually necessary in the economic life. You may say: How shall I as an entrepreneur get money from those who might lend it to me, if I am only going to pay them interest for such a short time? They will only wish to give me money on the assumption that they will get interest out of my business for as long a time as possible. Thus, you may find that it is not enough simply to let money grow old in the way described. This may lead you on to think out the method in greater detail. For instance, money issued today might be date-stamped, not with the present year but with a future year, in such a way that the value increased up to that year, and thereafter decreased.

In short, a living thing may realise itself in a variety of ways. By the act of grasping it livingly, you give it the possibility to realise itself in the most varied ways, just as a living human being can use his ability in various ways. This is the essence of a non-dogmatic concept. To make such concepts your own, especially in economics, is to see how well these things enter into real life. Only on this foundation will you be able to make proper use of what is given in the so-called economic science of today out of valid but only partial observations.

Take for example what is said of price. You will be told that the conditions determining price-levels are the following, so far as the seller is concerned: His relative need for money, the value of the money, the costs of production which he has to meet and the competition among buyers. But if you analyse these concepts you will always find that, though you can think about them rightly enough, you cannot enter with them into the realities of life. For you would first have to ask yourself: Is it an economically healthy state of affairs if it so happens that a particular entrepreneur is in need of money at a particular time and thereby, in accordance with his private need for money, prices rise or fall in a particular direction? Can the use-value of money, if we may call it so, work in a healthy way at all? Both things can work in a healthy and in an unhealthy way. Or again, speaking of costs of production, it may be desirable for the attainment of a healthy price not to think how the price will come out if costs of production are looked upon as something absolute, but on the contrary to think how the costs of production for a given article might have to be reduced so that it has a healthy price when it comes on to the market. In other words, you need to have concepts which really begin at the beginning. Just as a human being cannot begin his life at the age of 25, we should not let our concepts, if they are meant for real life, begin at some arbitrary point - for example, with the competitive relation between buyers or between sellers. After all, it may well be the fundamental error of our economic life that such excessive competition exists at all. These are matters of principle, which must be taken very much in earnest.

Quite apart from whether one or other of you may agree with particular parts of my exposition, the endeavour has been throughout to make our concepts living, for then they will show of their own accord how they need to be modified. What matters is that we should be brought on to the path of living concepts. Thus, we can say: If we have money that is used up, i.e. grows old, then, inasmuch as money comes into circulation and figures as purchase money, loan money and gift money, the specific qualities of money will bring it about naturally - if they are allowed to function in a purely economic and unhampered way - that the demand for young money will arise at one place and the demand for old money at another.

One ought to go on elaborating these things for many weeks, and then you would see how well they fit in with a sound economy. Wherever an illness arises in the body economic, you would see that it is just by the observation of these things that it can be healed.

What is it that really emerges when we think, in this way, that in circulating money we have a kind of reflection of that element of use and wear which in fact is present throughout the whole range of consumable goods - including the cultural sort? In a money which wears out we have a parallel process to goods, commodities, real values, which also wear out. What have we, in effect, if we perceive this parallelism - we can extend it over the entire world economy - between the real value and the token value? Truly we may describe it essentially as a kind of book-keeping system for the whole world economy. It is the world's book-keeping. When some item is transferred or delivered, this simply signifies the entry of an item in another place. In actual practice the thing is done by passing money and commodities from hand to hand. The principle is fundamentally the same whether we contrive to record the items in their proper places in an immense book-keeping system embracing the whole world economy, and so direct things simply by transferring credits, or whether we write out a chit and give it to the person concerned, so that the thing is done in external action. In the circulation of money we have in effect the world's book-keeping; this, as everyone can really see for himself, is what should be aimed at. For in this way we give back to money the only quality which it can properly have - that of being the external medium of exchange. Look into the depths of economic life, and you will see that money can be nothing else than this. It is the medium of exchange of services or things done. For in reality human beings live by the things actually done, not by the tokens thereof.

It is quite true that money can create a false impression of things done, and with the rise of a kind of dealership in money, the whole economic life can thus be falsified. But this kind of falsification, this counterfeiting, is only possible when we do not give money its true character.

It is important for us to see, as I emphasised in the last lecture, that different kinds of services must be judged in different ways with respect to the values circulating through the economic life. As we showed yesterday, that which derives from land to begin with, and on which labour is expended, corresponds to the picture: "Labour united with an object of land." In a certain sense, we can begin the economic process at this point. Here, we may say, value is created by the labour which I unite with a particular product of nature. But in the economic process there is also the contrary stream, which comes into play the moment there is freed activity. As soon as freed activity comes into play, another formula of valuation, if I may call it so, has to be introduced, namely: "Freed activity is worth the amount of labour which it saves to the person who contributes it." Take for example the artist who paints a picture and thereby provides a value, a value for which real interest is felt (otherwise it would not be a value). If the production of the picture and the existence of the artist are to be economically healthy, the artist must value it by reference to the amount of labour required to satisfy his own needs during the time which it will take him to produce a new picture in like manner. Thus, in the economic process freed activity and cultural products come to meet that which derives mainly from the elaboration of land, i.e. of manual labour, applied to the means of production. On the one side we must have labour uniting itself with the means of production, while on the other side labour must be saved or spared. Thereby the economic circuit comes into being with its two opposing streams, which must compensate each other in a healthy way.

The great question is: How shall they compensate each other? In the first place we need only bear in mind the universal book-keeping of our world economy. It is here that we should find the items on either side which must somehow be mutually balanced. And this would be the source of price. But the point is that the items in this universal book-keeping must mean something. Let item A correspond to what we may describe as "labour united with land" (L x W), and item B to "so much labour saved by service" (I - W) Every such item must have concrete meaning, which requires that it be at least made comparable by the economic system. We cannot simply ask: How many nuts is a potato worth? First we must say: "Nut" signifies a product of nature united with labour; "potato" signifies a product of nature united with labour. And then we can ask how the two values are to be equated. The problem is to find something which will enable us to assess economic values one against the other.

It becomes still more difficult if you take, say, a literary essay. The essay, too, must be, economically, worth the amount of physical labour upon some means of production that it saves, minus the very small amount of physical work spent on the actual writing. You can see that it is not altogether easy to work out how these things are to be equated or assessed as against each other. Nevertheless, by taking hold of the economic process from another angle, we shall find ways of reaching such an assessment. For on the one hand we have the physical labour spent on the means of production, including land itself. At a given time it is quite a definite amount of labour. That is to say, at a given time a definite amount of labour is needed to produce wheat over a given area, say x square metres, of land, taking "production" as ending in the moment when the wheat is in the merchant's hands, or at some other given point. Once more then, the labour needed to produce wheat can be given a magnitude. Properly regarded, all human economic service or achievement - of whatsoever kind - eventually takes us back to land. There is no other possibility. The farmer works upon land directly: One who provides, shall we say, clothing, does so indirectly; his labour will contain an element of "labour saved" to the extent that he applies intelligence to it. Nevertheless even his work has its connection with land. Everything, right up to the most complicated of freed activity, eventually goes back to land - that is, labour expended on the means of production. Think it through clearly and you will see that everything in economic life can be traced back in the end to physical labour on land. The process begins with land; where values are created by the application of labour; and it is these values - taken to some definite point still as close to land as possible - which have to be distributed over the whole of a "closed" economic domain.

Go back to yesterday's hypothetical case of a closed village economy. In such a self-contained village economy you have the manual workers, but I assumed that the only cultural workers were the parson and the schoolteacher and possibly the parish clerk. (It is a very simple economy!) Most of the inhabitants are doing bodily work on the soil; only, they have to do enough additional bodily work to provide for the needs - food, clothing, etc. - of the teacher, the parson and the clerk. Suppose the village economy consists of 30 peasants plus the three - what shall we call them? - "worthies." These three supply their cultural services. They need the spared labour of the rest. Suppose that every one of the 30 peasants gives to these three, or to each one of them, a token or ticket, on which is written so much, say, of wheat - that is, wheat elaborated to a certain point. Another member of the community might give a ticket on which something else was entered, something comparable to wheat for purposes of consumption. These things can be ascertained. The worthies will collect these tickets. Instead of going out into the fields to fetch their wheat, rye and beef for themselves, they will hand over their tickets to those concerned, who in their turn will do the necessary labour in addition to their own and will give them the product in exchange. That is a process which cannot help developing of its own accord. It cannot possibly be otherwise, nor does it make any difference if it occurs to some bright individual to introduce metallic coin instead of tickets. It amounts to this: Some kind of tokens must be devised, based on the stored-up material labour - labour expended on means of production, labour invested in economic values - and then handed over to those who need them, so that they can save themselves the labour implied.

Hence, you will see that money cannot really be any other than an expression of the sum-total of the means of production available in a given region - means of production, including in the very first place land itself - reduced to the form in which it can be most suitably expressed. This will relate the economic process to something which we can at least take hold of. For it is not possible to bring about an economic paradise anywhere on earth; and those who believe it is invent their Utopias without reference to reality.

It is so easy to say that an economy should be thus and thus. But an economy - including that of the entire earth, world economy - cannot be absolutely determined, but only relatively so. Suppose that in a closed economic region we have an area, Ar, of land. Now supposing all the people in this area are doing everything which it is possible for human beings to do, a different amount will then be available for consumption if B million people live there, than B^1 million.

Thus, it depends on the ratio of population to the area of land, and on how

much a given population can get out of its given area, for it is from the land
that everything physical ultimately comes. Take now the hypothetical case:
An economic area has a population of, say, 35 millions - the number does not
matter. What holds true, here, of a self-contained economic territory, is true
also of the world economy. Assume that the problem is to bring these 35
million people economically into a just relation. (I may not be putting it quite
clearly and precisely, but you will soon see what I mean). What would you
have to do if you wished such a condition to prevail among these 35 million
people as would bring about affordable prices, affordable, that is, to both
buyer and seller? You would have to give each one of them an amount of land
corresponding to one 35-millionth of the entire area available for production,
adjusted according to fertility and ease of cultivation. Suppose that every
child were to receive such an area of land at birth, to be worked by him in
perpetuity. The prices which would thus arise would be affordable prices for
such an area, for things would then have their natural exchange values.

Now the curious hypothesis which I have here put forward is nothing else
than the reality. The economic process actually does this of its own accord.
Of course you will not believe that I mean what I am now saying in any other
than a figurative sense. Yet these are the actual conditions. You can imagine
the entire area distributed among the people concerned, remembering that
they will also have to elaborate, in the proper way, such products as become
detached from the soil. You can imagine the entire area divided up among the
population, and it is in fact this which gives to each individual thing its
exchange value.[71] Indeed, it might well be that if in some place you were to
note down the actual exchange values, you would find a very close
approximation. But if you now compare this with ordinary present-day
conditions, you will find the price of one thing far above and the price of
another far below that level. Still, if you like to suppose a Utopia somewhere,
populated solely by newborn children (looked after by angels to begin with),
to each of whom you have given his piece of land, then, when they are able
to begin work, you will have produced conditions under which the natural
exchange values will arise. And if after a time prices are different, it can only
mean that one has taken something away from another. It is this kind of thing
which produces the various social discontents; human beings dimly feel that
here something works into the process which does not correspond to the real
prices at all.

If economic life becomes permeated with a way of thinking such as we have
here sought to adopt, the actual measures we shall take will bring about the

result I have stated. We shall find that our currency, representing, as it were, the day-to-day book-keeping of world economy, will have to be inscribed, let us say: "Wheat producible over a given number of acres", and this will then be equated to other things, with the different products of the soil being the easiest to equate. So you see where we must start from - our figures must mean something. It simply leads away from reality if money has inscribed on it: "So much gold". It leads towards reality if it has inscribed on it: "This represents so much labour upon such and such a product of nature". For we shall then have this result: Say all money is stamped "x of wheat", "y of wheat", "z of wheat.", etc. The real origin of the whole economic life will then be made evident. Our currency will refer to the usable means of production upon which physical labour is done - the means of production of the given economic region. This is the only sound basis of currency - the sum-total of the usable means of production.

An open mind shows that this is so. It may be objected that no one value can be precisely equated to another. But to a great extent this can be done. For since in this method of valuation everything is ultimately valued through consumption, the values of different kinds of services do not differ so very much from one another.72 However freed my activity may be, I need so much saved labour every year - namely, as much as I require to maintain myself as a human being. Moreover, by this means it will be evident how and to what extent those engaged in freed activity need something in addition, beyond what a manual labourer needs. And when the matter has become as transparent as this, it will be acknowledged precisely because it is transparent. Even today - though they become increasingly rare - conditions do exist in self-contained economies under which those engaged in freed activity receive all that they need; where the others give it them gladly, without even writing it down on slips of paper beforehand. In saying this, I do not wish to make an economic argument sentimental. I say it simply because this, too, is part of the realities of economics and because in any economic system one is after all always dealing with human beings.

When one attains in this way to a transparent relationship between all the members of an economic whole, each one in every moment will then have his connection with land, even in the money. The unsoundness of present-day relations stems from our remoteness from land; the connection having been lost. If we can bring it about (and it is only a question of evolving the necessary technique in the associative life) that money is denominated in terms of land, rather than the indefinable gold value, then we shall see directly

- in every-day business - how much a given cultural service is worth. For I shall know, when I paint a picture, that for me to have painted this picture so many people on the land, for example, have to work for so many months or years to produce wheat or oats, etc. Think how transparent the economic process would become. The ordinary way of putting it today would be to call it the substitution of a wheat-currency for a gold-currency. Yes, and that is just what we need. For by this means true economic conditions will be brought about.[73]

Once again I have placed a picture before you. I have to speak in these pictures, for they give the reality. What people generally have in their heads in economic intercourse today is not reality. He alone has the reality who in receiving a piece of money of a certain magnitude in exchange for something, knows that it signifies so much work upon the land. We must, of course, include in our calculations the work that is done on other means of production. These will, however, be equivalent to land. For the moment they are finished, and thus leave the realm of commodities altogether, they are devalued inasmuch as it is no longer possible to buy or sell them. They thus become equivalent to the means of production which we have in land directly. It is therefore only a continuation of the part which land already plays in the economic process, when we say that means of production should be dealt with in this way. Moreover, it is only in this way that we can have a clear idea of land itself, considered as means of production. You need only consider this: Even a given region of land may have to be worked upon to some extent before it is available as "land"- before it is fit for cultivation. Up to the moment when land - or a given part of land - has been cleared and can be handed over for use, during this period also, some labour must be expended on it. In other words, by the time this labour has been done, even a piece of land may justly be reckoned a commodity, an economic value, in the sense that it is land combined with labour.

Only by formulating the ideas in the way we have done will you get the concept "means of production" clear and transparent, and then be able to work it out in the most varied spheres. You will perceive, when for example an author writes an article, that its main economic value consists in the labour it saves; from which you would only have to deduct the minute amount of bodily work which the actual writing entails. Your concepts will be capable of differentiation in manifold directions so that you stand with them in very life, inasmuch as you are forming them out of life itself. And then, if for example you are concerned with some question of prices, you will no longer be content merely to trace it back to the immediate costs of production; you will have to trace it back to the primal phase of all production. Only then will you be able to trace them rightly up to any given point in the economic process.

In this way, I hope I have been able to give you an idea which will at least guide you on your way towards the cardinal question of economics, namely, that of prices. For to engage in economic activity at all is to bring about the exchange of products among human beings, and this exchange lives itself out in the forming of prices. It is the forming of prices that matters, and in this respect you do not have to go back to anything vague or indefinite. For you can always follow things back to the fundamental relationship of value which is brought about by the very fact of work upon the land, namely the proportion of population to a given area of cultivation. In this relation you will find that which originally underlies the formation of values: All the labour that can be done must come from the given population, while all that this labour can unite with must come from the given land. Everyone needs what this labour brings about and, as to those who can save themselves the labour on account of their cultural services, the others must perform it for them in addition to their own. Thus we arrive at the actual basis of economic life.

Looking at things in this way, we shall admit that even in our present highly complicated economic life, that which was universal in the most primitive conditions - where the simple exchange of goods (barter), shall we say, was the essential thing - still plays its part. The difference is that we are no longer able to see the connection. But we shall have it before us always, when the connection with land is expressed in our currency notes. Whatever we may do, the connection with land is always there - a reality we should not forget. Once more, speaking pictorially, let me say: While I am giving my pound quite thoughtlessly for this or that, there is always a little being[74] who writes on it how much labour actually expended upon land it corresponds to; for this alone is the reality. Here, too, if we would get at the reality, we cannot stop short at the outer surface.

Well, it has not been possible within this fortnight to give you more than a few suggestions to stimulate and guide you on your way. The most important thing of all is that you should perceive how, compared with the usual ideas, the ideal pictures we have evolved here actually represent something living.

If you have absorbed what is living in these ideal pictures, you will not have spent these fourteen days in vain. For it is this that weighs on one so heavily: Great issues are impending. Human beings are in need of free and clear insight into the essentials, for the healing of our civilisation's many ills. There is much talk of what should be done, but little will, alas, to dive down into realities and to draw forth from there the realisation of what should be done. We have gradually departed from the sphere of truth, and from the real life of rights - rights that spring forth from the very nature of the human being - and from that which must unfold in the human being if he is to be of value to his fellows - namely the genuine practice of life. From truth we have slid into the empty phrase; from the sense of right into mere convention; and from a practical hold on life into dead routine. We shall not escape till we develop the will to go down into the facts and to see how things are shaped in their own real nature. The many agitatory phrases in the world today, and the appalling harm they do, are a result of the fact that so few human beings have an earnest will to go into realities.

How important it is, then, that those who would be economists contribute to the healing and reconstruction of our civilisation. To this end, we must endeavour to make economics more than mere theory; something of real economic value, so that the labour we are being saved can be put to good use by those who relieve us of it, for the benefit and progress of humanity as a whole. I believe that in resolving to come here you were thus mindful of this task of the economist; and I hope that this has been confirmed in you by what we have attained, however inadequately, through our work together. I look forward to an opportunity of working at these things again another time.

ECONOMICS

The World as One Economy

The Discourses

1: **POINTS OF METHOD**
31 July 1922

The threefold social order[75] seems logical enough, but how realistic is it?

It would help to discuss this point more concretely. One has to bear in mind that economics as such is actually a very young science, hardly a few centuries old, and that, until the great Utopians came along, practically everything in it came about more or less instinctively. These instinctive impulses have, however, passed into reality.

To better understand this, consider the following: People today often say that our ideas about economics arise out of economic class differences, out of the productive processes and so on. Leaving aside the more extreme ideas, like those of Marx and his followers, even the most conservative teachers of economics say everything necessarily arises from the economic basis of life. But looked at concretely, the institutions which have created the present economic life are merely the result of the thinking of the Middle Ages, albeit in connection with different realities. Consider the economic consequences and the forms of ownership that have derived from the Roman concept of ownership, itself a purely legal category. Although influenced by the prevailing categories of the time, these things were not conceived scientifically but in legalistic, juridical terms. Later on the mercantilists and others arose, people who were not creative in this sense, but theoretical. For example, the advisers of Emperor Justinian - the men who created the *codex des corpus juris* - were much more creative than later teachers of economics. These men not only shaped the Justinian *codex*, but also had an influence on the Middle Ages. Inasmuch as the Middle Ages embodied impulses that arose in opposition to the Justinian *codex*, they therefore came about by reference to it.

In the modern age economists are no longer creative, but contemplative - an approach that began with Ricardo.[76] His "law of diminishing returns", for instance, is a very good example of a law that is correct but quite unrealistic. Experience continuously proves that, when technically intensified cultivation appears, this law is invalid; and yet if one takes into account all the factors considered by Ricardo, the result is exactly what he called the law of diminishing returns. In reality, however, the law proves to be false.

A more trivial example is Lasalle's "iron wage law".[77] I must say that I think it is scientifically imprudent when it is said that this law is obsolete because it has not been proven. Given Lasalle's way of thinking, and the conception that labour can be paid for, Lasalle's iron law of wages cannot but arise. Its logic is so severe, that, provided one shares the view that Lasalle had come to - that no one is interested in paying more than is absolutely necessary for the worker's keep - one has to admit its absolute correctness. Workers will not be paid any more than necessary. Fundamentally, as a matter of theory, one cannot escape this law. And yet members of the proletariat say it is wrong because it is not true that wages have been kept to a certain minimum, which is simultaneously the maximum, during the last centuries.

But why is the iron law of wages wrong? If the conditions had prevailed under which Lasalle formulated his law, the purely liberal outlook of the 1860s, then precisely this law would have entered social reality. As it was, a swing away from the liberal economy took place, so that even today men are still modifying the iron law of wages by enacting legislation which alters the reality that it would have otherwise given rise to.

Thus one can see that a law can be correct without being real. I know of no greater thinker than Lasalle. He was a very consequent thinker; only he was very one-sided. One can formulate natural laws when one observes them. One can also formulate social laws - but these are only valid as the expression of a certain tendency and, as such, are subject to change. Insofar as the economy is still based on free competition - which it is to a large extent[78] - the iron law of wages is correct. It applies so long as the entrepreneur is left in freedom. But for this reason, the purely deductive method of thinking is not possible in economics.

The inductive method, as used by Lujo Brentano[79], is even more useless. Induction states that one perceives economic laws by observing economic facts, an approach that completely contradicts the creative thinking I have elsewhere characterised. Unfortunately, in pretending to be scientific, modern economics bases itself on the inductive method and, for that reason, leads one nowhere.

Economics needs a descriptive method of thinking, which sets out from different starting points, allowing them to culminate in concepts. Even so, the concepts arrived at in this way tend to be one-sided, because one can never oversee all the factors involved. However, they can be verified by being referred back to the phenomena. One reaches economic conceptions by verification and modification of concepts in the light of experience. This is the descriptive method needed by economics.

In my lectures on economics I would like to develop such a conception by showing the factors involved in price formation. The usual method of economics is quite awkward because it has to assemble concepts out of an infinite number of factors, rather than proceed through imagination. With imagination, concepts modify themselves of their own accord. Fixed concepts, on the other hand, cannot be easily changed.

Take Gresham's law: "Bad money drives out good".[80] When bad money (money printed below value) circulates, it usurps the good money, which consequently goes into other countries. This too is an inductive law, based on experience. However, it is valid only as long as one is unable to define the meaning of money. As soon as one were able to define money, Gresham's law would be modified. It would not become entirely obsolete, however. Every economic law is valid up to a certain point; it is just that they are all subject to modification. It is for this reason that economics needs a descriptive method. At best, the inductive method of the natural sciences arrives at deductions, but in general such deductions have much less importance than is supposed.

Induction and deduction are not suited to economics. Deduction would only be useful to economics if it were possible to apply general rules to which social reality conformed. Oppenheimer, for example, makes a major induction with his idea of housing corporations, from which he deduces a complete social order. Many years ago, when Oppenheimer[81] was already the "housing man", he said, "Now I have the capital, we can found a new cultural colony." I replied, "Doctor, let's talk about this project when it has perished." For it has to perish. It is not possible to create a little area within the general economy, based on privileges derived from something different, without its becoming a parasite within the economic life as a whole. Such enterprises are always parasites. They last until they have taken enough from others; but then they perish.

Descriptive economics is only possible if one enters into the phenomena with one's thinking, especially as in economics one is constantly working from the past into the future. Moreover this working into the future means that human beings with their talents and capabilities are always entering in. All the time one is dealing with something alive and changing and one has always to be prepared, therefore, to modify one's concepts. Economics does not deal with substances, which one can shape, but with living human beings. It is thus a special kind of science, one that has to be permeated by reality. You will readily appreciate this point theoretically, and agree that it is difficult to work in economics. But beware even of accepting this. If you are considering writing a dissertation, you would be advised to consult the relevant literature of recent times. By comparing different opinions one can gain insight into economics. As a discipline, it is characterised by the most incredible definitions. Try, for example, to collect the different definitions of capital - put eight or ten of them together. One comes to my mind: "Capital is the sum of the produced means of production". I do not understand what the adjective refers to. The opposite is the unproduced means of production - nature, the soil, for example. The author of the definition probably also understands this to be the case, but he is unable to explain how the soil capitalises itself. Yet it does so. One cannot escape the fact. The problem is that our concepts need to be enriched, otherwise we see things too narrowly.

If you think it difficult to find reality in these observations, I would respond that reality could become very easy. You say the "threefold social order" is logical, but it is not at all logical. My writings on the threefold social order were not written from an economic point of view only, but were social too. This plays into their style and purpose and means that they cannot be assessed only in economic terms. Very few of my writings can be assessed in that way. In no sense do I regard them as being logically written. On the contrary, I very carefully tried only to give guidelines, examples, illustrations. I wanted to evoke a consciousness of what can be achieved if someone is responsible for the means of production only for as long as he is able to be, at which point it is transferred to someone else. I can readily imagine that what is thereby achieved could be done in different ways, but I only wanted to give indications. I wanted to show that one finds alternatives if the threefold nature of social life is given true effect - that is to say, if one really frees the cultural life, places the life of rights on a democratic basis, and allows the economic life to be represented by associations.82 I am certain that in this way the economy will take its right course - that the right things will take place in the economic life. I want to rely on people finding the right course of action. That is a reality.

My treatment of the concept of work (Steiner is here referring to Chapter 1 in his book *The Threefold Social Order*. - Ed.[83]) had to include a real concept of work in the economic sense. This concept has to be freed from everything that does not create economic values. Everything else has to be eliminated if one is to arrive at a description; and it is this descriptive method that matters.

To what extent is inspiration required for understanding economics?

Inspiration is not that difficult if one takes it seriously. It is not a question of discovering supersensible facts, but of making inspiration effective in the economic sphere. Consider the defining of work. I would first show how it is possible for the human being to do work that has no economic value. This is a truism, of course. A great deal of energy can be expended in talking, but this does not give rise to true economic values. Next I would show how work, even as it begins to have economic meaning, can have its value modified. Consider a lumberjack at work, work which is clearly value-creative; on the other hand, consider a cotton merchant, who therefore has nothing to do with wood-cutting, but who suffers from his work and cuts wood during the holidays for relaxation. Here the matter becomes more complicated. The merchant can, of course, sell the cut wood and receive an income from it. But you cannot assess this work in the same way as that of the lumberjack. It might be, for example, that the merchant would work less in the winter if he could not spend his fortnight cutting wood in the summer. Then you also have to consider the stimulation he derives from this work. The economic **value** of the wood cut by the cotton merchant is exactly the same as that of the wood cut by the lumberjack; the economic **effect**, however, which falls back onto his activity, is a very different one.

If the value of the merchant's woodcutting is that it affects his activity as a merchant, then one needs to examine whether this is also true when somebody uses a pedal bike for the sake of getting slimmer. The person concerned exerts himself, but there is no effect for the economy. Yet even here, one has to differentiate between someone of private means and an entrepreneur, since as a creator of economic value, the latter will become more efficient.

One has to approach the question of work gradually and by way of characterisations, during the course of which one arrives at the direct value of work and its indirect, reflected value. In this way, one will arrive at a descriptive concept of work, with which one can return to the lumberjack and

compare the meaning of the woodcutting done by the cotton merchant with
that of the professional lumberjack in the economic process. One needs to
pass from one step to the next, taking account of the effect at every step. That
is what I regard as realistic. This is Goethe's approach to the concept of the
archetypal plant. He drew a diagram, of course, but he meant something
continuously variable. My point is that concepts in economics are
continuously subject to change.

You will, of course, not be favourably looked upon with such concepts!
University lecturers will not allow them. They want to have definitions.
Nevertheless, I have yet to come across a rigorous comprehension of the
concept of work in economic teachings. One should characterise and not go
on talking negatively. For example, there is the argument that work cannot
be a criterion for price, because work is experienced differently according to
one's strength. You do find negative examples recorded. But the positive
aspect is missing, namely, that one reaches a characterisation of work in
which work ceases to have economic value in itself, but acquires its value
from its context. In this way work ceases to be something in itself and
becomes something that is totally within the economic structure.

Work is an economic element. It arises out of real human effort, but then
flows over into the economic process and thereby acquires various economic
values in very different directions. To value work one needs to speak of the
processes that lead to these diverse directions.

Inspiration is to find out how to advance from one to the other. Finding the
right examples depends a little on one's flair for such things.

**Is a generic term not necessary after all? Isn't the cause of the observed
effects the important thing in the descriptive method, as in the others?**

As far as effects are concerned, I agree that one has to get to the causes. But
just as in certain domains of nature one cannot find the causes unless one
proceeds from the effects, so to a much larger degree is this true of economics.
An understanding of causes does not help, if it is not derived from the effects.
Consider the immense effects of the war economy (referring to the First
World War - Ed.). If one was not aware of them as effects, one would not seek
their causes. It is a matter of acquiring a certain sense for the quality of the
effects, so that one can reach to the causes. Certainly, in practical life, one has
to arrive at causes for it is on these that the real economy is based. One learns

to assess effects, and by observing how they occur, one begins to recognise causes, which can then be corrected. It is of no value merely to recognise causes. One has to arrive at causes in such a way that one can say:- I have arrived at causes by proceeding from their effects. Knowledge of such immense importance as, for example, that the speech centre is in the left half of the brain, has only been realised via the effects; speech gone - left part of the brain paralysed. First you realise the effect. Only then is one led to an examination of the problem. In this sense, the method of referring back is necessary.

I cannot regard everything that has to do with art, religion or even sport from an economic point of view. I can regard certain aspects of these from an economic point of view, but not the whole.

I visit a place and find extraordinarily artistic buildings there - this, of course, is a utopia. But it is not just artistic perception. These artistic buildings are only possible on the basis of certain economic conditions. If I visit a place with many artistic buildings, I will immediately be able to visualise how the economy works there. And if I visit a place where so-called beautiful buildings are tasteless, I shall from that draw my conclusions about their economic circumstances, too. Even if I find only utility buildings, I shall get ideas about the economic conditions of the area concerned. I can conclude that at the place where I find artistic buildings, higher wages are being paid than at the place where I find none. In other words, there is nothing I can think of that cannot be seen from an economic point of view. Everything up to the highest realms has to be seen from an economic point of view. If an angel were to come down to earth today, then either it would have to appear merely in a dream - and be unable to change anything - or, if it wanted to appear to people in their waking consciousness, it would have to enter the economic life. It could not avoid doing so.

I admit that one can consider these matters from an economic point of view, but one can also consider them from a different point of view.

One enters a circle here. All one can say is: That to begin with it is necessary to base one's considerations on the economic point of view. It has only a heuristic, research value. But if you want to find real economy to its full extent, you cannot avoid describing economic effects from all sides. You have to describe the influence on the economic life of an area if it has 100 excellent painters or only ten. Otherwise one cannot imagine how the economic life is made up. I would not have emphasised this aspect so strongly otherwise. Precisely by doing so, one always comes to definitions which are not valid in some areas or which one has to modify considerably. It is impossible, for example, to define the income which a person should receive by pointing out that he should be able to claim what he produces himself. Such a definition actually exists; that one has the right to what one produces. It seems harmless enough and in certain respects it is correct. But the sewer cleaner cannot do much with it! In economics one should not abstract something from the totality of phenomena, but should arrive at it through this totality. The whole point of thinking economically is to be of help to those who cannot do so. But one must be aware of the fact that economic thinking must be more or less total, a thinking of a very comprehensive kind. It is much easier to think juridically which, indeed, is what most economists do.

Opinions about the "normal" are so divided in economics that it is difficult to know what normal is.

I have no interest to compete with the interpretations of "normal" and "abnormal". There is a saying: Only one health and countless illnesses. I do not accept that. Everybody is healthy in his own way. People come to me and say that there is a person suffering from heart-trouble, with this or that small fault and one should cure him. I have often said: Let him have his little fault. A doctor once showed me a patient who had injured his nasal bone so badly that one of his nostrils had become contracted and he could not breathe easily. The doctor said that he should be operated on, which would be very easy to do. I said he should forget about it! His lung was constructed in such a way that he should not get any more air; he was fortunate to have a contracted nostril. Because of it he could live another ten years; with a normal nose he would more than likely be dead in three years. From this you can see that I do not attach any importance to "normal" and "abnormal". I often say "a normal citizen" and what I mean is understood.

A question about the value of statistics.

It is true that statistics can be very helpful. But today the statistical method is applied externally. Somebody prepares statistics about the increase in the value of houses in a certain area and then compares these with those he did of a different area. But that is no good. Only when the processes as such are examined does this become valuable. For then one knows how to assess such figures. Otherwise a row of figures can seem to be quite different, but only because an unusual instance has been included...

Does inspiration enter into the gathering of figures?

Suppose you have three rows of figures and notice that, qualitatively seen, certain facts of the first row are modified by corresponding facts of, say, the third row. Here inspiration is at work. Certain numerical values may perhaps cancel each other out. In history I call this symptomatological observation. One needs to be able to assess the matter and in certain cases to balance contradictory facts properly against each other. At times economics is carried out in a most unobjective manner. One gets the feeling that statistics are dealt with in such a way that, for example, the preparation of a balance sheet by the directors of finance of the different states is done according to party politics. Where somebody wants to furnish evidence for a certain party line, numerical data are used that could just as well prove a different one. One's soul has to be impartial. Something elementary is required. In every science that deals with human nature - even in a science which teaches you how to treat and tame animals - your examples have to be capable of modification. This is especially so in economics. Here inspiration comes in. One needs to have it. I hope you do not mind my putting it like that.

I am convinced that many more of today's students could have this inspiration - after all it is not something flowing about in nebulous mystic heights - were it not, in the main, knocked out of them at school long before they go to university.

As university students today you have the task of recalling what was knocked out of you at school; to enter into a living scientific activity instead of today's lifeless one. I once spoke abroad with a number of lecturers in economics. They mentioned that on their visits to Germany their colleagues would invite them home, but never to their lectures. Impartial insight into these matters is really necessary today. Economics has particularly declined in recent times because people have lost creativity in regard to thought. Today people have to bump into facts with their noses if they are to believe them.

Currently one can read articles in the papers about the cultural blockade of Germany - something which of course has been developing for a long time. If we want to deliver the magazine *Das Goetheanum*[84] in Germany today then we have to supply one copy at the price of 18Marks! Think though of the technical and medical periodicals! This is an economic question, too. One can say that Germany is subject to a cultural blockade, because the denial of those periodicals helps lead to the stupefaction of Germany - but the blockade is of an economic character. In Russia it has already adopted a state character. There one can no longer read anything which is not sold by the Soviet state. At the most one might be able to sneak in a book here or there.

Would it not be useful for the observation of economic effects to proceed first from the observation of existing facts rather than from statistics?

One needs this approach even when one uses statistics, for statistics only enable one to substantiate matters numerically. It is obvious that when one goes to Vienna, one only needs to wander through the streets to gather information. One only needs to consider which flats friends inhabit now and which ones they inhabited ten years ago, and so on - step by step. One can make this type of observation in the most awful way. One can go and see for oneself that an entire middle class has disappeared. Economically speaking, it no longer exists, and it is terrible to see how those who made it up live now. One should work out from such facts, but the figures for them can still be very important as supporting evidence.

One needs something like a "good nose" for the real facts; once one can prove them numerically one can proceed yet further. Take, for example, the devaluation of the Krone in Austria. It is indeed ridiculous that the Krone has so little value today, and yet no one value can decrease without taking something away from the others. The victims of the currency, you will find, are those whose pensions and similar incomes have been devalued. This you can check statistically, and it is symptomatic that the calculation for Austria is already out of date, not to mention that for Russia. Austria should have the right to devalue the Krone further since everything is already exhausted, but it still does not declare state-bankruptcy. This, of course, can only be achieved by some kind of blockade. As soon as such a blockade is lifted, the people have to adopt completely different measures.

Is it possible for the state to seize upon existing wealth by means of monetary expansion?

Certainly the state can exist through the increase of money. But once the point is reached where its revenue is exhausted, unless this is provided artificially, the state could no longer really exist economically. Even if it were to print more banknotes, every doubling would lead to a rise into infinity. The state would have to isolate itself more and more.

Does the state not live off the capital invested in business?

Yes; but off the income therefrom.

What I mean is that it sucks out the capital and diminishes it.

Insofar as the capital bears income-character, yes. The state can, of course, live in this way, but it can no longer work economically. It is not an economy. The state can only live off something that has already been produced; it only lives off the old. In Austria the point at which the revenue is dead should have been reached long ago. In Germany it is still some time away. Most certainly Austria could not go on if it were not for some enforced legislation - concerning rents, for example. Currently in Austria, you do not really pay any rents - I think it is approximately 25 centimes for a three-room flat. The situation only keeps going because certain things are available for nothing. It is the same in Germany, where one only pays perhaps a tenth for one's accommodation. In Austria a certain section of society has fallen to such an extent that it can no longer even pay 25 centimes. People who had an income of 3000 Krone, for example, could perhaps have lived from that; but today that is worth only slightly more than an English shilling. Quite obviously one can no longer live from it!

Economic phenomena are in fact so horrendous today that one has the possibility of studying the laws of economics in a way that would help practically. This attempt failed in 1919; but at that time the currency crisis had not become what it is today (1922 - Ed.).

As further study we could discuss the question: What does economic thinking mean? And then: How does one get to a concept of work in the economic sense? It would also be good if somebody would work through quite freely in his own mind the concepts I have used already. And it would be a good idea to work out the concept of entrepreneurial capital. If one wants to characterise entrepreneurial capital in conceptual terms one has to contrast it precisely with mere income capital.

2: CONCEPTS OF WORK
1 August 1922

Work in terms of economics is human activity. In physics, as we know, work is defined in terms of its mechanical effect. Is every activity which can be put to economic use thereby work? No - in the end value can only arise through the consumer. If something has been brought about by work and is given a real economic value, then this can be regarded as economic work.

I would only like to give a small stimulus by asking what the position would be if, through discussion of these arguments, the following question arose:- Suppose in some way one relates work in the economic organism to work in the sense of physics. What is the position if one goes more thoroughly into the conception of work in physics? What you have said is right enough, but the physicist, in establishing a formula for work, will adopt the concept of mass, because work in physics is energy, a function of mass and speed. You will easily find an analogy for the latter in the economic process. But the peculiarity of the formula for work in physics is precisely that the concept of mass is introduced into it, mass which is defined by reference to weight. The concept of work in physics, therefore, has weight replaced by mass and speed. Were one to go along with your analogy, it would become a question of finding out if it is necessary to introduce into economics something like the concept of mass or weight. Were one to do so, one would have to look for the equivalent of mass in the economic process. My point is that such a discussion would give rise to this question.

An understanding of the nature of work involves acknowledgment of the consumer. The entrepreneur presumes this idea of acknowledgment. The fact that anything is purchased at all is in itself acknowledgment.

Because your concept of acknowledgment is not primarily an economic one but is more philosophic, it is necessary to give it economic weight; to show that it has economic meaning. Acknowledgment as such - for example, that a housewife realises she needs something before she buys it - is little more than a judgment. Economic considerations only begin when she realises she can now buy this particular item. It could easily be the case that the item is of the very best, yet cannot be bought for economic reasons, that it is too expensive. Without economic qualification, acknowledgment is a philosophical category. The concept of economic activity would clarify this.

How, then, is economic activity verified by acknowledgment?

Acknowledgment as such can hardly be an economic category because it is subjective. Of course, subjective elements play into economics, but one has to show how such things become objective. Assume that two people have totally opposite opinions about an item for sale. A "yes" may lead to economic success; a "no" to failure. The economic aspect arises where these judgements lean on the one hand to success, on the other to failure. Acknowledgment itself can only be a philosophical concept. Although it can of course slide down into the area of private economics, it has yet to enter the realm of economics proper.

I would understand economic activity to be an anticipation of the physical expression of a verification acting as an initiative (Ugh! - Ed.).

It may be that we are dealing here with something apart from the subject of this discussion, something very different to economic thinking. Your formula does not show that you have considered the matter economically. The formula is of course praiseworthy, but it belongs more to the philosophy of economics. It seeks in a rather scholastic way to discover a concept of economic activity that gives it metaphysical justification in terms of a complete world order. If that is what you are aiming at, then you are on the right path; and it would be very interesting to discuss the matter. But if you ask yourself whether what matters isn't that a number of people - who are after all present-day people - bring something into the economy out of their thinking, something that could contribute to economic recovery, then your formula amounts to very little.

Naturally, it could help people to learn to think better, but the real need today is to make economics as such really fruitful. In natural science and medicine it does not matter greatly whether or not one has a methodology. There methodology is of less value than treatment techniques, research instruments, etc. In economics, however, methodology is of first importance because it is what we think that becomes practice. Otherwise economics would follow Brentano's approach and be purely empirical. It would not become practical. Today the need is for economic thinking that can be put into practice. It would be of great interest, therefore, to work through your definition word for word. But it belongs more to the philosophy of economics than to economics itself.

The previous speaker sought to devise concepts of work in a way that could help anyone wishing to evaluate work in an association. That was his direction and that should be our direction once, as a worker, we are inside an association, for example. We need to assess things in terms of economics.

All human activity that directly or indirectly produces value is economic work.

Something more needs to be considered if one wishes to achieve practical economic thinking. To become clear about this, let us make an analogy with natural science. As long as one observes only generative processes, that is, processes that go in a certain direction, the complete process of the human organism remains incomprehensible. A real understanding of the total process is only possible once one starts to consider the decomposition processes in our bones and our nervous system, and in our blood, where they are alongside growth processes. Within the human organism there are quite definite decomposition processes from chyle, to lymph formation, to the creation of blood. Then there are the processes connected with breathing. These processes represent a balance between growth and decay, while the processes in the bones and nervous system are decidedly processes of decomposition. Devolution as opposed to evolution.

We can only reach a real understanding when we arrange our concepts so that we see, for example, that the liver process is a combination of growth and decay, or that what is in the brain is not construction but disintegration, and that it is on this that consciousness depends. Then one gains an understanding which enables one to enter reality. Practical understanding is not achieved by holding on to a definition on a basis of abstract, step by step, purely dialectical logic.

Thus in economics it is necessary to consider not only the creation of values, but also their consumption - that one speaks of real destruction up to a certain extent, as I have done. It was said that the demolition of a house has a value, too, because the demolition means that something productive has been created for somebody. One can of course see things like this if one remains within an abstract development of concepts. But for practical economics much depends on how one connects the economic process to the production and consumption of values. And it is, of course, necessary to show that work has meaning for both processes, otherwise one cannot get an adequate concept of work. If work were not also involved in the consumption of values, one would be unable to work in the economic sense. One has to include this in one's concept.

I think this matter will be of great significance as far as the production and consumption of values is concerned - because values exist to be consumed, and if they are not, an unhealthy tendency arises in the economic process. The process is disturbed by too much production, because, to put it figuratively, the stomach of the economic life becomes too full.

Should we not form the concept of work in such a way that work is understood to be activity suitable for an enclosed economic organism?

It is a matter of understanding the thing in its reality. Undoubtedly the over-production of umbrellas can be a process of decomposition; but as far as the work done is concerned, it is quite definitely a creative process. The consumption is not necessarily achieved by what you define as work. One cannot call the over-production of umbrellas destructive if one wants to think the matter through with regard to work.

We have to be aware of the fact that in economic observation it is necessary to characterise, to try and reach a concept by identifying it from different points of view, so as to reach a judgment that is truly alive. Abstract definitions are of no value. One has a concept of work: Work as human activity in its economic aspect, work as the economic activity of the human being. But how does such a definition differ in the economic sense and in the sense of physics? There is no reality in such an economic definition. If a physicist defines work as a function of mass and speed, then one has something real inasmuch as mass can be weighed. If a physicist wants to define speed then he sets down a definition. This definition serves only for communication, however, for the physicist is fully aware that he thereby only indicates something that needs to be looked at. A concept of speed is possible only through observation. The physicist's definition is the measurement of speed. He will never think that it is an explanation, but thinks - whether correctly or not, I do not wish to examine here - that he gives a real explanation when he explains work as a function of mass and speed.

Were one to do this in economics it would be a question of taking hold at the right point. If at a certain point I give my explanation of work, for example, in such a way that value is created by it - value arising as a function of labour and land, or arising out of intelligence and land - then you have work inside the transformation which is taking place. This is however, a qualitative explanation of work while the moving body experiences a change of place. The measurement of the physicist is the real nature-substance. I, however, aim at a definition which in fact corresponds to such a real definition of physics. If I try to define work on its own nothing particular is achieved for economics. I have to realise first that work as such only becomes an economic category once it is brought into relation with the nature-product. If one makes such a definition then one gets into a kind of conception which will set one back at a later stage. The classical physicist's definition of work as a function of mass and speed loses its meaning completely in the face of modern ideas of ions and electronic processes, because here the concept of mass is removed. One is only dealing with acceleration. Here the physical process emancipates itself from ponderable mass, just as, in my view, capital emancipates itself from cultivated nature and fulfils an autonomous function.

In other words, one enters an area which justifies itself from every point of view. That is the peculiarity of real thinking, one thinks more than is actually contained in definitions. That is what I want to point out. When I speak economically, I try never to approach a concept from where one cannot. I cannot approach "mass" directly in physics either, but only its function. That "mass is the sum of matter" is also only a word definition! Just as little would I consider it meaningful to define the concept of nature, work and capital one after the other, but would approach them from where the realities are; not nature as such, but cultivated nature; not just work, but organised work; not just capital, but the capital that is taken hold of by the human spirit and set into economic movement. To grasp matters from where they are - that is what I think is necessary in economics today.

Unrecorded question.

I would like to point out that the differentiation between mental work and physical work is not really justified. If one tried to define mental work and physical work one could not help finding anything else but a slow transition from one pole to the other, but no real opposite. Physiologically, there is no real opposite. That these matters have been considered wrongly can be seen from the fact that people have always erred about the recreational effect of gymnastics. Today one knows that gymnastics do not have the recreational effect that was attributed to them earlier on. The pupil will not work more through so-called mental work than through gymnastics. It is, of course, always a question of thinking about it in an economically fruitful way.

Question about the relationship between economic and biological thinking.

Economic activities are to a very large extent analogous to biological entities. One can verify that very easily if one tries to establish the economic value of work: For example, book printing. Let us assume that a poet considers himself to be a very great poet and also manages to get his lyrics published, be it through patronage or financial support or whatever. And now the paper-worker, the type-setter and a certain number of people who, according to Marxist principles, perform real productive work, produce this book of lyrics. Now let us assume that not one copy is sold but all are pulped, thus giving one the same real effect as if they had not been produced in the first place. In this case one has basically generated work for no purpose whatsoever. Now, however, one first has to find out whether what the Marxists say is to a large extent nonsense or whether it does not have meaning after all. And there one will notice that the biological approach offers a certain analogy. One could, of course, say, that in biology one is able to consider the whole entity which stands in front of one while in economics one only deals with tendencies and the like. But, I ask you, does one not also face tendencies in nature? Consider that, out of countless herring-eggs, only a few become herrings, while the majority are simply destroyed? It is a question of whether those destroyed eggs have any importance in the entire process of nature, or whether they merely follow a different direction in the overall biological process. For that is in fact what happens. There would be no herrings and many other sea creatures, did not so and so many herring-eggs simply perish. Furthermore, one is not yet standing on the ground of real observation if one says: "Well, eggs perish - and so on." One is then obliged to say: I am confronted with an evolution here. The egg originated and perishes through something. The processes only head in different directions and the herring only continues the formed tendency of the egg. Nowhere can one in any way say that the herring has more right than the egg to cease existence. And now one has an analogy with perishing work and perishing economic entities.

If one maintains analogies in one's way of thinking between economic and

biological thinking then one will come across countless points. But this goes
unnoticed because we have neither an ordered economic thinking nor an
ordered biological thinking. If biology were to begin to develop true thinking,
then that would be very similar to economic thinking. One needs the same
abilities to pursue biology in a real sense, as one needs for the pursuit of
economics.

**How does the comparison with herring-eggs justify the remaindered
poetry?**

It may be that the people employed to do that would, if they were not
employed for this work, find employment somewhere else, in which case not
enough might be derived from human activity. Like herring-eggs, human
activity, too, needs to be "wasted" occasionally and this "wastage" is not
without economic effect. It is necessary but easy to say, "let sleep be rest, let
life be activity". But from a certain point of view sleep is much more
important for life than being awake. The same applies with this example. One
can of course, say:- I want to apply it in a more useful way. But the question
is, is it more useful if what is produced is a surplus of umbrellas? To begin
with these are temporary aids; however, in an unhealthy economic process,
to abolish work might have a disturbing effect. It would look different if one
were to think clearly in economics. To do that one would need to create
enormous ingenuity - but here we go beyond ordinary economic observation
- to utilise the surplus working-time thereby created for those people who
could be put out of work. If one would think healthily in economics,
something would emerge immediately that one would probably welcome.
But people cannot imagine that it would be necessary to teach those who
became unemployed what it means to save time. Because it would hardly be
necessary for a person who now works eight, nine hours to work for more than
three or four hours. If things were thought through sensibly in economic
terms, people would need to work much less than at present. And into this
time would enter what corresponds to the perishing herring-eggs. At present
people waste so much in work that has to perish again anyway.

**Thinking in biology means having a visible object with defined
boundaries to think about. In economics one has to characterise what
one is thinking about.**

In biology, too, you only have a "visible object with boundaries" in a relative
sense. You do not have it, if you observe world formations through a

microscope, where one considers more the individual phenomena arising out of a larger context. One can say one has a clear object in a drop of blood. But the moment that one looks at it through the microscope, one will see it differently - in one cubic millimetre of blood there are five to six hundred red blood particles and all are active. This is certainly visible to the eye through the microscope and it looks very similar to that which one can see if one observes a limited economic process somewhere. Imagine one goes to a particular stall at the market and observes how the stall-keeper stands, how his goods are laid out. There are the customers, he passes the goods over and they give him money. If you now imagine all this pressed together into one, like something dense, something belonging together, then there is no real difference. One can also understand economics within a limited area just as relatively. If one observes the stall-holder with all that comes with it, then that is only relatively different to, for instance, the English selling opium in China and observing everything that belongs to that. I cannot see why one has no object there.

The point is that one does not know where economics begins and where it ends.

One also does not know where biology begins. It is a different matter if one rides the comparison to death. All I am saying is that what enables one to understand the nature of life also enables one to understand economics. There is only one thing necessary. And there the content of what you said may apply:- in the observation of a nature-object the object comes towards you, while in economics the subject has to a certain extent to go to meet the object. In economics one needs what yesterday I called "flair". Biologists can get by with little flair, working only with methods. But a certain flair is essential to thinking economically.

It seems to me that the economic process came about without the thinking being economic; that the thinking has still to become economic. It makes no difference whether the economy runs in a healthy way or not. Therefore, I should be able to speak of an object in economics in natural scientific terms.

You are right. The difference is that in economics it is necessary to proceed from a certain subjective comprehension of what happens outside in the world. This subjective way, however, is easier in economics than in biology. In biology one always stands outside the matter one studies. For example, if one studies a cockchafer, one does not become a cockchafer. One always has to stand outside. But in economic observations one is to a much lesser degree outside the matter. One can always muster up enough humanity to understand the worker very well and also the entrepreneur. Such normal, human sympathy replaces what is external notion in biology. To this extent you are right. But on the other hand, in my opinion Goethe[85] gave such a good definition of the drawbacks of the concepts of trade precisely because he had advanced a long way in his biological observation. With Goethe you sometimes find particularly striking economic ideas. This has something to do with his morphological-biological observations. In nature biology takes the part of something that pushes you if you do not have a certain flair yourself; in economics you need to generate this by yourself.

There are theorists who say there are no economics because there is no economy. Spann expresses as much.[86]

Spann is very much admired and he is considered to be a very special light by some intelligent people in Vienna. I have not concerned myself with him, however, and cannot offer too much of a judgment about him. But what these very intelligent people say has not made an awful lot of sense to me. It is but mere witty dialectic to say there is no economy. There are also people who say "there is no life, only mechanism."

We should next make specialised observations. Somebody should try to show more concretely where economic utilisation and devaluation processes are necessary.

50 tailors had to sell their own wares, they could not do so as cheaply as dealers, because it is time taken away from suit-making itself.

But surely the cost of distribution is saved if the tailor does without the dealer?

That would be a relevant consideration if trade weren't cheapening. But it is, and for this reason it is of no consequence if the tailor keeps the suit in his house.

Suppose the cost of production to be 100. The trader adds on 20, but depresses the price to 110, with only 90 for the tailor. If the tailor refuses to sell to the trader at this price, he will be 10 better off.

One has to consider the entire balance sheet of both tailors and traders in order to see the real effects. One can't see them from comparisons of single items. The complete balance sheet would show that because division of labour increases work efficiency, the individual disadvantages himself by returning to older economic conditions. Admittedly these things are difficult to see in a single transaction, but they do become visible when seen on a larger scale.

This is even clearer in the ready-made clothes industry.

Certainly. Naturally, one has to examine the precise reasons. The effect under discussion is minor in the case of the tailor and dealer when the transaction concerns whole suits. But it will be much greater when tailors are each making particular parts of suits. Obviously, the tailor is a radical example, but my purpose was to illustrate a principle.

Why is this principle not applicable to farming?

I didn't say that. What I said was that people tend to produce less and less for themselves nowadays with the exception of farmers, where it is natural to provide food for oneself. Here it doesn't matter, because the usual economic process today is so widely altered anyway in farming. But if there were a true relationship between agriculture and non-agriculture, then it would matter. Today's extensive price manipulations obscure the true nature of this relationship - a point we shall take up in the next few days. If one examined the balance sheet of an overall economic area to observe the balance between farming and industry, one would see that farming supports industry by all manner of "underground" arrangements. Under associative economics, there would be quite different allocations of labour in town and country, for example. People underestimate the difference associative economics would make. For this reason it is not easy to answer such a question as, "Why is Der Kommende Tag not an association?"[87] It is not enough to reply: Because it is not big enough to have a definite influence on the economic process directly. What is it that "Der Kommende Tag" wants to do that is different from other companies? To undertake reform from the side of the workers. And yet to achieve this everyone would have to leave the unions. But so long as the workers in the company choose to strike as in so many other companies, there is nothing one can do. One thing above all would come about under associative economics - quite a number of factories would move into the countryside. Village economies existed for very good reasons. They were once the only form of economy, then came the market - both quite accurate terms. So long as the market is surrounded by a village economy it is a harmless form of economic life. But as soon as the town economy develops, the entire producer-consumer relationship is radically changed. A market surrounded by villages is regulated in effect by natural clear producer-consumer relationships of supply and demand. But in town economies these relationships become confused and obscure. Nowadays one can maintain clear producer-consumer relationships only by way of associative economics. Other details could be indicated about this from the point of view of the threefold social order, but it is not easy to speak about these things, because one is reliant on intuition to a large extent, in an age that demands "proof" - despite the fact that no-one demands proof that he will be hungry tomorrow. Experience tells one that one will be hungry tomorrow, not proof. Similarly, a real economic science would enable one to know what will happen. Were this not so, what value would there be in economics? It wouldn't be productive.

Tailors cheapen production by division of labour. Is this true also for the production of buttons or similar things.?

As a boy I lived in a village, which had its own cobbler. He only dealt direct with his customers. He made every part of the boots himself and then delivered them himself. Division of labour begins when the delivery is done by someone else.

Is it also cheapening for me to produce buttons myself?

If one doesn't actually need the buttons, one would lose considerably.

I am assuming that I do need them.

Then the question is what one needs the buttons for. On this will depend whether they have a value and thus whether one loses or not.

I intend to use them up.

In agriculture different considerations come into play. If the division of labour were brought through it would be valid there, too. However, in farming one hardly has the opportunity to turn to account the cheapening effected by the division of labour.

Bread is still very close to farming. But if it is not distributed as widely as possible it becomes expensive.

What about fashion goods?

With fashion goods one is no longer talking about economic matters, but aesthetic ones. It can be that the division of labour should not be applied into every corner of life, as this could restrict cultural life. There is a price on aesthetics, of course, but I do not want you to think that I am fanatical about the cheapening effects of the division of labour.

What happens if there are dealers in excess of the number that can be economically justified?

In what I have said I have assumed there are only as many dealers as are economically justified. It is a matter of getting the optimum.

Can one fix the number?

If economic life is conducted reasonably, the number of dealers will be established in the same way as the number of producers. But this is rare nowadays. Much unnecessary work is done today, and also people act under disguised economic relationships. This could all be different.

4: **VALUES**
3 August 1922

Can one still speak of value once goods have fulfilled their purposes? What happens when goods are newly introduced into the economic process? Does the demolition of a house represent devaluation by labour? Does such devaluation have any economic meaning? Can one speak of devaluation through labour only if new values are not created?

Express your views about this! Subjects will arise like mineral coal vs. brown coal. Someone might regard mineral coal as more valuable than brown coal, but he would need to argue his case. Another, rather daring, thesis might argue that mechanical work does not increase price. But putting forward exceptional cases, such as submarines, does not help. It is a matter of bringing about economically necessary devaluations through labour in the course of the continuous economic process.

One needs to learn to speak of valuation and devaluation through labour, in a totally economic sense. Economically speaking, when machines are devalued, they are consumed. The question is not whether the aim of work is devaluation, but whether labour can bring about the devaluations that are deemed necessary.

The devaluation of values through work is meant to make way for higher, intermediate values.

Consider the simple very ordinary example of the bobbin. The bobbin is wound by work and the result is a product. But to continue its work, the thread has to be reeled off. In cases of intermediate work such as this, the work has to be undone, so to speak.

Does the same apply when a train is relocated, for example?

Yes. If one moves a train from one place to another one destroys one value and creates another. Such processes tend to go unnoticed, but they occur everywhere. The coal shoveller on the train is another example. One may argue that this is a continuous process, but it isn't. It is done in stages. The cost of the two could be compared.

Packaging is another example.

Certainly, and a very striking one. For here the concepts of use and wearing out do not apply as they would in the case of a razor blade, for example.

To collect, sell, recast and re-use old iron - does this constitute devaluation?

This is equivalent to the utilisation of refuse. One could not call it devaluation.

But the one process is completed!

Yes, and then one discovers that one can re-use a product of nature. We need to employ the criterion that labour is necessary to cause devaluation. The melting down of old iron is not as such a process of decomposition. But I recognise these are subtle matters, capable of different interpretations.

Is the mere squandering of grenades in wartime devaluation?

Yes, but only for the labour.

Is armament production creative of value in the economic sense?

Not if the production only creates reserves. Then it is destructive, unnecessary work.

Do you mean that the excessive consumption (i.e. physical destruction - Ed.) brought about by war is a deficit?

The abnormal consumption of war can be likened to the man of private means within an economic community. Such consumption can be seen as economically justified if the land yields more than the rest of the population can use. Then it can be said to be a positive thing, bringing economic balance. Reasoning in this way, people can and do provide justification for military economics. Employment is provided, for example. But the fact remains that nothing is really produced thereby.

Can one compare military economics to the cauterising of wheat?

The school of Rodbertus[88] puts forward this idea, ranking defence among the
factors of production. It depends on one's picture of economics. One could
do without defence, but not so the fire engine... or breakfast. But if one
believes the armed forces to be necessary, they can only be a consumer in
economic terms.

But this, as I say, depends on one's view of what is necessary in life. Concepts
of usefulness play in here, and these are labile.

**In the case of power turbines, mechanical work saves labour. But can it
not also be said that mechanical work has been performed by labour?**

Think of a set of scales, with different length arms. Leverage enables a heavy
weight on one side to be balanced by a lighter weight on the other. In a similar
way, all mechanical work represents a certain quantum of labour. It is simply
that the proportion diminishes by virtue of economic leverage in this way.
But such things do not belong in the economy, where the amount of expended
work relative to performance is functionally determined by non-economic
circumstances.

Does mechanical work raise prices?

If you consider work in its full context, then you have to work out a quota
everywhere.

How does devaluing work enter into the economic process?

Suppose one has a shaving salon large enough to require one employee in
particular to sharpen blades - this illustrates a continuous economic process
within which devaluation takes place. The work of the blade sharpener would
need to be shown differently in the balance sheet to that of the shavers. Both
are working in the ordinary sense, but economically the sharpening process
is a negative.

**What happens with devaluation, then? Does the lack of a counter-value
make it a gift?**

Only the signs change. In a continuous economic process value creation is positive and devaluation is negative; while, if nothing happens, one writes nil.

When a new machine replaces a process, the product is cheapened by the saving of labour. Whether the work creates or consumes value is of no importance.

Yes, one can always bring out the same. Even so, the distinction between value creation and devaluation remains. The question is simply whether it is necessary to work to effect devaluations, which have already materialised in the economic process.

Question not recorded.

In order to remove any unclear concepts, it will be necessary to consider the economics of drinking tea, supposed by some to be work.

Surely tea-drinking is not work?

When one eats food one creates the values necessary for further work; just as machines create further values.

It is not possible, however, to include in economics what happens to the human being - that leads to Marxist theory. The suggestion, I think, is that drinking tea could create economic value and is, therefore, work in the economic sense.

If a cultural worker is supported by economic values, the result will be an increase in his mental alertness, which in turn will ray out into the economy.

Yes, but this cannot be included within the economic process without something else. By itself, drinking tea is not productive. The tea would only be productive if it were indispensable to production.

Tea drinking enables further tea production.

Proper economic values cannot be assessed in this way. Consuming for the sake of production is not really an economic question.

Surely the tea picker is no different to the doctor or cobbler, whose services enable one to work more than if one were ill or unshod?

Put like that, then tea becomes a value in the economic process when it is picked. But does value arise or vanish in the same sense in the course of consumption?

It will vanish, be devalued.

I would say, revalued.

But then every type of consumption would have to be described as a transformation.

I meant transformation into energy.

In that case we move outside economics into science, by introducing a natural, as distinct from an economic process. When tea is drunk, economic value disappears from the economic process. Now suppose that tea does make a person fitter, more able to work. In itself, that increased propensity has no value. But if it is expended on nature, then the creation of values begins anew. In other words, the effect of tea on the drinker has no economic significance. Such a process has to be excluded from economics, just as does the value of land.

Of course, one can include the value of land, but only analogously. Soil is made fertile by the passage of worms through it, but that cannot be included in the economic process. Fertility as such and work as such, have no economic value. Value arises only in connection with working on nature or improving work by inventiveness. Economics cannot be understood if it is allowed to embrace human and natural processes.

How is one to understand gifts in this connection?

Here one can speak of devaluation. As long as one has only human capabilities in mind, which the gift is intended to support, one is not as yet in the economy. With a gift, the value disappears, economically speaking - to reappear later elsewhere.

One can nearly see how the gift works on.

That which works on is generally not quantifiable. Were things not so, one would have to include diligence, for example, as an a economic factor, but this would be an economic fiction, nay an economic impossibility. One might reprimand one's workers morally if they were lazy, but economically it is a question of whether they have produced anything.

Can one only speak of work in an economy subject to division of labour?

Work, in the economic sense, begins when men produce for one another.

Can one speak of work in a primitive economy?

Only in the sense that within a family, the various members work for one another.

So, how does one arrive at a concept of work at all?

In economic terms, very easily. Work arises when nature is transformed by the human being for the purpose of being consumed.

Does it matter if it is not consumed?

It has at least to be consumable in order to have a value.

Does value only arise by reference to products also in the case of the mental organisation of work?

No, because the "object" of intellectual work is classification, division of labour, and so on.

Then it does not come within the concept of work?

It is a secondary concept. Work is human activity expended on a nature-product to make it consumable. This is a finite concept. By intelligence one can divide this work but the resultant structuring of work has moved away from the product. It is a mere division of work.

But what if devaluation by work is included?

Devaluation is only negative in terms of the value. As far as making something consumable is concerned, one does not go backwards. One only reverses the direction with gifts.

But in making something consumable, there is a return from a higher process to a lower one.

First you wind the bobbin. That requires work and creates value. Then you unwind it. You destroy the value, but the product is made usable thereby. Work is a matter of creating a usable product. This concept embraces such intermediate steps as unwinding the bobbin.

Useless work therefore has to be described as work.

If one wants an economic concept of work, work has first to be defined. But economic work is not yet a value. Remember that economics is concerned with values; work is secondary.

Teachers also perform work.

That is a major question; not at all easy to answer.

I mean freed activity, cultural activity.

That belongs to devaluation as such, not devaluation through work.

But the teacher is producing into the future.

This leads one to consider the concept of work further. Naturally, one needs to describe teaching as an economic value of high degree. But does an economic concept of work really apply to teaching? To be sure, the teacher physically walks about, speaks, and so on. A type of work is being performed, but this is not what counts economically. Economically, it is the teacher's organising activity that matters and which enters the economic process. Fidgets can expend a lot of work to little productive effect. But quiet, tactful instruction can have a greater result. It is the effectiveness that matters, not the energy expended.

Even in work there are those who try hard and achieve little, and those who try little and achieve a lot.

This demonstrates the emancipation of work. Manual work is tied to nature, mental work is free. And with mental work, the teacher's physical "work" is irrelevant. What counts is his capacity, his education. Not his physical work.

Why is freed activity devaluing?

It is devaluing in the sense that it uses up values that have been created. Except that it belonged to a different folk character, the Romans had a very subtle, instinctive economy. They spoke not only of bread, but of bread and games and provided for them economically. They said:-just as a loaf of bread has to be consumed, so the production of bread has to be expended in the work needed to perform the games. It is a reciprocal consuming because, as everywhere in an organism, one finds reciprocal creation and destruction. So here, too. So it is that freed activity does not continue the economic process, but leads it back. That is why I have always shown the economic process as circular - land, labour, capital. (See Sketches 3 - 5.) These three work back in the process and cancel it out.

Can one include private economic work in your idea of economics?

One has to! Within the private economy definitely.

I mean, I cannot include private work in the concept of economics.

That is because the word is not precise enough. Because one is terming a collection of private businesses as an economy. One needs a better concept.

Is work only the activity directed toward a certain object to make it consumable?

Yes. In economics the task is not to find abstract, philosophical definitions, but to formulate "applicable concepts". Economists such as Lorenz von Stein[89] may formulate wonderfully clever concepts, but these tend to have philosophic, not economic use.

5: THE MONETARY SYSTEM
4 August 1922

What is the cause of the post-war (First World War - Ed.) **exchange fluctuations? Are certain personalities behind them?**

Whether certain personalities are responsible is hard to say. They may be a part-cause. But it is very difficult to identify main causes in such things. Many and different factors are at work in determining exchange rates. The main factor affecting the recent exchange losses is the discrepancy that has now become possible between gold currencies and paper currencies.

Nowadays gold currency is of little consequence in countries with weak currencies. In contrast, in those countries with strong currencies and where gold currency still exists this naturally gives such countries a credit advantage. Above all, the currency question is a credit question. So that when credit weakens in an economic region, one can have recourse to gold and reduce the credit in conformity with stock exchange rules.

But we should not overlook the rather senseless internal economic actions that take place. There can be no doubt that much of the German Mark's current slump is due to internal speculation in Germany and its gold sales to foreign countries. Such things eventually cause a currency's value to fall sharply. The same has happened in Austria. Events in Russia are less easy to assess. But in Austria and Germany the problem began with the reduction of gold reserves, the weakening of credit conditions and internal speculation. In Germany currency speculation has taken the form of exporting gold. In Austria foreign reserves are being held back, so that the Austrian currency is made even more expensive by Francs and Dollars already in Austria, although this would not be possible if the highly valued currencies were not already on the rise. But in such conditions, the process continues inside a country and thereby the problem can become boundless. But the current evils were first set in train when, in Germany during the war, gold was collected in large quantities by the state and then paid out of the country. So that the German people now have no gold left. That is the essential factor to observe.

To do so one only need compare the post-war gold reserves of the Reichsbank with the gold stocks of the German people before the war.

Of course, other factors were at work but these are difficult to identify. It only needs the currency of one country to be held back, for exchange rates to be affected. Even though this may happen outside them one can bring about acceleration or delay in this way and thereby force down the value of the poorer currencies. In this way, individual personalities can easily damage a state. How much is due to a country's own action, however, is hard to say. Nevertheless, you would be shocked by the huge sum attributable to individual speculation.

Some people say that the reason for currency-misery lies in the change in the balance of payments between the richer and the poorer countries. And for Germany reparation payments have only worsened matters. As a consequence the balance is in favour of the Allied Powers.

That could never have led to the degree of devaluation currently being experienced in Germany and Austria. It is not true that the discrepancy between gold and paper money is only a superficial aspect of the balance of payments. Before the war paper money was backed by gold. The gold-backing of currencies is an economic fact and a relationship that essentially prevents inflation. Remove gold, and inflation begins. Recent currency devaluations are the result of believing one can dispense with gold. But so long as, due to England's power, the gold standard is still in force, the first consequence of reduced gold reserves is the rise in the price of gold, which directly undermines credit. Thereafter, in the realm of credit, the balance of payments becomes problematic. But the process does not begin there.

The reason for the currency devaluation can already be found before the war. During the war it was said of Germany that she would perish due to the financial straits she was in. This could not actually happen while the war was on, however, but could and did happen afterwards. As soon as the borders were a little bit open, a flood began. The economics of the war manifested themselves, amid many other factors.

Mere balance of payments figures do not help one become clear in these matters. The figure difference is not the issue. The point is to know what the payments represent in real economic terms.

When gold goes out of a country its effect is to devalue the currency so long as the gold standard continues.

In view of the colossal upheavals in recent history one can understand this idea. And given current economic conditions - founded as they are on the gold standard - it is undoubtedly the case that goldless countries depend on the gold reserves of others for the value of their products. And the value of their money is similarly determined. But the very magnitude of recent events is beyond the comprehension of most people and thus they tend to assume "very mysterious causes". But today's currency devaluations are not that mysterious. Indeed, the main problem is to get people to assess recent events correctly. Since the war I have frequently said that it was like living through four centuries in as many years. Now if we had lived through several centuries we would expect many changes to have taken place, especially in the language. But people still speak in 1922 the language of 1914, unaware that the changes wrought by the war really were centuries long. This is the problem.

Historically viewed, one usually overlooks the time-scale of economic changes. For example, during the 15th and 16th centuries in England, wheat price fluctuations were as great as 20 times the lowest price. The time-scale alone allowed this considerable fluctuation to occur without tumult. The difficulty today lies in the compression of 400 years into 4. People do not reckon on this qualitative aspect of life. And so they don't notice until after the event the effect that money can have. People only have an instinctive sense for the state of their wallets. And they only notice things after the event, through the medium of the loss of currency value.

Take Russia, for example. Consider the whole Russian way of life permeated throughout by the sentiment of "Father Tsar" right up until Lenin. The Russian currency devaluation is only a barometer for whatever has taken place. It is not so difficult to understand such things. Their effects are terrible, to be sure, and will worsen further. But they can be understood nevertheless out of the course of other events.

Do we already effectively have world economy today?

One cannot put the matter quite like that. To begin with the war represented the transition to world economic conditions. One has only to consider international cheque arrangements to see even before the war that there was a high degree of world economic transactions. But people's thinking did not match these events. Old definitions of national economies continued to be used, hindering world economy and causing all manner of torment by the erection of customs barriers everywhere. Those since created by the Treaty of Versailles are only a continuation of the problem. Rather than think, people preferred to alter facts, by setting up customs barriers whenever there was a problem.

And yet world economy exists to a large extent despite the customs barriers. Our local tram fares are affected by events in America, and were so before the war. The real value of things has for some time been determined world-economically. But now all manner of barriers have gone up because of the war, causing all manner of economic disturbances. This is retrograde in terms of pre-1914 economics.

But still people refuse to think things through. Versailles is based on national economies. The complete dismemberment of Austro-Hungary, for example, in no way accords with economic facts, neither in the case of her shipping prices nor the price of her coal. It accords with absolutely nothing. This was the cause of the final chaos - the frantic attempt to overcome new facts with old thoughts, despite the fact that world economy was already extensively present. The very currency fluctuations we experience today prove the existence of world economy.

When America lends to Russia to finance her economic development, the result will be that Russia will get the money while America retains ownership title, but will not get the money back in any way.

If America were to resolve to do this, no matter in what way, it would be a gift. Out of the huge lending that has taken place a gift has to come about. But America, clearly, will not decide to do this until Europe guarantees to desist from further military and economic entanglements. America's economy would undoubtedly benefit from her helping, but she will not because Europe appears to her as worthless. Americans fear every loan and will continue to do so until Europe can re-establish personal credit. Rathenau and Wirth were problems because they were connected to pre-war circumstances. All such people, in both defeated and victorious nations, need to disappear from the scene before credit ratings can be restored. Real estate credit is non-existent. New faces are needed. Then a slow recovery in our currencies would begin and once begun, would call forth a totally different mood. Other factors would come into play and an upward movement would occur. But right now morale has fallen too low.

A recent opinion poll on the causes of currency-misery came up with quite contradictory answers.

All were probably correct in that people were referring to their specific experiences; but these are necessarily partial. This itself illustrates the need for associative economics. One individual alone cannot make extensive economic judgments. I am reminded of Edison, a man who can think thoroughly economically, when he spoke of how he interviews prospective employees. He asks less about management than about whether the applicant has remembered what he learned in school and whether he is open-minded. After all it makes a difference whether a book-keeper can tell wheat from rye or knows what a sunflower looks like. People think it doesn't. But it does. Despite this "grain of salt" example, Edison strikes me as extraordinarily economical. It shows to what extent his mind has understood work.

What do present economic necessities demand of those who believe a new economics must be founded?

In my lectures I'm endeavouring to give partial answers to this question. The important thing to understand is the transition to world economy from the national economy that has been so effective in the last fifty years or more; that one understands that the old economic categories are no longer valid and that a new economics needs to be created and that this can only be created out of thinking.

For example, prior to the conditions of world economy, the different national economies lay next to one another, as it were. Before that they were quite separate - as in times when one could still simply take over areas. Distance is not important. Imagine when Franconians moved into still uncultivated areas of France. They contrasted with the West Goths who entered an already developed area. But the greatest example of separate but related economies is that of England and its colonies, especially India. These separate economies were brought together by peaceful conquest. That is a first step. The second concerns adjoining yet independent economies. And the third is the creation of an economically -closed area. Today we need to be aware that beneath all the recent and current upheavals the fact of world economy is demanding to be recognised.

An interesting example of how impractical people can be is Spengler's book *The Decline of the West*,[90] which includes a chapter on economics. A man with excellent insight, but no idea of how things are in reality. His examples never accord with reality. In the second volume, Spengler's economics is specially bad because, while he understands well enough how certain ancient economies worked - agrarian economies, for instance - and also modern economies, he separates the two. Even a man as ingenious as Spengler does not recognise that the ancient form of economy, permeated by material money, lives on today as the money we buy goods with - "purchase money". Spengler believes we only have "function money". He fails to distinguish between these things, and in consequence creates a lavish array of coquetishly-tailored concepts that are splendid to look at, but muddled. Such ideas are a real danger for those not taken in by their splendour. But it is our task to follow conditions with our thinking.

The three stages of economic development exist today as a threefoldness in the economy, but this is hidden from us because we use one kind of money for everything. Take the argument between the nominalists and the metallists. The former believes money is only a token, its value residing not in its substance but in the figure imprinted on it. The metallists take the opposite view. People debate such concepts without considering that metallism expresses a reality in respect of agriculture, and the functioning of money in the economy, while nominalism corresponds to the reality of industrial and cultural life, economically speaking. And between the two there is their intermingling, of course. It simply does not do to prefer simplistic explanations, when in reality life is such a complicated affair!

I cannot reach an understanding of the reciprocal movement of Elaborated Land - Labour - Capital. After all, the means of production have already been transformed. (The questioner is referring to Lecture 7 and Sketch 4. - Ed.)

The reversal does not refer to the fact that the means of production are produced, but that they produce. Their transformation only has a meaning when the means of production cease to be commodities. They remain commodities right up until they are used to produce something. At this moment the economic flow reverses; the means of production are separated out from their circulation as commodities. In my book on the Threefold Social Order I pointed out that at this juncture the means of production blend into land because they can no longer have a price attached to them. They are economically equivalent to land and therefore return to land.

Does the fact come to expression in the balance of payments?

You mean the disappearance of the value of the means of production? Only in exceptional cases. It would if someone were to set up a factory, by realising a sum of means of production, then become ruined, and another person carried on - someone more adroit and successful. If the two balances were put together a partial devaluation would be observed, wherein the second person had acquired the means of production for a reduced sum. There would be a gift element. On this basis the means of production would be accounted as cheaper. Current accountancy practice could demonstrate this.

Those are exceptions, of course. Today the abnormal is the norm.

Yes, but were one to proceed generally on this basis it would lead to an economic monstrosity, because the means of production would pass over into rents instead of nature, and yet rents only come about through the investment of capital.

Unrecorded question.

One must not forget that it is quite different, economically speaking, when capital is in an enterprise than when it is not. A completely different force is at work when money is invested than when it is not. It is merely deceptive the way things are done today. You may ask: Where, then, are the capitals, the loan-capitals, which are not in enterprises? They are merely to be found as production and as ground rent. And if someone wants money just for himself he would have to withdraw it entirely from the economic process for a period, thereby causing tension, and then release it via a different value. However, he would lose out because money is being progressively devalued, otherwise it is not conceivable that the process takes place at all, and that relationships change.

If one were to take hold of the economy in a healthy way, the right relationships would emerge. Today it is often quaint how wages are dealt with. Higher wage demands increase production costs. Wages then appear too low - and so it goes on, whither no-one knows. People throw sand in their own eyes when they act in this way. Associative economics, on the other hand, leads only to real wages, wages which c<u>an</u> come about. Not that "wages" is the right word, of course. But false, economically unreal, wages could not come about.

Why do wages have to "come about" at all"

Consider, a worker who receives an average 2F a day. You may say that is a very low wage. How can this become a very high wage without it amounting to more than 2F?

By products becoming cheaper.

Not until then will you get the final values. Then you will see that all I have said is real. The cart does not always have to be before the horse. One need but ask the question in this way: We pay 2F. But how will the 2F become worth twice or thrice their value? One must proceed from out of dynamic, not static relationships. People always expect movement out of stasis. But the fact remains that the mere putting of 5F in my pocket has nothing whatever to do with economics!

Will money gradually lose its value, even as purchase money?

As purchase money it keeps its value until the end. The question is more a technical one of circulation, and of how this happens. It is not easy to form a picture of money's gradual loss of value. To do so would require an extraordinarily bureaucratic apparatus.

I would like to stress that I do not wish to agitate, only to say what the reality is. I am of the view that it is not possible to use the economy to establish heaven on earth. We must seek the best possible situation, of course, and it is important to ask why we have less than this today. This is due to the fact that the individual factors of the economy cannot give effect to their own value. For example, non-manual workers today are not appropriately paid, economically speaking. They receive either too much or too little, and in consequence constantly seek to redress the balance, thus disturbing the economy. What is needed, Förster apart[91], is to ensure that prices reciprocate not only goods, but cultural life as well.

This necessitates the ageing of money. It is merely a question of how to do this. Now one can only give outer effect to the gradual devaluation of money by stamping money, the fully-stamped notes being processed by officials. But this necessitates a very complicated bureaucracy. So it is not a question of outer devaluation, but of guiding money through the real course of economic events. This can be done by first giving all types of money the form of a bill, that is, with an expiry date. Such a date cannot be abstractly chosen, of course, but has to be estimated out of the facts at the time of issue, and then modified according to what happens. (Similar to today's techniques of debt-rescheduling. - Ed.)

This would represent a world economic form of the ancient Hebrew custom of cancelling debts at Jubilee Year. This is very similar to the ageing of money. Debt-remission removes all harmful loans and investments. The point of Jubilee Year was that it was the seventieth year. Admittedly, it was fixed *a priori* - as befits a patriarchal age and society - and would not suit world economy, but it corresponds to a life reality nonetheless - the life-span of the human being. Gift capital in youth, loan capital in productive life, and trading capital in retirement; reflecting the fact that in youth the human being consumes, in middle life he produces and in old age he graces.

In world economy *a priori* arrangements would not be possible, of course. The seventy year period would be considerably longer. But it should be clear that money's devaluation would be effected gradually through economic intercourse itself, because the initial year would be shown on the note. In real economic circulation such money would have a lower use-value (but NOT purchasing value). The older it becomes the less its use-value, and this would convert it into gift money, to be re-issued as young - that is, "new" - money again. Moreover, in this form of economics it would be clear that labour has its highest value in connection with nature-products, although associative price formulae would not result in all this value being paid over to the worker. Part would be so, of course, but the rest would move on in the economic process. Thereby the individual could not enrich himself at another's expense.

How can money be used in different ways if its purchasing power is constant?

If an enterprise is set up with young money it can be planned over a long term. With old money it cannot be.

Unrecorded question.

Do you mean that once one has acquired means of production then one has this instead of money and that the money now belongs to someone else? Well, of course, the money would remain in the means of production, but it can become transformed. Not if it were used up, of course; but if its circulation were ensured. This would not involve great bureaucracy; the associations would arrange for the same-dated money only to be used in enterprises with a like basis.

The money, therefore, merges with the means of production. This does not contradict the other law, whereby means of production as such lose their former value as commodities. These laws coincide at this point. These things can be found today, but they are masked. Money lent for production does not return, it stays there. But we insist on selling the means of production so that the money in it is constantly made young again (never gets old). However, if one imagines the means of production as something one does not sell, then the money stays in, and neither ages nor gets younger. Real thinking would never lead to a question such as: How does one make money keep its age? One would say, it must be that way. We simply have to formulate the reason why. This is an outer, technical matter.

Naturally, one could point out that speculators could evade such things. But then speculation in an associative economy would be no easy thing, with money having expiry dates. Speculation relies on the supposed permanence of the value of money. In reality money loses its value anyway. Otherwise the Pomeranian farmer would not be right who asks: How large is the Russian national debt? I need only invest a small amount of capital at interest, with interest chargeable on the interest, and in time repay the debt. This could never happen because all those responsible for these sums, which after all require security, would go broke. In some way or other the guarantors would disappear and the Russian state wouldn't see a penny even after hundreds of years.

Pure money loses its value. If we grasped such things with our common-sense we would do less harm. That is why I am not concerned to agitate, but to draw attention to realities, to things that are already there to be seen. In this way world economy can be helped to healthy expression.

How do you see the relationship between money and the state?

In terms of what I said yesterday (Discourse 5) such a thing as a state bank would not arise. A form of bank would arise between those who have received gift-money and those who create new funds through their work on nature. This process would be removed from the state. The economy must administer itself on a basis of such laws as the rejuvenating of money. That is, on a basis of laws belonging to the economic life, not those belonging to the state. Were this to happen quite other conditions would arise than are possible under fiscal economies, where the exchequer usurps the associations.

What, then, would be the basis of currency?

All paper money would tend to look the same. Modern currency differences are arbitrarily created. Money would become uniform, and the substance it was made of would be a matter of indifference, because it would be metallistic in character when young, nominalist when old. Money would be in constant flow ("currency" perhaps?! - Ed.) and would be completely adapted to the nature and needs of the economic process.

Did you not earlier uphold the usable means of production as the basis of currency?

Consider what gives value to fixed money in a period of time. It derives from the usable means of production. If there were very little usable means of production it would have to be converted very quickly. Money would pile up everywhere and purchase money would return through the means of production and so on. But if there were a large amount of usable means of production, the cycle would be different and the money would have greater value. In this sense, money derives from the means of production.

Would one need to use some solid material like gold?

As far as I can see, the actual substance used would be immaterial. The date would determine the value; this could be printed on paper as readily as on gold. Special economies might require gold but not world economy generally. One needs to think of money more as a form of book-keeping, recording in minute detail every transaction. The material the date is stamped on is not important, except perhaps in the aesthetic sense.

Would gold not provide a certain standard?

This cannot be. And even if it could, book-keeping would show it. All forms of money transactions are book-keeping. It's just that money changes hands, instead of entries changing from debit to credit columns.

It shouldn't be gold, because it could be hoarded and thus used to get round devaluation.

Assuming there to be a buyer for the gold. He would have to be there and the purchase would have to be worthwhile. Superfluous, or, rather, unhelpful calculations would have to be made. One could, for example, make the gold into a piece of jewellery and use it deceptively.

One needs to see things in terms of the economy itself. Then it will become possible to evaluate things properly; while today we are hampered by partial observations and inadequate guesswork as to how to handle the economy.

Which type of capital arose first? Trading capital or industrial capital?

Trading capital came first. Indeed, it is the essence of economic circulation. Even today in primitive "village" economies where there is little industrial capital, craftsmen earn hardly any more than farmers. But traders are always setting money aside; hence they are able to lend. And this process continues because capital comes about only because it is needed. Industrial capital only comes about as a third stage and is so connected to habits that rational bases for it cannot be found.

Should Switzerland go in the direction of national economics or world economics? Is there not a tendency in many countries to revert to national economics?

You mean that Switzerland entered into world economy too soon and this turned out not to be in her favour? One cannot say that, because Switzerland has not been able to put her world economics to the test in a natural way. The so-called "benevolence" of her neighbours today is an unnatural outcome of the war. If Switzerland had been able to develop as she was doing in 1914, world economics would have been to her advantage. Naturally, the same problems would have resulted, of drifting into associative economics. But as the matter stands today, it has to be said that little depends now on Switzerland. Today we must turn our attention to the world at large and the conflict between national economics and world economics. Today the world economy is everywhere disturbed by political considerations and nationalism. These things press the economy backwards. Switzerland is not a useful example here because she is politically powerless. Politically, Switzerland says what is asked of her.

America is quite different. With her decisive tendency to promote national economics and retard world economics - a tendency that may eventually prove very difficult to overcome. Compare this to, say, England as she is currently organised. England is only a national economy in a pseudo sense. Her economy is part of a world economy and as such could give rise to world economy more directly. England's economic connections with India, Australia, South Africa and so on, stretch all over the world and in their very nature tend toward and require a spirit of world economics. Even America will have to comply with such realities eventually. If England went now in the direction of national economics she could not develop any further. Switzerland doesn't count; one needs to look at the real antagonism between England and America.

I cannot imagine how the value of the diamond in the crown of England derives from labour and not from its rarity. (Referring to Lecture 5. - Ed.)

I say this on the basis that values can only be created by the application of either human labour or human intelligence. And thence through the process of the division of labour. Given this, if one sets out to explain the value of the diamond in the crown of England one has to do so by saying that, if it is possible to separate values from the economic process and make them one's own, then this necessarily means the value is held back. So a person can hold on to a million, he can even put it in his socks. He can even regard his hoarding as some other activity and attribute value to some other product instead of money, and allow his money back into circulation. He can go on in this way and invent a concept like "rarity" to explain his actions. But this is all in the mind. The reality is otherwise. It is not rarity, but the fact that values are withheld, removed from the economic process.

Comments on the threefold social order: The impossibility of realising it; its being used or understood as three divisions; the difficulty of clearly seeing the boundaries of the different spheres and the probable restriction of economic life to technology.

The thinking of those who think in this way is not sufficiently trained. And that is the main problem. We do not train ourselves to think properly, and can only form concepts that are neatly laid one beside the other. But consider the human being himself. He has a threefold organism of nerve, rhythmical and metabolic systems. The eye could not function without the optic nerve and the nervous system generally. But the nervous system is fed at night by the metabolism and continuous respiratory processes ensure air enters the optic nerve.

The same applies to the social organism. It is necessary that two other systems play into the economic organism. But just as this interweaving does not lead one to doubt the position of the human head in the human organism, so one need not see threefoldness as divisions. I have always spoken against this idea. The cultural organism will be based on freedom, but it must have an economic dimension. How else could professors eat? Equally, the economic life has a cultural aspect. And so on. Those who object to this are those who think in terms of divisions. I even found one person lecturing on the three parliaments! But that is to imagine an impossibility. Only the state, the rights life can have a parliament. The cultural life must be founded on the free individual, and the economy on a basis of associations. The different functions flow together in parliament, where the right rules for the conduct of the social organism as a whole will arise.

Does the value of the diamond in the crown of England correspond to the tension between the stone and the desire for luxury?

The matter can be explained precisely in this way, only by a different path. The tension which arises through consumption is always the tension between labour working on land, and intelligence organising labour. One should not speak one-sidedly about the value of the diamond in the crown of England. What is this stone really worth? It is only of value in a very specific, but not economic sense, because of the prevailing culture. Value is attached to it. Now suppose it is bought at the asking price and the seller uses the proceeds to have work done, it would be as if a snowball had caused an avalanche. In such a case there is no reason to alter one's formulae. A rarity-product is equivalent to an enormous amount of work. This comes out of its economic context.

NOTES & BIBLIOGRAPHY

RUDOLF STEINER, ECONOMIST

(1) *The Economic Consequences of the Peace*, J M Keynes, The Collected Writings, Macmillan 1971.

(2) Latest edition entitled *Towards Social Renewal*, Rudolf Steiner Press, London 1977. See also Note 11 and, for a fuller introduction to Rudolf Steiner's ideas, *The Social Question*, New Economy Publications, 1991.

(3) See *A Brief History of Der Kommende Tag*, Emil Leinhas, New Economy Publications, 1978.

(4) *The Consequences of the Peace for Economics*, Christopher J. Budd, New Economy Publications, 1979.

LECTURE 1

(5) Schmoller, Gustav, von. 1838 - 1917. Economist.

(6) Roscher, Wilhelm. 1817 - 1894. Economist.

(7) Beaconsfield, Earl of; Benjamin Disraeli. 1804 - 1881. Writer and English statesman.

(8) Richter, Eugen. 1838 - 1906. Liberal politician.

(9) Lacher, Eduard. 1829 - 1884. Liberal politician.

(10) Brentano, Lugo. 1844 - 1931. German economist.

(11) Here and in the next paragraph, Steiner is referring to the sociology he sought to introduce based on the latent dynamics between the economic, political and cultural domains of society - what he called the threefolding of social life. In English this conception is variously referred to as the "threefold social order", the "threefold commonwealth", and the "threefold state". Whatever name is used, it refers to the new paradigm, in accordance with which humanity's social evolution is now proceeding, but which remains unrecognised. People remain stuck in the sociologies that pertain to the separate national existences that the advent of a single global economy has rendered obsolete.

(12) Readers can best understand what Steiner had in mind here by referring to his comments on John Maynard Keynes and his book *The Economic*

Consequences of the Peace. See *Steiner on Keynes,* New Economy Magazine, Sept / Oct 1992.

(13) It is interesting to note in this connection that Isaac Newton, the originator of the spectrum theory of light, was also master of the Royal Mint in England. As such he was directly involved in the form and conduct of the economic life of his day.

(14) Adam Smith. 1723 - 1790. Best-known for his *Inquiry into the Nature and Causes of the Wealth of Nations,* 1776.

LECTURE 2

(15) Steiner uses the term "nature" where in classical economics one usually says "land". This confronts one with something of a conundrum. To stick rigidly to "nature" runs the risk of getting lost in the vaguenesses of "alternative" economics, since nature in these ecologically-minded times and as understood in the English language connotes "landscape" far more than "economic category". My preference is always to use "land" where Steiner uses "nature", in order to emphasise the need to deepen our understanding of traditional concepts in economics. The need is to come to a deeper, strictly economic, understanding of a term such as land, rather than to embark on a search for seemingly more easily understood expressions. The same can also be said of "labour" and "capital". If we deepen, by making strictly economic, the meaning we give to these terms, we will transcend the narrow confines of materialist economic thinking, which is seldom purely economic, comprising frequently concepts about economic life that are in themselves more often juridical or ethical than economic. We will in the process avoid the other pitfall awaiting today's economist - that of abstractly stretching the language of traditional economics, by inventing further categories, such as "information". The reality is one of three categories - land, labour and capital - to which threesome all simplifications or extrapolations always return. It can also be argued that land, labour and capital are better translated 'nature-man-spirit', this being a more faithful rendering of what Steiner had in mind. I have in fact done this in my book, *Prelude in Economics* (New Economy Publications, 1979); however, the result does not sit fully happily in the English language as used in economics. In the end, I have resolved on a combination of "land" and "nature" using these terms separately or synonymously according to my sense of what the reader's requirement would be, bearing in mind however that this is a treatise on economics and some effort on his part to grasp difficult ideas is assumed! I make no apologies for any awkwardnesses that result from this approach.

Indeed, this problem provides *par excellence* exactly the kind of exercise on which can be honed the economic thinking Steiner so strongly argued for. (16) Steiner's expression was originally in the singular - "a good". Another conundrum for English-language economics, since, although English speaks happily of "goods", meaning (in terms of Steiner's thesis) products of nature worked on by labour, it does not allow "a good". The logical word would be "elaborated product", but this is somewhat unwieldy. For the most part, I have used the plural "goods" or the awkward alternative "elaborated product" as befits the text. The thing to remember is that accurate economic thinking does not necessarily confine its articulation to the current scope of the English language. In particular, as is made clear later on, words often used in English - such as 'goods', 'body' - tend to connote physical things, whereas they can have, and in economics they very much do have, a supra-physical meaning. The terminology of economics is affected all the time by the fact that in reality it refers to a realm that hovers, as it were, just above or, better put, is implied by its physical counterparts. For example, though we have all seen the price of something marked on a label, who has ever seen, let alone touched, a physical price?! The need to think concretely in terms of this implied realm is reinforced by the use I have made on occasion of "a good". The aim is thus to refer not to its physical existence, but to its economic significance.

(17) In this passage and throughout this treatise, Steiner uses the word *Arbeit*. This can be translated "work", of course, but here the conventional economic term "labour" has been adopted and retained. That said, the word labour is used with a specific end in mind, namely to refer to the kind of work more associated with manual effort. It is indeed difficult to use the term labour in a wider, more generic sense - to refer to the whole range of economic activity that the human being can perform, from the coarser, physical type needed to work the land, hunt, mine coal or make things, to the intangible, but no less economic, work of a teacher or an artist or, indeed, an entrepreneur realising a hunch. It is one of the challenges facing modern economics to devise a concept of human effort that correctly expresses how, in the direction of physical toil, it takes on a manual character (labour) while in the direction of mental or inner processes it becomes rarefied and seemingly non-existent - as when an inventor first conceives a new device. In the further course of the lectures, Steiner places great reliance on this intangible pole of work, frequently using the expression "spiritual work". In this translation, I have retained this expression only where I could find no other, more English and more economic term. Wherever possible, I have called the intangible pole of work - "freed activity". Steiner's conception of economic life centres on a

progression through hunting, farming, manufacturing and teaching, in which human endeavour moves away from the land to less coarse aspects of economic life, such as cultural activity. In this process of abstraction, the more rarefied one's connection becomes to the material world (represented by land), the freer it is from land's constraints, and the more self-supported it is by its very intangibility. A hunch, for example, is dependent for its successful realisation on the imagination and "nous" of the person who has it. The "feel good factor" - to use modern jargon - and similar phenomena are dependent on invisible things like confidence, and expectation. Although a literal translation would have "spiritual work", I find this has connotations in today's language that contradict what Steiner meant. "Freed activity", on the other hand, means essentially intangible activity - like that of the teacher - which nevertheless has clear and powerful economic effect.

(18) Again, the German *Geist* does not translate very readily. In English "spirit" is bedevilled by nuances of spiritism, spiritualism and so forth. Wherever the sense allows, I have used intelligence instead, although I am aware that this word does not always work either! In certain situations it can convey something disconnected from life, abstract and, in the perjorative sense, intellectual. I have risked using intelligence as much as possible, meaning by it the positive and very real element in the human being through which his inner life, however defined, expresses itself. Only where unavoidable, have I used "spirit", and then on the understanding that English-speaking readers will imbue this word with a concreteness not usual to it. "Spirit" in Steiner's usage is shorthand for all that arises through the human being by virtue of the fact that he is a thinking being with many varied and developing skills and talents. The entirety of this activity and its results makes up his spiritual life.

(19) "Rent" is meant here in the strict economic sense, the value that emerges from land. This, the economic meaning of rent, hovers above the usual one, normally understood in terms of landlord-tenant relationships and as the money paid for the use of a building or piece of real estate. The two are not, however, synonymous and any economist worth his salt will mark the difference!

LECTURE 3

(20) This use of the word "interest" is important. How often it is said that one or another policy is determined or thwarted by the "vested interests" of certain parties. Yet we all act in protection or furtherance of our economic interests. From the social point of view, the challenge to modern economics

is to show how economic interests can be contrasting or conflicting. In this passage, Steiner makes a beginning in this direction, albeit *en passant*.

LECTURE 4

(21) At this juncture, it is wise to pause for thought - economic thought, of course! Steiner uses two words - *Arbeitsteilung* and *Arbeitsgliederung*. The second does not translate directly, but needs the intermediary of a picture, as do all real economic concepts. Without them economic science falls prey to abstract, merely intellectual ideas. To our ordinary way of thinking, the picture associated with "division of labour" tends toward that of conveyor-belt production in modern industry. It tends to be the idea of a merely physical splitting-up of the work process into separate parts. Thus, instead of the cartwright, one person makes the wheels, another the axles, and so on. This picture is not incorrect, but its implied separateness is real only because such a separation can be effected in the physical world. It is possible to assemble a cart out of its constituent parts and to make these parts separately. But beware transferring this atomised aspect of division of labour in respect of physical products, to the social aspect of those who thus do the work. The human beings involved should not in the process be seen as, let alone become separated one from another. Just as the parts of a cart do not come into their own until they are united into the cart as a whole, so the division of labour must not be allowed to be an excuse for atomised economic existence. The term does not mean division in the absolute, fragmentary sense possible in the physical world, but more the sharing of the burden of a common task. We cannot easily get round the phenomenon that the naming of this process occured when economic thinking was too narrowly focussed. It is an example - a very fundamental one - of the problem facing economists, the need to think more widely, to base their consciousness on wider phenomena than those afforded by the somewhat blatant appearance of industrial capitalism on the essentially agrarian stage of yesteryear.

(22) This and, the shortly to follow, "debtor" are meant in a functional economic sense, not perjoratively.

(23) Steiner's expression is *geistige Schöpfer*, "spiritual worker", that is, one whose work is what in Note 17 I have called "freed activity". I do not want to lend further currency than absolutely necessary to the term 'spiritual worker' because on two counts I think it detracts from the overall economicness of Steiner's approach. Firstly, as already mentioned, "spiritual" lacks concreteness and, moreover, tends to mean anti-economic, opposed to economics. Secondly, "worker" belongs too much to the factory

syndrome, class theory and the, increasingly anachronistic, scenario of the working class. Without in any way denying or decrying the very real problems that these things refer to, Steiner's economics is intended to go beyond the capitalism that so ill-treats people. He does so precisely because he does not build upon the understandable, but nonetheless erroneous, ideas that evolved to become the Marxist perspective.

(24) By using the word "transfer" I have exercised my editorial prerogative. Steiner actually says: "...what on the one hand is *lent or invested* capital, through the very fact that it becomes *owed or borrowed*." However these expressions lead one far too quickly into jurisprudence, on the one hand, and a profound mis-reading of what he later describes as "loan money". The identification of lending and loans - as understood by the modern mind, schooled as it is in the practices and ethos of today's financial system - with Steiner's concept of "loan money" has become a great obstacle. Above all, it is just this sloppy synonymity - in itself an example of NOT thinking economically - keenly fostered alas by many adherents to Steiner's approach, that prevents people from seeing and experiencing the kind of capital and its effects that Steiner, precisely at this juncture in his lecture course, is endeavouring to draw attention to. "Transfer" is thus used deliberately to avoid a premature confusion between jurisprudence masquerading as economics, and economics proper.

(25) A passage that will smack to some of dangerous economic elitism, seemingly suggesting that capital should only go to the clever people in society. But this is not at all what Steiner has in mind. To begin with, he is not equating capital with income. He is assuming that society will support every human being economically (albeit not necessarily by identical means or in identical measure) and that this is a separate issue from the use we make of capital. Indeed, assuming that revenue generally comes from productive and profitable use of capital, Steiner is simply saying that, generally seen and economically speaking, humanity's capital, if wasted, will not be able to provide the revenue that humanity as a whole needs, however that revenue is shared out. Indeed, the very fact that capitalism does not administer capital in the way Steiner suggests, cannot be unconnected from its increasing inability to finance real human needs.

(26) One might perhaps prefer to say satellite, instead of balloon, since satellites are indeed used today to scour the earth as a whole. Technology is abreast of the economic reality of the world as one, but economics still lags behind, remaining wed to the kind of thinking Adam Smith exemplifies. This lack of a global approach to economic life on the part of economics has a further, disconcerting consequence in that it is hindering the development of

the idea of the world as humanity's joint common wealth. The absence of such a conception means that, because the several nations who predominated economic life at the start of the 20th century did not, when they could have, combine to create a single global economy for the whole of the human community, the active idea behind today's *politique* is that one nation should prevail over the rest. The absence of an awareness of our one-world economy and the pursuit of global hegemony permeate our social life with a permanent, chilling tension. Psychologically, at least, we live in a state of imminent conflict, for ever under the threat of global economic war and, indeed, for ever presented with isolated expressions of this condition everywhere throughout the world and throughout recent history. Much is made of the ideological, non-economic character of these "trouble spots", but take away the markets thus being sought and the access to cheaper labour, take away the addictive dependency on the arms industry and the huge profits made by those who bank-roll the combatants, take away the monopoly-seeking interests of trans-national corporations - and what is left? Precious little indeed! As to ideology, the most real ideology of this century has been that, not of socialism, but of self-determination, national liberation, overcoming colonialism. But in every case, these attempts by the peoples of the world to take their rightful place in the human community have been opposed directly because of the sharing of resources and markets that they imply. In most cases such struggling peoples - from Algeria to Viet Nam - were forced by the West into socialist ideas because these, indeed, seemed to explain the actions of the West; but this socialism was always for the most part incidental and often not present at the outset. The West, throughout this century has refused the shift in paradigm which is responsible for the emergence everywhere of nations seeking no longer to be colonies.

LECTURE 5

(27) Meaning credit intended to finance what the individual as such, from out of his capacities, can realise.

(28) Note: this discussion of interest is in regard to the lending of money at interest to an individual, this being, for the most part, how most individuals experience the provision of capital by others. It is a very moot point whether this parochial, near-to-hand experience has a general applicability today. I doubt it. Many individuals have capital by way of inheritance, savings or capital gains - that is, they experience themselves as the producers of it and do not pay interest on it. Also, corporate financing - the far greater motor of economic life - is conducted extensively on the basis of invested capital,

where the return is not a percentage of the principal regardless of the capital's productivity, but a proportion of any profit derived from its use, and that only after the charging of costs. By using the example of interest on private loans, Steiner runs the risk of diverting his reader's attention from the economic point he is seeking to make, because of the "household" experience that the reader may be supposed to have more to hand. It should also be pointed out that the example of personal credit refers to the capitalising of production or business and not, as modern practice might lead one to assume, to the financing of a house, the purchase of commodities or the funding of debt.

(29) "on land" = credit charged to the land. It may be used to acquire land or to provide security for money used for other purposes. Either way, its economic effect is that its value is substantiated by the value of the land thus financed or taken as collateral.

(30) The capitalisation of land. The following is an attempt to show the calculation Steiner alludes to:-

i)   Assume:-

      a) Uncapitalised price of land is 100,000
      b) Interest 5% p.a.
      c) Term 20 years

      Therefore:-

Uncapitalised value of land	100,000
Interest	100,000
Capital value of land	200,000

ii)   Now, assume interest @ 4% p.a., then:-

Uncapitalised value of land	120,000
Interest	80,000
Capital value of land	200,000

(31) Though he doesn't say so, in this passage Steiner knocks away one of the main props of today's non-economic, capitalistic consciousness - in which we all partake. For the capitalist idea rests full square on the notion that

capital can be amassed irrespective of the economic effects of doing so. People do not think - or if they do, they quickly forget - that when capital is not worked on further in the economic process by conscious means, it is indirectly devalued, by economic effects which seem to come from the periphery. Thus we live in an age which devotes all its energies to amassing capital, while blaming the economy for the very obvious, very real and very serious devaluation that amassed capital experiences. The sooner our thinking, not to mention our actions, comports with economic reality in this regard, the better off we will be. The solution to the devaluation of amassed capital is certainly not to amass even more! (The same goes for the folly of trying to maintain the value of money by artificial means.)

(32) This is a cornerstone consideration. The land reformers Steiner refers to are those such as Henry George and Damaschke who seek to socialise rent and thereby make equitable today's economic life. As far as Steiner's thesis goes, while the aim of such things is laudable, the economic effect does not achieve it. To socialise rent is to transfer the income from land - whether healthy or usurious - from the private to the public purse. All manner of social difficulties attend this scenario, but for the purposes of this note the point is that, economically speaking, the aim should be to prevent untrue rents arising in the first place - that is to say, the rents which derive from the capitalisation of land. This, however, is the eye of the needle for economic thinking, through which few, if any, have yet passed. For what, in our propertied, mortgaged society, are we to make of "land"? Where does it start and stop? Is it the topsoil, which can be worked by a farmer, or the subsoil which cannot? On the other hand, subsoil can be excavated to provide the foundations of a building. So, is "land" then the physical land on which the building stands regardless of its substrata, or is it more the leased area to which one has exclusive or shared right of use, whether by payment of a capital sum, or a rent, whether owned "outright", mortgaged, leased or simply rented? To exercise one's mind on this point and, what's more, to structure one's economy in accordance with the "correct" solution to the problem, would be to pass through the eye, humps and all! It is indeed a need of the times that people begin to do just this. (See also Rudolf Steiner's *Sociology of Land*, New Economy Magazine, Sept / Oct 1991.)

(33) Steiner's work was founded to a large extent on the simple precept that the method of natural science, namely careful observation of external phenomena, could be applied to non-sense-perceptible phenomena. While the method would remain constant, the content and nature would change. The scientific method applied to the natural world is *natural* science; applied to the world beyond the physical it gives rise to *spiritual* science.

(34) Steiner treats this idea of "association" in many places, chiefly in his book *Towards Social Renewal* (see Note 2), but also in a series of lectures entitled *The Social Future*. For those wishing to see how Steiner's concept of associative economics has been developed since these lectures were given, and how it relates to today's market economics, see *Beyond the Market*, Gaudenz Assenza, New Economy Publications, 1992.

(35) I have used the word "independent" where others might have used "free", because Steiner's concept is not of liberation or unconcerted conduct. It is not *laissez-faire*, autonomous action that recognises no constraints other than those forced upon it. Steiner's concept of freedom, whether it be applied to capital, the individual human being, or, as here, the economic life generally, is not separatist or anarchic. However free the human being may be, he belongs to a community, and freedom does not imply the flaunting of this fact. By the same token, capital may become free at a certain point in the economic process - that is, it achieves an existence in its own right. But this does not excuse it, remove or estrange it from the economic process as a whole. On the contrary, its independence arises precisely because it can now play a causal part in that process, whereas so long as it was being created it was essentially an effect. Similarly, Steiner's idea of a self-directing, autonomous - here "independent" - economic life does not mean an economic life that separates itself off from considerations and constraints of might and right, culture and politics. It refers to the need to redefine the cultural and political context of economic life so that it may unfold in accordance with its own nature. Independence, as used here, does not therefore imply incoherence or selfish conduct. It means that when something is independent it can, of its own accord, and out of its own nature, contribute something new to society, whereas previously it depended on that society for its whole existence.

(36) In the intervening years since 1922 the State has, of course, come to play very much this tyrannical role, both in the extreme Soviet sense and in the subtler job-creation mode of the West. This process is fuelled by another tyranny - that of "the market". Without something of the kind envisaged by Steiner, labour is transplanted willy-nilly these days, in accordance with the exigencies of public policy or the vagaries of the market. In the process, no thought is given to the real welfare of the workforce, nor are prices stabilised in any long-term sense. In this one can see how tragically events have developed, compared to the real potential we have to resolve them.

(37) "Freed activity" as introduced in Note 17.

LECTURE 6

(38) Reader beware! As pointed out in Note 24, "loan" as used here does not equate with a bank loan, for example. "Loan" is meant to refer to an economic category that hovers above, includes, but is not synonymous with, the loans we more usually speak of. "Loan" as an ordering concept, not a financial instrument. Bank loans can indeed, and often do, have a non-loan character. They become gifts when remitted in the face of over-indebtedness, for example; purchases when the cost of the loan is as great as the return it provides - that is, when the borrower's profit is soaked up by economically excessive interest charges, which transfer away from him more value than he has been able to create.

(39) In the original Steiner simply says capital "... must be given an outlet into free cultural institutions." I have altered this section in order to make clear what he means by "free cultural institution", a concept he otherwise introduces without warning or direct explanation.

LECTURE 7

(40) Steiner speaks of *Handwerk*. This could be variously translated as craft, artisanry; with its corollaries, craftsman, artisan. A truer economic translation, however, is manufacture - the creation by the human being of artefacts, regardless of whether these tend more to the artistic or the industrial. "Manufacture" is thus used here in a very wide sense, to mark the economic progression Steiner makes from hunters who simply take what nature gives them (leave aside that culling, for example, borders on farming!), farmers who have to labour extensively but do not create artefacts (again, leave aside any artificiality introduced by the genetic engineering of plants and animals), manufacturers who make things, the "ingredients" of which originate in land, but which are economically speaking the product of labour and intelligence, and so on, until one arrives at, say, a teacher or preacher, whose material product is negligible, but whose economic effect is nevertheless very real.

(41) Tread carefully! "Borrow" can lead the mind immediately into the landscape of today's methods of transferring the use of capital from one person to another. The economic point Steiner is making is that capital is not a commodity to be used up or an asset to be owned, but an enduring reality. The question is how to make this capital available to individuals so as to maximise its fruitful use, and how to transfer it from one individual to another. This happens inefficiently and inequitably through the "capital

market" today, from which it is borrowed by those who can afford to do so. But what Steiner has in mind cannot come into full focus until one imagines what agency would supersede the capital market, when the borrowing of capital would take on the economic colour Steiner attributes to it, not the colouring of right and might it currently has.

(42) Steiner introduces the concept of human will here by way of extending the concept of freed activity. He means by this that the human will is not conditioned only by the human being's external environment. It is self-subsisting, latently free, and thus able to follow the requirements of its own nature and needs. The more one moves away from land-connected activity toward freed activity, the freer the will implied by this activity.

(43) Steiner is referring to the economic dislocation in Germany after the First World War.

LECTURE 8

(44) Economic thinking will not, however, lead to the idea that an economic association can be made to exist merely because it is given that name. The name can be as readily attached to a cartel. The point is that a certain way of working and a certain overall aim is implied, which can be called associative economics. Merely calling a thing an association will not achieve what Steiner has in mind. If used in the abstract, the term is of little use because it becomes detached from the entirety of what Steiner is talking about. Indeed, today's economic life includes many phenomena that could with justification form part of an associative economics, but which do not use its terminology. (See *Beyond the Market*, New Economy Publications 1992.)

(45) Steiner was speaking in pre-"market" times.

(46) In the producer's case the demand appears to be demand for money; in the consumer's case it is a demand for commodities. - Ed.

(47) And this pre-Keynes!

LECTURE 9

(48) Unruh, Hans Viktor, von. 1806 - 1886. Politician and writer.

(49) Siemens, Georg, von. 1839 -1901. Banker; Gwinner, Arthur, von. 1856 -1931. Banker.

(50) Hilferding, Rudolf. 1877 - 1943. Financial theorist and statesman.

LECTURE 10

(51) Forster, Friedrich Wilhelm. 1869 -1966. Pedagogue, pacifist.

(52) Space does not permit a full commentary on this idea, with which, admittedly, the medical profession does not necessarily concur. It is, however, a fundamental observation and tenet of Steiner's analysis of the human being, and the analogy it provides for understanding humanity's social organism is thus one that he places great store in.

LECTURE 11

(53) The region in Gaul and Germany founded by Clovis and reigned over by Frankish kings from 500 - 752 AD.

(54) This does not, of course, refer to the British political philosophy, but to the political idealism that blossomed in Germany in the mid-19th century.

(55) Eric Roll describes the Mercantilist school "as a phase in the history of economic policy, which contains a number of economic measures designed to secure political unification and national power. The building-up of nation-states is put in the forefront, and monetary, protectionist, and other economic devices are regarded merely as instruments to this end. State intervention was an essential part of mercantilist doctrine. Those responsible for government accepted mercantilist notions and fashioned their policy accordingly, because they saw in them means of strengthening absolutist states against both rivals abroad and the remnants of medieval particularism at home." (P. 49, *A History of Economic Thought,* E Roll, 5th edition, Faber and Faber, London 1992.) It should also be added that many of those who advanced mercantilist ideas were also commercial capitalists whose interests depended on the furtherance and application of such ideas.

(56) Hume, David. 1711 - 1776. English philosopher and statesman.

(57) Marx, Karl. 1818 - 1883.

(58) What seemed radical in 1922 has now, of course, become the norm.

(59) Although it doesn't say so directly, this is clearly a no-frills explanation of protectionism - a prophylactic for decline, not a spur to fresh growth.

(60) And this was said in 1922, not 1992!

(61) The Physiocrats - a school of thought that came to the fore in Paris in the 18th century - held that "agriculture was the only genuinely productive sector of the economy, and the generator of a 'surplus' upon which all else depended. Agricultural production was alleged to be unique; a farmer could plant one seed and, in due course, reap twenty. A manufacturer, on the other hand, could register no similar multiplication in the physical product; he simply altered the shape of the material inputs on which he worked." (P.19, *A History of Economic Thought*, W J Barber, Penguin Books, 1967.)

(62) This helps to throw light on what is becoming one of our greatest problems, and the cause of great potential instability. The transfer of manual

work to "foreign" workers in places like Germany and Switzerland, the requirement of the Single European Act to allow free movement of labour, and the desperate economic circumstances of Eastern Europe are all factors leading to deep-seated social tensions.

(63) It should be noted here that Steiner is referring very strictly to the production and consumption of *food*. In doing so, he may give the impression that those who do not provide food are somehow beholden to those who do. But one can see that this is not the case, as soon as one realises that food producers also need telephones, machinery, education, health care, and so on. Steiner's argument at this stage is not, therefore, a social one, but a strictly economic one.

(64) It is this fact that actually finances the extensive social security systems of our time, for example. The economic problem is not lack of abundance, but mal-distribution, inequitable distribution of wealth.

LECTURE 12

(65) Spengler, Oswald. 1880 - 1936. Philosopher and historian.

(66) Known as "scrip", such schemes have been tried several times in this century, usually in times of economic depression or when attempts are made to create localised currencies. They are usually very effective in stimulating exchange, but, conflicting head-on, as they do, with the modern banking system, they have nearly all come to nought - either being terminated by legal means, or remaining experiments. Nowhere have they effected widespread change - neither in the consciousness of the time, nor in the way the world's economy is structured. In Steiner's terms they correspond to purchase money, although they usually lack the breadth of perspective and thus the exact meaning he gives the term. Nevertheless, they demonstrate the practicability of such things, but also the very real opposition they face from those whose economic interests are vested in today's financial system, dependent as it is for its profits on sustaining the intractability of modern economic problems - problems to which it is directly party.

(67) It follows from this, of course, that the whole matter of balance of payments - which so overhangs our lives today - will fall away and become seen for what it is - a nonsense brought about by the unreality of nation state economies in a time of world economy. We do not, after all, trouble ourselves with the balance of payments between counties or states, departments or cantons.

(68) The question of things becoming dearer is, of course, the problem of inflation. In Steiner's terms, notwithstanding every government's aim to be

rid of it, the persistence of inflation can be readily understood as the masked expression of aging money. It illustrates Steiner's claim that the real nature of world economy will out, but in a way that causes chaos. The chaos is not, however, within the economic process as such, but in our conception of it, and consequently in the form through which we force it to come to expression.

LECTURE 13

(69) This is not an obscure or fantastic notion. Today's largely secular culture - and certainly the "amoral" science of economics - may no longer be inspired by a sermon. But the phenomenon referred to by this clerical example is real nonetheless. From post-war "music while you work" programmes to today's permanent broadcasting of popular music in factories, offices, on building sites and in all manner of work places, from Volvo's experiments with the use of colour and pictures in the work environment to the humble device of the tea-break, who can deny that physical labour unto itself does not feed the human being. If physical labour is all he does, he tires at it, does it less well. It loses in productivity, thereby making for more expensive products. The aim of all these things is to inspire the human being, or at least to stimulate him to continue. Manual labour loses its effectiveness unless fed all the while culturally. Indeed, the end of the week, the pay packet, the distant holiday - all these phenomena are essentially there to keep up our flagging labour. The fact is that labour unto itself palls. It is culture within it, as it were, that maintains or enhances its productivity, making products cheaper, which is the converse of, or another way of saying, that culture saves labour. The idea is, of course, extended in that of "labour-saving" devices, which are the embodiment of inspired thought, clever design and so on. And it is corroborated by the fact of leisure time, at least among those populations who experience it. Steiner's references may be old-fashioned (although he makes it clear that he is describing a "primitive" village of yore), but the validity of his concept is not lessened, gainsaid, or refuted thereby. The fact remains: The economic value of freed activity consists in the labour it has saved.

(70) Caution should be exercised at this point in one's interpretation of Steiner's thesis, lest one, simplistically in my estimation, thinks he means by "work on the land" only agricultural work. To think that way runs the risk of giving to the farmer or the farming community a "special case" status that may be used to lord it over the rest of society, or to excuse it from the exigencies of economic existence. I do not believe any such thing, neither in theory nor in practice, is intended by Steiner. On a more technical level, for him to suggest primacy of agriculture is to prefer agrarian economics over

monetarism, to argue for wheat rather than gold. Lecture 14 notwithstanding (see Note 72), the drift of all he says in his lectures contradicts this outcome: He seeks to resolve the contrast between wheat and gold. To this end, agriculture (for this is the economic category, not farmers) is seen by Steiner in a specific context, outside the process of trade as such - a given for that process. By the same token, however, human intelligence is also a given. Treating agriculture as it should be treated economically - as something outside the economic process - is not the same thing as endowing the farming community with special status, which in reality is a kind of latter-day physiocratism (see Lecture 11, p. 142.).

LECTURE 14

(71) Reader beware! There are, of course, schemes today which aim to solve certain economic problems by dividing up a farm, say, or a rainforest, into little areas - each one sold or owned by an individual. Such schemes are sometimes thought to be illustrations of what Steiner is here saying. But are they? The picture of land divided up among the entire community dependent on it is an ideal one. It also assumes a lot else in respect of forms of land tenure, access to capital, allocation of means of production, and so on. And it is a picture that belongs to conditions prior to division of labour. Move off this base-point - as we must if we are to talk about today's circumstances, and something far more subtle needs to be envisaged; something far less rustic and evocative of days gone by. Something more technical, more having to do with the denomination of money, and a radical reappraisal of land tenure than a mere tinkering with things that, after all, continue to belong to the external aspect of the capitalist, non-world economic scheme of things.
(72) Don't let this remark pass by un-noticed. It refers in effect to the seminal economic text of Aristotle, the grandfather of economics - grandfather in the sense that modern economics tends to date itself from the "scientific" period. Judging by the fleeting, if any, reference Aristotle is given today, economics has difficulty placing its parentage in antiquity. Nevertheless, even if one cannot contemplate an economics starting so far back, in deference to intellectual history, Aristotle's observations need taking into account. In the Nichomachaen Ethics (Book 5, Chapter 5.) in particular, he sets out why, as Steiner puts it, "everything is ultimately valued through consumption, that is, by demand." Even Marx paused at this signpost in Das Kapital (Vol. 1, The Commodity, p. 151, Penguin, 1976.), though I fear he read it wrong, or that someone had turned it to point in the wrong direction. The relation of Steiner's approach to economics and Aristotle's own thesis is dealt with in

detail in *Rudolf Steiner and Aristotle, Fellow Economists*, New Economy Publications.

(73) Yet, in Note 69 I said that Steiner was not advocating a wheat standard! Of this I remain convinced. To keep track, as it were, of the economy's foundation on land does not imply a wheat standard, but a technical continuum in the metamorphosis of money from its primitive form to the sophistication of which Steiner speaks. I recognise that there may be those who say that I am in this way contradicting Steiner, claiming he meant things which he didn't say. I leave it to the reader to judge, but in my assessment Steiner's remarks on nature currency at the end of the course - when read literally - neither flow naturally from nor naturally reinforce the preceding development of his thesis. Indeed, in Discourse 6 (p. 223.), when asked about the basis of currency, he does not directly talk of nature-currency at all, but of book-keeping. The point is that the world's book-keeping (money) needs to keep track of the economy's land basis: The question is how? Although one tends to think, for example, that gold and wheat are polar opposites, how do we assess the value of gold? We do so by reference to the Troy ounce, an ancient measure that holds one ounce of gold to be equivalent in weight to 480 grammes of wheat! I have considered this whole matter in "Of Wheat and Gold" (New Economy Publications, 1988.), which book I mention here not in order to promote its sale, but because I have tried through its pages to get to grips with what I experience as a not altogether happy conclusion to Steiner's overall line of thought. Indeed, I suspect it is a kind of snag, or knot, which, had he reconvened on the subject, Steiner would have smoothed away, or undone and retied differently. As I say, the reader must judge!

(74) Steiner's word was *Dämon*. In German this does not have the negative connotation given it in English, even though OED gives "a being of a nature intermediate between that of goads and men." To convey this neutrality, I have used the neutral "being".

DISCOURSE 1

(75) The "threefold social order" refers to Rudolf Steiner's overall approach to sociology and economics. He published various writings on social questions, key among them in English is the book *The Threefold Social Order* (see Note 2).

(76) Ricardo, David. 1772 - 1823. English economist.

(77) See *Ferdinand Lasalle - Initiate of Social Reform*, Mervyn John, New Economy Magazine, April 1985.

(78) Steiner was speaking in a pre-Keynesian era, when the state kept out of

the running of the economy and, insofar as it had an economic aspect, was expected to balance its budget and leave those responsible for the economy to get on with it. He would be dismayed at the present-day conduct of the economy by the State. He sought for the separation of state and economy, but in such a way that the economy would be run altruistically for the genuine benefit of everyone, with individualistic *laissez-faire* capitalism giving way to associative economy. [See also Notes 34 and 45.]

(79) See Note 10.

(80) Sir Thomas Gresham. 1519-1579. Founder of the London Stock Exchange.

(81) Franz Oppenheimer. 1864 - 1943. German economist and sociologist.

(82) In Steiner's view, the world's economy needs to be organised on the basis of associations, focussed on specific areas with reference to their true economic boundaries, and managed by those competent to do so. Associative economics is the antithesis of the nation-state economics that prevailed instead. (See also Note 44.)

(83) See Note 2.

(84) A journal concerned with Steiner's work, named after the building in Switzerland that became the centre of his activity.

DISCOURSE 2

(85) Goethe, Johann Wolfgang, von. 1749 - 1832.

(86) Spann, Othmar. 1878 - 1950. Economist and sociologist.

DISCOURSE 3

(87) See Note 3.

DISCOURSE 4

(88) Rodbertus, Johann Karl, 1805 - 1875. Economist and politician.

(89) Stein, Lorenz von. 1815 - 1890. Law professor and sociologist.

DISCOURSE 5

(90)*The Decline of the West*, Allen and Unwin, Abridged 1961. See Note 65.

DISCOURSE 6

(91) See Note 51.

NOTES

NOTES

NOTES

NEWECONOMY PUBLICATIONS

***

* = Rudolf Steiner Archive Series

NEWECONOMY MAGAZINE
Economic Commentary with a Difference / Bi-monthly

BOOKS

Prelude in Economics / Christopher Budd
History of Money / Gerard Klockenbring
Of Wheat and Gold / Christopher Budd
Beyond the Market / Gaudenz Assenza

RESEARCH PAPERS

Rudolf Steiner's Conception of Money* / chb
Central Banking / chb
Aristotle and Rudolf Steiner - Fellow Economists* / chb
The Consequences of the Peace for Economics / chb
A Brief History of "Der Kommende Tag"* / chb & jcl
Eastern Europe's Quest for Democracy / chb
Rudolf Steiner's *Economics Course** / chb
Islamic Economics and Capitalism / chb
Rudolf Steiner's *The Social Question* * / chb
UK Local Government Funding / chb
Human Rights / Don Cruse
Autonomous Economics and Europe's Central Bank / chb